"The major cause of divorce isn't problems with finances, in-laws, parenting or sex. The major cause is that couples don't know how to deal with conflict around those issues. This long-overdue integrative resource is an invaluable tool and should be in the hands of every counselor. If you want to help couples take their marriage from good to great then you must read this book. It will be required reading for all of my students."

GARY J. OLIVER, Th.M., Ph.D., executive director of The Center for Relationship Enrichment, and professor of psychology and practical theology, John Brown University

"The institution and even the definition of marriage continue to be in turmoil and the subject of debate and controversy within our culture today. Yet the Scriptures portray marriage as a beautiful metaphor of the union between Christ and his bride, the church. As such, couples face not only the challenges and obstacles inherent in any human relationship but must also contend with the spiritual forces of darkness that seek to destroy this image. Discord, pain, misunderstanding and hurt are inevitable. *Counseling Couples in Conflict* offers a solid integration of biblical principles and counseling skills with clinical theory that helps foster relational wholeness. Practical case examples are utilized throughout to illustrate key points and provide a balanced model for restoration. Whether a pastoral counselor or a professional mental health clinician, this book is an essential resource for anyone doing marital work."

ERIC T. SCALISE, Ph.D., LPC, LMFT, vice president for professional development, The American Association of Christian Counselors

"*Counseling Couples in Conflict* is a clearly written and helpful book based on a relational restoration model. I highly recommend it for pastors, Christian counselors and lay counselors who are involved in helping couples."

SIANG-YANG TAN, Ph.D., professor of psychology, Fuller Theological Seminary, and author of *Counseling and Psychotherapy: A Christian Perspective*

"Addressing the concerns of professional counselors and pastoral counselors alike, Sells and Yarhouse offer a biblically based, theologically grounded and therapeutically sound model for working specifically with couples in conflict. I recommend this book for beginning counselors and for seasoned colleagues in the field. It definitely has a home on my bookshelves."

VIRGINIA T. HOLEMAN, Ph.D., professor of counseling, Asbury Theological Seminary, and author of *Reconcilable Differences*

COUNSELING
COUPLES
IN CONFLICT

A Relational Restoration Model

James N. Sells

& Mark A. Yarhouse

IVP Academic

An imprint of InterVarsity Press
Downers Grove, Illinois

InterVarsity Press
P.O. Box 1400, Downers Grove, IL 60515-1426
World Wide Web: www.ivpress.com
E-mail: email@ivpress.com

InterVarsity Press® is the book-publishing division of InterVarsity Christian Fellowship/USA®, a movement of students and faculty active on campus at hundreds of universities, colleges and schools of nursing in the United States of America, and a member movement of the International Fellowship of Evangelical Students. For information about local and regional activities, write Public Relations Dept., InterVarsity Christian Fellowship/USA, 6400 Schroeder Rd., P.O. Box 7895, Madison, WI 53707-7895, or visit the IVCF website at <www.intervarsity.org>.

Scripture quotations, unless otherwise noted, are from the New Revised Standard Version of the Bible, *copyright 1989 by the Division of Christian Education of the National Council of the Churches of Christ in the USA. Used by permission. All rights reserved.*

While all stories in this book are true, some names and identifying information in this book have been changed to protect the privacy of the individuals involved.

Design: Cindy Kiple

Images: Frederic Cirou/Getty Images

ISBN 978-0-8308-3925-4

Printed in the United States of America ∞

Library of Congress Cataloging-in-Publication Data

Sells, James Nathan, 1958-
Counseling couples in conflict: a relational restoration model/
James N. Sells and Mark A. Harhouse.
p. cm.
Includes bibliographical references and index.
ISBN 978-0-8308-3925-4 (pbk.: alk. paper)
1. Marriage counseling. 2. Pastoral counseling. 3.
Counseling—Religious aspects—Christianity. I. Yarhouse, Mark A.,
1968- II. Title.
BV4012.27.S46 2010
616.89'1562—dc22

2010040606

| P | 20 | 19 | 18 | 17 | 16 | 15 | 14 | 13 | 12 | 11 | 10 | 9 | 8 | 7 |
| Y | 29 | 28 | 27 | 26 | 25 | 24 | 23 | 22 | 21 | | | | | |

CONTENTS

ACKNOWLEDGMENTS

THE FIRST ACKNOWLEDGMENT IS THAT this book does not have a dedication. It's hard to dedicate a book on marital conflict. The only suitable choice would be our wives, Heather Sells and Lori Yarhouse; however, dedicating a book on marital conflict just doesn't have the zip that dedicating a book on marital bliss would have. To protect our marriages from conflict from which there may be no return, we will pass on that option. Yet at the very outset, we must acknowledge the importance that others have made in the formation of this book—both in its ideas and in its creation. Heather and Lori have been instrumental in influencing the way we have come to think about marriage. The experience of relational grace has been our greatest teacher.

We are both grateful for the contribution made by our colleagues at Regent University: to the president, Dr. Carlos Campo, to the dean of the School of Psychology and Counseling, Dr. Bill Hathaway, and to the professors, staff members and students who have stimulated our thinking, helped us hone our ideas and offered relentless encouragement—your provision is on every page.

This is the second book that we have coauthored together with InterVarsity Press. Thank you to Gary Deddo, our editor, and to the IVP Academic staff. This book was placed in good hands.

Jim: John Beckenbach and Shawn Patrick are every professor's hope for graduate students. Our work together has grown from student and teacher to research collaborator to friend. Thanks for the contribution you have made as to how I think about marital conflict and its restoration. Mark Nelson prepared the index. My grad assistant Emily Hervey and student services coordinator Ann Marie Hohman were vital in preparing the manuscript. Likewise, graduate students Arlene Malone, David Olges and Emad Fahmy made suggestions to help the ideas in this manuscript fit together. And each in their unique way, Mark Reh-fuss, Elisabeth Suarez, Lee Underwood and Scott Wykes have encouraged me to "profess."

Mark: I would like to express my appreciation to Jill Kays, Rob Kay and Heidi Jo Erickson, my research and teaching assistants for the last two years. They are excellent assistants and have provided much-needed support. Also my colleagues at Regent—including Bill Hathaway, Jen Ripley, Glen Moriarty, Vickey Maclin, Joseph Francis, Judith Johnson, Lynn Olson, Linda Baum and LaTrelle Jackson—have made being a Christian and a psychologist meaningful to me in very practical ways.

Finally, there are scores of couples with whom we have shared many significant moments. It has been a gift to watch the process of marital restoration, and on occasion, it has been an honor to be present with them in the sorrow that is felt when a marriage is dissolved. Their joy and their pain have been our teacher. The fingerprint of each couple is present in these pages.

INTRODUCTION

THIS BOOK IS FOR PASTORS and Christian counselors who work with couples. These couples come seeking a trusted ally, guide, encourager and helper. You are prepared with two essential tools. First, you have a developed perspective of what marriage is supposed to be. Through your study of Scripture and of human development, you understand the importance of marital strength to the family, church, community and society. You have some idea of what a good marriage looks like. Second, you come with the compassion of a servant. You see the pain on their faces, hear the disappointment or despair in their voices. This is part of your calling, to render care to those who are discouraged. You identify with the calling to bring good news to the afflicted and to bind up the brokenhearted as described in Isaiah 61.

Yet even with those essential components, you may find yourself underprepared to work with couples who are stuck in patterns of anger, hurt, discouragement and frustration. Compassion levels are high, but progress is slow. You likely have a vision for what marriage is to be for those who seek your assistance, but do not have the resources or training to help them get there, or get there quickly. And that lack of growth can put a damper on the enthusiasm you have for this important work. We have seen many people in the human caring professions avoid direct work with couples—the "let's roll up our sleeves and get to it" work—because they lack knowledge of theory and tactics to help couples heal from relational wounds.

We approach this task with you as two psychologists who work with families and who seek to integrate our Christian faith with the practice of therapy. Our goal is to offer our knowledge of the therapeutic process, drawn from multiple family systems theories, including Contextual, Emotion Focused and Object Relations Family Therapy. Beyond knowledge, we aspire to help the reader to have success in working with couples who seek relational renewal and restoration. You, as a pastor and/or Christian counselor, are in a unique position to render care, facilitate healing and impart the grace of God to couples in pain. Marital restoration is complicated. Injuries are usually not superficial. Problems are usually not simple. Resolution is usually not instant. But we offer a glimpse of God's vision for what marriages can be and a strategy for success.

This book will be presented in three parts. Part one will address the presteps to conflict resolution. We first consider the condition of marriage in twenty-first-century North America. Marriage has experienced significant challenges within the culture.

In chapter two we will explain the complexity of marital conflict. Seldom are marital conflicts simple to understand and easy to resolve. If that were the case, we would not be needed. In fact, there are usually three fights occurring simultaneously, which creates a "two steps forward, three steps back" experience that can exasperate the best counselors.

In chapter three we introduce the concept of Us. The foundation of successful marriage is the structure upon which a marriage is constructed. Counselors, we believe, move too quickly beyond instilling a vision for the idea of Us, and attend to the details of the fight. Without ensuring the couple has a "big vision" of marriage, the counselor is at risk of painting over rust—it works for a while, but the corrosion quickly returns.

Finally in chapter four we emphasize the importance of boundaries and professional limitations for pastors and counselors. While pastors and counselors may have a ministry mindset, the practice and conduct of counseling is best managed through a set of limitations that build objectivity and promote fairness.

Part two will focus on the cycles of conflict and restoration. Imagine two concentric circles—a small circle inside a larger circle. Most marital conflicts cycle through the internal circle that is driven by pain, defensiveness and injury. But couples can process their conflicts through the outer circle, consisting of grace, justice, empathy, trust and forgiveness. Chapters five, six, seven, eight and nine will explain the process that either perpetuates relational conflict or alters its direction away from dissension and toward reconciliation.

Finally, part three will examine the application of the conflict-restoration cycle. While every couple fights uniquely, there are patterns that emerge in similar circumstances. In these chapters we will consider the emergence of marital strain around sexuality (chapter ten), parenting and child rearing (chapter eleven), sexual infidelity (chapter twelve), divorce and blended families (chapter thirteen), and substance abuse (chapter fourteen). In each of these chapters we consider both the issues that emerge that are often commonly associated with each theme as well as the common factors associated with the relationship conflict-restoration cycles described in part two.

Throughout the book we want to convey the importance of your relationship as pastor/counselor to the couple. Effectively addressing marital conflict requires more than teaching reflective listening and paraphrasing skills. There is a powerful mentoring relationship formed between the couple and the counselor.

Part One

THE PREFACE TO MARITAL COUNSELING

MARRIAGE AT A CRUCIAL STAGE OF EXISTENCE

The First Bond of Society is Marriage.

CICERO

TAESONG-DONG MIGHT BE THE VERY worst place to live on the face of the earth. It is the lone village in South Korea that nestles next to its North Korean "sister city" Kichong-dong. No one actually lives on the North Korean side, but in Taesong-dong about two hundred farmers go about their work tending fields as their ancestors have for centuries. They do so with more than one million armed soldiers surrounding them with explosive firepower to seriously affect the quality of the next crop! They stand between two warring powers, quietly going about their business, hoping that they are not destroyed because those around them cannot get along.

We see you, as pastors, professional therapists and lay counselors, sitting in a similar spot, though slightly less lethal. You are placed between two parties who have declared war on each other. Tension is often thick when each side meets in the neutrality of your office. Everyone knows that a misunderstood gesture here, or a comment poorly chosen there, could ignite the standoff that has existed for years.

Those who work with couples know from experience the "cold war" of marriage. Whether or not they are familiar with the data on marriage, pastors and counselors meet every week with couples whose marriages reflect the changes in our culture. It may feel like a siege. The definition and value of marriage has changed for many, pitting one side against the other. Marriage counselors sit in the middle of the fight. Couples come to pastoral counselors worn out by the standoff that has occurred within their home. They may be separated and considering whether reconciliation is ever possible. Other couples may sit down with a pastor and are essentially asking permission to pursue a divorce or have made up their minds that it is inevitable. Some are dealing with the common concerns of financial stress, communication problems or sexual difficulties that place a strain on the marriage. Still other couples may be dealing with the immediate concerns of perhaps sexual infidelity, pornography use or the ubiquitous press on couples for their time, as they balance over-scheduled lives that keep them from enjoying the marriage the way they thought they would. Amid it all sits you—the pastor, marital therapist or lay counselor—armed with a white flag and the hope of the Christian message, being charged with the task of bringing peace to opposing forces.

THE STATE OF THE UNION

What is the state of our marital unions today? What are marriages today struggling with, exactly? How bad is it? Can counseling make a difference in families? If so, how? These are the kinds of questions that can really get a pastoral counselor thinking. It is important to get a sense for how things are, while recognizing that it is only one part of a larger story. So while we will look at the state of the (marital) union, we want to remember that there are many benefits to marriage that will also be important for the counselor to keep in mind.

As we'll demonstrate, there are two conflicting realities in regard to our culture's attitude toward marriage. The first is that marriage is seen as a passé institution that restricts individual happiness. The second is that first-time married couples report the highest degree of personal happiness compared with single, cohabiting or divorced adults. We see data that offers discouraging evidence of the state of families in the twenty-first century, but we also see ample evidence in the research data that suggests the merit, worth and vitality of marriage and the benefits of marital intervention by pastors and professional and lay counselors. This evidence suggests that the craft you practice has a positive, immediate and lasting effect on marriages. Furthermore, the data suggests that rebuilding marriages has a positive effect on subsequent generations of marriage—far beyond the issues that husbands and wives must address, but literally on the second and third generations.

The state of divorce. When we look at rates of divorce, we can say that young married couples in their first marriage have about a 40 percent divorce rate.[1] The divorce rate rises for those who marry again. The divorce rate is also affected by level of education: those with a college education have about a 30 percent divorce rate compared to about a 60 percent divorce rate for those who do not complete high school.[2] Other factors have been studied that are connected in some way to an increased likelihood of divorce, including living together before marriage, having religious differences, marrying at a younger age, and having seen one's parents' divorce.[3]

Looking at divorce by itself doesn't tell the whole story. Our culture is changing; the way that we see marriage and divorce has shifted. We can see differences in attitudes toward marriage, in whether it is valued as an important arrangement or whether it is something people feel much less passionate about. If people feel rather casual about relationship commitment, they might be less likely to value marriage as a place where such commitment is required. Also, if people focus more on what they believe is best for them, they may put more stock in self-interest over something like marriage with the creation of a new relationship, one that demands sacrifice through placing others before oneself.[4]

Marital cynicism. As to marriage, cynicism abounds. The humor of Johnny Carson still reflects a pervading attitude of our day: "If variety is the spice of life, marriage is the big can of leftover Spam." Our culture questions a lot of traditional structures and sources of knowledge. This is partly a product of our age—we live in a postmodern society that not only questions but openly challenges traditional views and norms. We are also at a place where we have seen the casualties of both poor marriages and broken marriages, and we may be witness to more people wondering whether "any couple can make marriage work as a life-long union."[5]

Some experts on marriage have pointed to the appeal of "serial monogamy,"[6] or what we refer to as the "*Seinfeld* effect." Do you remember the popular sitcom from the 1990s? The message was loud and clear that marriage was devastating to a person's freedom, friendships, social life, sex life and so on. The cultural and social changes represented in a show that derides marriage impact our society by contributing to decreased expectations that people marry. The benefits of not getting married can frequently be romanticized.

Perhaps related to this is the idea that people today possess greater wealth and can live independently. Individuals are able to make ends meet, and therefore do not value or need marriage the way they might have even thirty years ago. Some women and men may give serious consideration to divorce in life circumstances in which divorce would not really have been a viable consideration only a few short years ago.[7]

That is a sobering view of marriage. We could focus our attention on rates of divorce and cultural messages that devalue marriage. We could join in with the cynics who question whether any marriage can last, let alone a sizable percentage of marriages. But we find it more helpful to reflect on how marriage has remained in many circles a desired social institution. Despite all of the threats to marriage, why has marriage remained an ideal that so many people ascribe to? Why do we celebrate when we come across announcements of thirty- and forty- and fifty-year anniversaries?

Marriage as a desired social institution. Marriage remains one of the most stable and desired social institutions and the one place of interface between religious and secular entities, as most people who marry do so within a church environment.

What is the appeal of marriage? Judith Wallerstein and Sandra Blakeslee have a helpful book titled *The Good Marriage: How & Why Love Lasts.* In it they discuss how people look for a love that lasts, and that this is true even in cases of longstanding marriages that unfortunately end in divorce—people continue to look for sustained relationships. Not only does marriage protect us from loneliness, but marriage and, by extension, family, provide a sense of meaning and continuity:

> A man and woman in a good, lasting marriage with children feel connected with the past and have an interest in the future. A family makes an important link in the chain of human history. By sharing responsibility for the next generation, parents can find purpose and a strengthened sense of identity.[8]

Perhaps now more than any other time in human history, people are able to choose marriage or not, or they can choose marriage for a time and then decide whether to continue in it or to dissolve it.

Wallerstein and Blakeslee point out the changes in support for marriage over time:

> Think of marriage as an institution acted upon by centripetal forces pulling inward and centrifugal forces pulling outward. In times past the centripetal forces—law, tradition, religion, parental influence—exceeded those that could pull a marriage apart, such as infidelity, abuse, financial disaster, failed expectations, or the lure of the frontier. Nowadays the balance has changed. The weakened centripetal forces no longer exceed those that tug marriages apart.[9]

Despite these changes, marriages remain an attractive institution to those who are married and to those who are single. Why is it valued so? It may have to do with some of the benefits experienced in marriage. These benefits appear to come through changes people experience when they marry. Marriage seems to change people. It reorients people's goals, and it can transform people's experiences.[10]

When it comes to goals, marriage helps people think about their future. It helps them make better choices about health-promoting activities, including diet/nutrition and financial decisions, such as saving for the future. Marriage gives people a better sense for the part they play in their own future.

Marriage also affects one's well-being. People who are married report greater life satisfaction. They are happier. They are less depressed and less anxious. They enjoy greater sexual fulfillment. They have decreased rates of mortality.

The following benefits to healthy marriages were also recently summarized on the U.S. Department of Health and Human Services website:[11]

- Women are more likely to have a better relationship with their kids, be emotionally and physically healthier, and be better off financially. They are less likely to get a sexually transmitted disease, be a victim of a violent crime, or to be in poverty.

- Men live longer, are physically and emotionally healthier, are better off financially, have greater stability at work and greater income, have a more satisfying sexual relationship, and have better relationships with their kids. They are less likely to commit a violent crime, attempt suicide, contract an STD, or abuse drugs or alcohol.

- Good marriages are also good for a community. Married couples tend to be better educated, more likely to own their home, and have higher property values. They also have lower rates of domestic violence, crime, teen pregnancy, and need for social services. They are good for communities.

A GOOD MARRIAGE

There is no one type of good or healthy marriage. They come in different shapes and sizes. In one report,[12] however, healthy marriages held many things in common, including a commitment to children, satisfaction, communication, conflict resolution, faithfulness and emotional support.

Types of good marriages. In their book *The Good Marriage,* Judith Wallerstein and Sandra Blakeslee identify four different types of good marriages: romantic, rescue, companionate and traditional.[13]

The first type, *romantic marriage,* is characterized by enduring memories of excitement and romance. The second type they call the *rescue marriage,* in which spouses benefit from a kind of healing of prior emotional pain or loss from earlier in their lives. The third type, *companionate marriage,* is one in which couples are able to strike a balance between their commitments to their careers and to their marriage and children.

The last broad type of good marriage identified by the researchers is referred to as the *traditional marriage.* This is one that maintains more of a traditional divide between public and private domains, with the man functioning as breadwinner in the public domain while the woman has more responsibilities in the private domains of the home and childrearing.

Creating a good marriage. In their study, Wallerstein and Blakeslee identify nine tasks that they advise couples to take on to create a good marriage. Some of these overlap with what is referred to as the family life cycle. For example, the first two tasks are: separating from the family you grew up in, and forming a new family together. The third task is to become parents. As the authors put it, "Children brought special meaning to the lives of happily married couples."[14]

The fourth task is to cope with crises. Although crises take many different forms, ranging from unemployment to health concerns such as cancer, it is important to turn toward one another and toward a good social support network rather than away from one another or in pain in isolation from potentially supportive relationships.

All meaningful relationships create opportunities for conflict. The fifth task of a good marriage is to be a place in which it is safe to have conflicts; a place in which the couple has built "a relationship that is safe for the expression of difference, conflict, and anger."[15] Early conflicts can establish key insights into the sources of different values and expectations, as well as the experience of safety and trust the couple has in one another.

The sixth task identified by Wallerstein and Blakeslee is to create and protect a fulfilling sex life together. There is also a great deal of variability here; couples create their own sex life, and it becomes a place of transparency and vulnerability, but also an opportunity to express and experience trust and safety while drawing together in meaningful ways.

The seventh task is sharing laughter and interests. Being able to laugh together is an important part of a good marriage, as is having a genuine interest in one another. Some interests are done by each spouse individually, while other interests are shared. Couples can enjoy both individual activities and shared activities; both kinds have the potential to make one another interesting.

Providing one another emotional nurturance is the eighth task of good marriages. This involves offering and accepting "comfort and encouragement in a relationship that is safe for dependency, failure, disappointment, mourning, illness, and aging—in short, for being a vulnerable human being."[16]

The last task identified by Wallerstein and Blakeslee is preserving a double vision, by which the authors mean carrying "in one's head a simultaneous vision of past images and present realities. It involves holding on to the early idealizations of being in love while realizing that one is growing older and grayer and cannot turn back the clock.[17]

So there are good marriages out there, and there are marriages that are in trouble. How do good marriages end up in trouble? Well, for starters, not all marriages that are in trouble were at one time good. In other words, marriages start off in different places based on the people who form them, the circumstances in which they were formed and many other factors. Marriages can sometimes really struggle, and we have a good idea how they could do better if both partners are willing to address those concerns.

WHEN COUPLES COME FOR HELP

Many couples seek out pastoral care or counseling precisely because they experience conflict in their marriage. Indeed, in terms of mental health referrals, marital conflicts have been reported to account for 40 percent of all counseling referrals.[18] Couples seek out pastoral care and counseling precisely because they want relief from relational conflicts.[19] They are often looking for someone who can step in and settle a dispute—ideally by agreeing with the one partner over the other. Perhaps they are thinking, *If I can just get our pastor to convince my husband of how right I am about our finances, he'll finally come around!* or, *If my counselor hears my side, she'll agree with me that my wife is being selfish on this one.* The position that caregivers are placed in is often felt to be precarious.

Predictors of success. Yet, as pastors and counselors consider the challenge of addressing marital conflict, we want to offer encouragement: there are important predictors of success in marriage counseling. For example, Carroll and Doherty conducted a meta-analytic study comparing couples who participated in premarital counseling preparation compared to those who did not. (A meta-analysis is an advanced statistical procedure in which all of the results of all of the studies on a given topic are combined.) They found that premarital counseling—the work that pastors, marriage therapists and lay counselors do with couples in preparation for marriage—increases the chances of a successful outcome by about 30 percent.

Similarly, Shadish, Ragsdale, Glaser and Montgomery conducted the same type of research on the effectiveness of marital counseling. They found that the positive effects were moderately strong and that no one treatment approach proved to be more effective than others. In other words, we know what you do can make a difference in the lives of couples.

We also know that there are factors or characteristics couples possess that make it more likely that they will succeed in turning their marriage around. Five major factors have been identified:[20] couple commitment, age, emotional engagement, marital traditionality, and convergent goals. We can talk specifically about ways to tap into these factors in the course of pastoral care or counseling, but for now it is enough to point out that couples who are committed to staying in the marriage tend to improve more than those who are really there to decide whether or not to divorce.

Younger couples tend to have better outcomes in marriage counseling than older couples, which probably reflects that the problems are being addressed earlier in the life of the marriage, before having a chance to really take root.

Couples who have strong positive emotional connections tend to do better in marriage counseling. They are emotionally engaged with one another and have positive emotional responses to one another. Typically these connections are based on shared interests and activities.

Those who tend to be more egalitarian in their marriages tend to benefit as a result of marriage counseling. This may be the result of having more flexibility around roles and responsibilities, how household or family duties are negotiated and divvied up, and so on.

The last factor is convergent goals, or the idea that a couple has similar values and aims in life. When couples share similar values or life purposes, they tend to benefit more from marriage counseling. Practically speaking, it may be to the benefit of the pastor or counselor to help the couple identify common values and goals that both can get behind.

We believe that another factor has an important outcome effect on marriage—the attitude and outlook of the counselor. Not all marriage counselors are equal. We draw a parallel to an athletic event, like a soccer or basketball game. Athletes can be overwhelmed with the speed of the game. The ball is moving so quickly that by the time an athlete reacts, he or she is playing behind. Couples counseling is much like that. With two emotionally charged spouses who have inside knowledge into how they play the game, counselors can easily feel overmatched. So, essential to the process of offering effective care is the ability to take control of the game. To some, that mistakenly means to dominate, control, direct and coerce. That is far from what we mean by control. We believe that control comes through important attitudes and abilities—beyond the obvious requirements of clinical training and spiritual maturity—that are essential in maximizing your effectiveness in helping couples. We will list four important marital counseling skills, which we will revisit throughout the book.

Marital counseling skill 1: Accepting what individuals choose to do with their lives. If you could reduce family counseling to one essential message to represent the whole of mature marriage and family functioning, it likely would be the ability to manage boundaries. Yet one of the most difficult challenges for counselors and the most frequent error is the mismanagement of the boundary between your vision for their marriage, and the individuals' decision to act in what they perceive to be their best interest. It is not that pastoral, professional or lay counselors frequently make the obvious errors and form unethical or immoral relationships with clients; we are speaking of more subtle boundary violations that are driven by our common commitment to assist couples in being successful in their marriages. The line between counseling and ministry becomes blurred, and in the process we lose our objectivity and judgment. An example of this boundary issue might be the pastoral counselor who is awakened in the early morning hours with the thought of a couple on the schedule for that day. Or when a counselor is inclined to ruminate over a session with a family that has occurred the day before. Like the parent who is worried for the well-being of his or her children, we might be drawn to pray, think or analyze, and may be grateful to God for drawing clients who have become dear ones to our attention. Seldom in these moments are we alarmed that our thoughts, which interrupt other activities, might be a signal that we have occupied a parentified role in our work as their counselor. "Working overtime" outside of the session is often a key indicator that the separation between the counselor and the family has become too tight. The passion for successful therapy can easily shift from their success as a couple or a family to our success as a counselor. We might feel the need for their marriage to turn around, and that becomes the driving force and even the obsessive expectation.

In truth, counselors are and should be passionate about marriage and ardently strive for its maturation. But we must do so for their benefit, not as a reflection of our need to succeed. And when clients choose to divorce, separate, see a different counselor, or passively deny suggestions and assignments made in therapy, we must be careful to reasonably assess our involvement in their decision, but to leave it as their decision, which we must acknowledge, respect and release from our control.

Marital counseling skill 2: Being comfortable in the front lines of marital conflict. Our colleague Dr. Don Pruessler works with adolescents. He is known to say, "I love working with kids; the angrier they are, the more I like working with them." This attitude needs to be ours to be successful marital counselors. The pain expressed between intimate partners often provokes the counselor to shut it down prematurely. An error that we can easily make as counselors is to misread anger and make it the problem, rather than to see anger as the declaration that a problem exists. Consider anger like a flare gun. It can ignite the sky, and all who see it know immediately that a crisis exists on the sailing ship from which it was fired. When rescuers come alongside the ship, they do not say, "Don't you dare fire those flares!" Rather, they immediately recognize that a state of emergency exists and respond immediately by learning the nature of the crisis.

For a counselor, anger serves as the indicator of crisis. It is possible that anger can be used manipulatively for one person to get their way. But this is only successful when we are intolerant of anger, not when counselors permit it to be expressed so as to explore its causes. The more immediate problem is when counselors shut down the expression of emotion that makes them feel uncomfortable, forcing the spouse to resort to less obvious, but more destructive ways to declare perceptions of unfairness or injustice.

Marital counseling skill 3: "Having no dog in the fight," or don't get trapped by taking sides. It is very easy to be drawn into the conflict by siding with the spouse for whom we have the strongest affinity, or who draws from us the most empathy. Counselors need to be careful to build relationships with both spouses with equal proximity and distance, encouragement and confrontation, affiliation and separation. This becomes a magnified challenge when there is an obvious "bad spouse" such as the one caught in infidelity, addiction or substance abuse. While it may be true that the problems of one individual may have a more substantial effect on the marriage than the other, it is also true that both play some role in the conflict. Truly innocent parties we have yet to see.

Counselors can often identify the subtle ways that couples will seek to enlist support and alliance. We might quietly root for the underdog or be intimidated by the power of the "big dog." Both become severe errors to carefully avoid. Later we will underscore the importance of "multidirected partiality," the key construct in Contextual Family Therapy that emphasizes the vital importance of holding relationship with both partners in balance. This is not to suggest that counselors consider all marital sins and shortcomings as equal. No one believes infidelity to be morally equivalent to tardiness in paying the bills. However, the emphasis in marital counseling is that all have sinned; that is, both have contributed to the marital condition and each must focus on the assumption of that to which he or she is responsible.

Marital counseling skill 4: Seeing both the forest and the trees. All counseling is complicated. Marital counseling is complicated multiplied by two. Events are occurring simultaneously, pushing and pulling the dialogue in conflicting directions. It can feel like one is fighting a forest fire—one minute counseling while the couple cooperates in resolving an issue, then with a sudden change in wind or humidity, the fire is out of control. We shall discuss in the next chapter the details of why this occurs. But suffice it to say for this brief summary that counselors must be cognizant of events occurring at different levels. The big picture—the forest—must always be held in view. The big picture might be the broad and general goals the couple seeks to master. While maintaining perspective on the horizon, the counselor must also be able to focus on individual trees, specific violations and injuries that have taken root in the foreground. These important events eventually grow into a component of the forest; therefore proper management of these small saplings helps determine the makeup of the forest.

In the chapters that follow, we will tie some of these suggestions in with how we understand the multiple layers of marital conflict, ways to foster a biblical perspective on intimacy in marriage, and the overarching approach we recommend for navigating and resolving marital conflicts.

NOTES

[1]Raley, R. K., & Bumpass, L. (2003). The topography of the divorce plateau: Levels and trends in union stability in the United States after 1980. *Demographic Research, 8*, 245-60.

[2]Ibid., p. 255.

[3]Ripley, J. S. (2003). Introduction: Reflections on the current status and future of Christian marriages. *Journal of Psychology and Theology, 31*(3), 175-78.

[4]Edwards, K. J. (2003). It takes a village to save a marriage. *Journal of Psychology and Theology, 31*(3), 188-95.

[5]Stanley, S. (2003). Strengthening marriages in a skeptical culture: Issues and opportunities. *Journal of Psychology and Theology, 31*(3), 224.

[6]Parrott, L., III, & Parrott, L. (2003). The SYMBIS approach to marriage education. *Journal of Psychology and Theology, 31*(3), 208-12.

[7]Browning, D. S., Miller-McLemore, B. J., Couture, P. D., Lyon, K. B., & Franklin, R. M. (2000). Feminism, religion, and well-being. In *From culture wars to common ground: religion and the American family debate* (2nd ed., pp. 157-89). Louisville, KY: Westminster John Knox Press.

[8]Wallerstein, J. S., & Blakeslee, S. (1995). *The good marriage: How & why love lasts.* New York: Warner Books, p. 5.

[9]Ibid., p. 7.

[10]Waite, L. J., & Gallagher, M. (2000). *The case for marriage: Why married people are happier, healthier, and better off financially.* New York: Broadway Books. (See chaps.

4-7 in particular, as we highlight several of the main findings in this section.)

[11]Wilcox, W. B., Gottman, J., Waite, L., Glenn, N., Nock, S., Galston, W., & Wallerstein, J. (2005). Benefits of healthy marriages. In *Why marriage matters: Twenty-six conclusions from the social sciences* (2nd ed.). Retrieved from www.acf.hhs.gov/healthymarriage/benefits/index.html.

[12]Moore, K. A., Jekielek, S. M., Bronte-Tinkew, J., Guzman, L., Ryan S., & Redd, Z. (2004). What is "healthy marriage"? Defining the concept. *Child Trends Research Brief.* Retrieved from www.childtrends.org/Files/CT_HealthyMarriage.pdf.

[13]Wallerstein & Blakeslee. (1995). *The good marriage.*

[14]Ibid., p. 70.

[15]Ibid., p. 143.

[16]Ibid., p. 239.

[17]Ibid., p. 322.

[18]Donavan, J. M. (1995). Short-term couples group psychotherapy: A take of four fights. *Psychotherapy: Theory, Research, Practice, Training, 32*(4), 608-17.

[19]Worthington, E. L., Jr., & DiBlasio, F. A. (1990). Promoting mutual forgiveness within the fractured relationship. *Psychotherapy, 27,* 219-23.

[20]Jacobson, N. S., & Christensen, A. (1996). *Acceptance and change in couple therapy: A therapist's guide to transforming relationships.* New York: W. W. Norton.

2

THREE FIGHTS IN ONE

Just when I thought I had the couple's fighting under control . . .
he said . . . then she said . . . then bedlam!

COUNSELOR IN SUPERVISION

MOST PEOPLE HAVE EXPERIENCED the frustration of blowing out birthday candles—not the annoyance that comes from needing to produce more wind to extinguish the annual increase in firepower, but rather the aggravation that occurs when we discover that we are trying to blow out those trick candles, the ones that reignite. It was funny the first time. But by middle age, it's just exasperating. We blow and blow and blow. The candles give us the impression of victory, then *poof,* the wicks burst again into flame.

Marriage counselors and pastors often feel a similar exasperation. When sitting with an angry couple, there may appear to be progress made toward building understanding, respect and regard for each other. Then *poof,* an inadvertent word, a look, maybe even a sigh or smirk provokes the couple to relationally combust. This repeated occurrence produces in counselors confusion, self-doubt and a frequent preference to avoid working with couples altogether. We often hear comments from pastors and counselors such as, "It seems as if we take two steps forward, then three steps back. . . . Why is this so hard? . . . How did I get stuck in the middle of this mess? . . . They didn't teach me this in graduate school or seminary! . . . How can I get out of this without them doing violence to each other, to me or my office furniture?" A pastor once commented about marital counseling, "Working with conflicted couples is where angels fear to tread."

We cannot say if indeed angels feel trepidation when placed between conflicted spouses. However, we can say, as Everett Worthington did, that "most counselors dread dealing with troubled marriages even though troubled marriages often form the majority of their caseload."[1]

To explain a primary reason why working with conflicted couples can be so discouraging, let's go back to the birthday candles, in which a second source of heat reignites the wick after it is blown out. Imbedded in the fibers are fine strands of metal made of magnesium. Those metal fibers stay hot for a few seconds after the flame is blown out. They reheat the wick to its combustion point, and *surprise!*, the candle reignites. It is similar with relational conflict. There are additional sources of heat that have an unexpected effect on the relationship— while one issue may be contained, other factors continue to apply heat to the relationship. When a counselor attends to just one dimension of marital "heat," the result is an appearance of progress that is interrupted by another conflagration. Frustration, discouragement and hopelessness are the frequent products.

THREE "HEAT SOURCES" TO ADDRESS

There are three factors, or three sources of heat, that ignite the "conflict candle." Counselors must attend to all three at the same time when working with couples. The first is the current conflict theme. The second is the couple's history with the conflict theme. Finally, each spouse has a family tradition that they carry into the marriage from their respective family of origin. These three components must be understood, communicated and managed by the counselor in order for the couple to avoid being yanked back into conflict while in therapy.

The conflict theme. The conflict theme is usually easy to identify. If you are to ask either partner, "Hey, what's the problem?" it is what you would get as a response. Commonly the conflict theme has two versions—his side of the story and her side of the story. But it is still the same story. The conflict, then, is what they are yelling about *right now*.

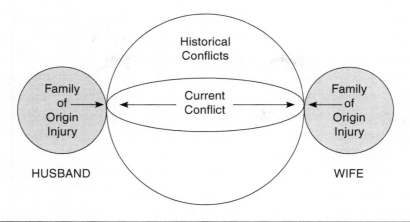

Figure 2.1

It is the fight about the bounced check, childcare, dirty laundry and why they are not stopping to ask directions. These themes can be about little aggravations; they also can involve large and significant differences or violations. The conflict theme usually rests between people—counselors must integrate "his problem" with "her problem" to form "their problem."

Mike and Janice are fighting about family scheduling. Janice's perspective is that Mike is unreliable and even inconsiderate of her by his failure to be at home when he says he will. Mike frequently fails at being home at the designated time for dinner or to transport one of their children to a lesson, practice or event—requiring Janice to cover for Mike's broken promise. His frequent tardiness sets into motion a number of events that are often embarrassing or upsetting to her.

From Mike's perspective he is caught between multiple demands that he can't control. He is a plant manager for a tuna packaging company. He is frequently called upon to solve problems. These unexpected problems occur when the day shift is ending at the plant and the next shift is coming to work. This is also precisely the time that Mike is trying to leave work and meet the family for dinner, or to transport a child to the event of the day. He sees Janice as failing to understand his responsibilities at work as he tries to balance them with his commitments and responsibilities as a father and husband.

The issues of schedules and timeliness are relatively small, benign topics when they are not in the heat of the conflict; Mike and Janice both acknowledge that the problem is not a big deal. They are not fighting over infidelity, abandonment or violence. Rather, their frustrations remain on the nuisance and annoyance level. These problems do not drive couples to divorce court, but they do rob couples of daily satisfaction and are the hairline cracks in the relationship that can open to gapping fissures.

These conflicts are intensely felt and usually successfully addressed by marital partners demonstrating the fundamental relational skills of listening, reflecting, understanding, planning and implementing. Most couples are able to resolve these differences by not entangling themselves with other factors. Pastors and counselors usually feel very successful in working with couples on this level because the cognitive-behavioral communication models of counseling are very effective. Couples are usually open and responsive to the direct admonition from Scripture regarding how they are to change their actions or attitudes in order to create a more successful family.

When a couple does not manage a "normal life problem" by successful resolution with their own resources, a counselor is wise to consider the possibility that there is another source of heat not being accounted for in their discussion. Or if the emotional reaction to the topic is disproportionately intense—such as the slamming of doors or the toaster across the kitchen—one would have to assume that there is more here than just a mere annoyance from a delayed schedule.

History with the conflict theme. Pain has a memory. Usually there is more to a couple's conflict than the actual argument topic such as schedules and arriving home on time. Spouses have a history of causing injury to one another. That repetition builds expectations and a response pattern within each partner.

In athletics, the term *muscle memory* refers to a set of movements that are learned then practiced over and over, like shooting a free throw in basketball. The brain habituates the body to the movements that have been rehearsed. So a basketball player can line up at the free throw line and shoot a basket with his or her eyes closed. Since the movements are memorized, one doesn't even have to look. Conflicts in marriage are similar. Once they have been repeated multiple times, our brains learn to recognize the cues previously experienced and react to the other person out of anticipation. In these situations, it's like couples can "fight with their eyes closed." They each have been there before. It is possible for a couple to become quickly embroiled in a fight without much buildup, expectation or intent, as if they were sent there at the blink of an eye. This may be why James, the brother of Jesus, encourages us to be slow to speak and slow to anger. He was referring to the natural tendency to react to conflict because of preexisting circumstances. Christian counselors see this phenomenon playing out in their offices. In a flash the conversation turns from pleasantries to hostilities. The counselor who hasn't had opportunity to experience the history of conflict in the relationship is the one caught most off guard.

To make sense of the influence of the historical conflict on the relationship, let's return to the story of Mike and Janice. Mike has regularly placed his work and personal interests above the family interest, and Janice is suspicious when circumstances emerge that cause Mike to be absent at family events. It doesn't take much to place Mike and Janice into conflict because any single small event has a "muscle memory"—that is, it is attached to other events that have a lingering effect on the relationship. Their brains do not need to build new paths to understand an event. Those paths are already cut—and they lead right to the memory of pain and disappointment. So Mike and Janice are able to skip a number of mental steps and go right to a defensive, self-protective perspective. It's as if a part of their brains are saying, "Don't wait for all the facts to come in; you must act now to guard yourself from hurt."

For the counselor, if a couple's circumstances evoke intense emotion, then it can be surmised that something about the event is threatening their Us. They perceive danger, anger, pain and insult. The self-protective "fight or flight" responses have been signaled. One or both become hypervigilant, extra sensitive, aware and guarded.

In this case, Mike has frequently placed his interests above those of Janice. His actions on any one occasion were never so flagrant to justify an intense reaction, but to Janice their accumulative effect creates a severe imbalance in her thinking about relational fairness. "Mike's needs trump Janice's needs . . . Mike is first . . . Janice comes later . . . What is important to Janice is not as important to Mike." These residual thoughts prove to be an accelerant to the normal disagreements that occur within their relationship. The result of this established pattern is that Janice will react to new occurrences of the same old injury with an exponential intensity. She is not just fighting one event of unfairness, but an accumulation of events. Likewise, Mike will become hyperreactive as well when arguments over "a little thing," like coming home slightly behind schedule, occur with regularity. Neither Mike nor Janice is necessarily operating with an awareness of the accumulated effects of these quarrels. But they both find it disturbing when they become embroiled in fights with lightning speed.

Family-of-origin conflict tradition. A third and very significant source in Mike's fighting pattern has nothing to do with Janice, and likewise, much that Janice was fighting had nothing to do with Mike. Individually, both become propelled from forces exerted from their families.

From their respective families each learned a pattern of acting, reacting and interacting with events, circumstances and people. Early in life we all learn a set of rules about how to respond to situations. Included in those instructions are implied ideas about how others are to act and how we can all best get along together. Neither Mike nor Janice was present at each other's "school." So neither was privy to how their partner was instructed, mentored and graded by their respective teachers. And their curriculums were different, often drastically. We can observe the lessons learned by the way they responded to their pain and the pain of their partner.

When Mike encounters pain, he pursues a course of independence and self-sufficiency. This came as little surprise after listening to Mike talk about his childhood experience. "When you ask about my needs, I have to admit that I almost have no idea what to say. I don't mean to make myself sound 'needless and perfect.' I know that I carry worries and feel anger and resentment—but beyond that I don't really know what I need. I think that I was encouraged not to have any needs by my parents—you know, be available to help others but never ask for help for yourself. That's sort of the way I grew up."

Likewise, Janice interprets the circumstances and events within her marriage by following a set of cue cards first recorded in childhood. Her parents were legally divorced when she was an adolescent; emotionally, they were divorced long before that. "I never remember my parents hugging each other . . . you know, real hugs. I remember them expressing the perfunctory kiss once in a while. But I never saw them be happy with each other. I remember trying to make it happen. As a little girl I once had my mom on my right and my dad on my left, and I took their hands and joined them together. I was the matchmaker. I wanted them to be in love, but was afraid that they weren't, and I was the good girl hoping that I could please both of them." Janice went on to say that they were pleased, generally, but that she always had a longing for something more, a quality of love and acceptance from them that never seemed to make it over to her side of the fence. She spoke of a prevailing sense of being alone and having no one there to comfort her.

Mike and Janice operate through a "social genetic code" that influences their behavior. That is, they each carry a predisposition to certain behaviors in certain situations, through an experiential grid formed through their experiences with family. It guides the way they interpret others' behaviors and select their own. However, we do not want to imply or suggest that the cause of our marital conflict rests with our parents. That is both simplistic and errant.

We often think of language as a metaphor to explain both the positive and negative influence of families. I grew up in an English-speaking home. English was imprinted on my brain in early childhood. I used English as my operating system to understand all of life's problems. English was a very useful tool and it has served me well, except when I have traveled to non-English-speaking countries. Using English as the tool to understand events, engage in relationships and guide behavior was not as useful there.

In the same way, parents give us a set of tools designed to manage pain. And they teach us what to do when others with whom we live experience and react to their pain. Mike and Janice learned to speak a relational language. When they married, they began a "multicultural" experience. They formed a hybrid culture consisting of both the old and the new. This culture was a fusion of each family's traditions and rules. The relational language that was learned as a child was a helpful starting place for their marriage—but it was not enough because each was in a new "country," developing new patterns for life. Relationally speaking, they became multilingual. But the old language, the old culture and the old relational rules can never be erased. If Mike and Janice learn a dozen new languages, their first language will remain English. Likewise, the patterns learned in childhood are never forgotten. They are the "first language."

An odd reality is that when anyone is in conflict, when there is an emotional exchange and when there is a need for self-defense, the person will speak in the relational language of childhood. A person who speaks two languages will normally revert to their mother tongue in an emotionally charged situation. And so, whenever we are on the defensive, we "speak" in our primary relational language.

COUNSELORS AND THERAPEUTIC FRUSTRATION

Imagine that Mike and Janice are in your office. You are ending a great session. The couple appears to be making progress in communicating their perspectives about the fight they had yesterday over Mike's failure to make it home on time. (Notice that the word *fight* is singular, because everyone is focusing on solving the presenting problem as if it were a discrete event.) You are employing interventions appropriate to the problem presented. The couple is listening to one another, reflecting, acknowledging and so on. You employ a short-term, solution-focused or cognitive-behavioral approach. Together they identify times when they managed their relationship appropriately. You work with them to establish commitments regarding how each might avoid creating the circumstances that have occurred in the past, and the session ends successfully with a plan for them to follow. As you wrap up the session, Mike says, "Can you believe this big fight comes out of such a small issue?" Unintentionally, the candle which had been successfully extinguished just burst back into flame! Janice says, "Maybe it's small to you, but to me, it's pretty important. It's about whether I can trust you to keep your word. It's about whether you will put your wife's and kids' interests in front of your own. No, Mike, if you think this is a small issue, then you just don't get it."

The shock wave from this relational explosion leaves you flat. What was looking to be a successful ending has just been decimated. And you're not quite sure what just happened or what to do next.

First, let's go back and rethink what happened. Mike and Janice were showing signs of success in attending to the conflict theme. They listened to each other and respected the legitimate issues that both raised regarding their scheduling conflict. But there was another dimension to the injury that was not addressed—that of the history of injury occurring in the relationship. Janice's response might have seemed to you and me a bit over the top. That is because we are thinking her reaction was just about the argument over the latest scheduling snafu. But it wasn't. She was reacting to the dozens of accumulated cold dinners, disappointed children and last-minute alterations in the evening plans. Janice was tracking the conversation on a different path than you were as the counselor. She was drawing from a history that made the current conversation only a distant hope. Her experience said, "Watch out; be skeptical."

A common response is to transfer your feelings back to the couple by labeling them as "bad," "uncooperative" or "not really serious about making progress." Another is to become discouraged with the process of couple therapy all together.

A different path is to understand these frustrating experiences by thinking through the three levels of conversation that just occurred and to integrate these levels as part of the couple's learning process. Mike made a statement that he probably thought to be an innocent commentary on what was happening to them. He was operating on the conflict theme level—he was focusing on the immediate issue of the argument that stemmed from their latest spat. Janice, on the other hand, did not receive his comment as limited to the present tense. She reacted intensely because she has years of experience with feeling neglected by Mike's "little mistakes."

Furthermore, Mike comes from a family in which he was appointed as the "conflict minimizer." So for him to gain closure to the conversation, his job is to make the problem smaller and more manageable before you end the session. Janice is experiencing this conversation differently. Something triggered her. She was calmed and encouraged by the counseling session, but when Mike made his comment, her emotions just popped. Janice had heard Mike promise that he would be home on time on hundreds of mornings. His repetitive failure to keep those little promises has made her highly doubtful that he will change.

What occurred, in classic systems thinking, was that the three levels of this conversation were not being equally respected and addressed. While on the surface it appeared that there was agreement, in reality, they were talking about the same thing but on different dimensions. The counselor and the couple allowed their thinking to become linear and one-dimensional. It is common to apply a one-dimensional solution to a three-dimensional problem, and then become stalemated. At times, this failure is a result of ignorance—we just didn't understand all of the factors that contributed to our pain. At other times couples can use the three dimensions to strategically bend the conflict toward someone's favor. Spouses can escalate any simple conflict by using aspects of the three levels of conflict.

Here is how it can happen. A basic military strategy in battle is to know the enemy in terms of position, numbers and weaponry. Then resources can be effectively deployed to counter the enemy's strengths and capitalize on its weaknesses. This is how battles are won—both military and relational. Conflicts usually begin with an accidental encounter; they are seldom planned. Couples don't anticipate having a fight next Tuesday at 7 p.m. Rather, they stumble into conflict while on "routine patrol." Conflicts usually are initiated by differences in will or opinion. Soon after engagement in direct fire with the enemy, both sides employ strategies to protect themselves. As the battle continues, it becomes more complicated. Both sides have time to call reinforcements and to direct their resources toward protecting their respective flanks and gaining the upper hand in this skirmish. Each person calls upon more and more resources to sustain the effort and overrun the enemy.

Fighting influenced by their respective families of origin and by their history serves to complicate their present conflicts. They function like diversions that require a distribution of resources that might weaken the defenses on either side. Soon, they can't decide what the fight is actually about or where it is occurring. They have lost sight of the original issue and are engaged in an offensive and defensive struggle on multiple fronts.

RESOLVING THE MULTIDIMENSIONAL FIGHT

When working with parents of adolescents, we often find ourselves encouraging parents to "be smarter than your kids." By that we do not mean to imply that parents have less intelligence, but rather that parents can easily misunderstand the complications of family conflict and become pulled into arguments because they don't fully understand the factors that are creating the situation. In the same way, counselors must be smarter than their clients, not that they are to be more intelligent. Rather, it means to stay above the fray, to not be pulled into the emotional components of the arguments, so that you can listen and watch for the emergence of these three sources of relational strain and attend to each as you hold the other two at bay. This means that when the fabric of a relationship begins to unravel as you sit with a couple, you are able to stop the destructive process and help them constructively bring restoration to the marriage. The counselor can take an active role in preventing further injury and in altering the destructive patterns the couple exhibits. The counselor is to be diligent in anticipating chances for either the husband or the wife to redirect the conflict into another dimension. The counselor's ability to recognize and catch the shift will prevent the couple from exacerbating and deflecting their progress. Now that you know the goal, let's examine the process.

Therapeutic authority: Establishing control of words and actions. A few years ago, a Christian counselor sought consultation with Jim regarding a challenging couple. She said that a consistent pattern for the couple with whom she worked was to turn to rage when the conversation in therapy began to touch on the historical injuries. "We just can't get to talking about the things that brought them into therapy because one of them will become so mad that somebody will walk out."

The counselor was asked the rhetorical question, "Whose office is it?"

"Well, it's my office," came the obvious answer.

"If it is your office, then you set the rules, and you enforce the rules. Are their behaviors—verbal or physical—outside your bounds for acceptable behavior in your office? Would the couple act this way in church? What about in the waiting room of a doctor's office or in a restaurant? If the couple is becoming angry, provoking one or the other to pull the power plug on the session, then they are in control of the hour."

The first task to any conflict intervention is to be in charge of the room. By that you are committing to protecting both individuals from harm when they take the risk of repairing the relationship. The counselor's primary ethical obligation of "do no harm" is best fulfilled when you can ensure the protection of both the powerful and the underpowered from incidents of injury. From the beginning it is imperative that your first duty be to establish your authority as the marital counselor. Jim uses the following statement in the first session:

> You have come to me, a marital counselor, with the intent to improve the quality of intimacy that exists between you. Evidently there has been a pattern of injury demonstrated by both of you that brings you to this point. I work for both of you to accomplish that task, which means that at times I will try to block behaviors and words that I fear will have a detrimental effect on your goal of marital restoration. You can trust me to not sit passively and watch you destroy your marriage when you have enlisted my service to help you heal it. If there comes a point when your goal has changed, and you no longer want to restore and enhance this relationship, please let me know, for that will change the way that I act in providing marital counseling for you.

This step of establishing boundaries by the authority of the counselor is crucial to the therapeutic process. More often than not, counselors are skilled in being empathic and understanding, but they are not skilled in exercising their role of guardian and protector. Marriages thrive in environments of love and trust. Counselors must replicate both love and trust within the office. Love is experienced through empathy and understanding. Trust emerges with safety and authority. Teddy Roosevelt's principle "speak softly and carry a big stick" has application in settings beyond international diplomacy; it is important in marital diplomacy as well.

Multidirected partiality. Immediately tied to establishing the therapeutic role of authority is to establish the therapeutic role of counselor. Marital counseling involves a professional closeness that is difficult to define. We choose the word *mentor* to maintain the professional separation that exists between counselor and client, but we believe that marriage counseling involves a quality of professional intimacy that is not contained in the less personal terms of *patient* or *client*. The therapeutic relationship that a marital counselor develops with a couple exists in that sacred space between two lovers. It often includes the most personal and intimate of details, which include their spiritual, emotional, sexual and relational existence. Clergy functioning in the role of counselors will likely prefer the term *pastor* to describe their work—we identify closely with this role as Christian counselors but recognize the existence of a thicker boundary between the counselor and the couple. The boundary is defined by the counseling profession's code of ethics. The relationship is, at its core, an economic/service provider relationship rather than a ministerial relationship. This distinction has an effect on the manner in which Christian counselors can "pastor" couples with whom they work.

This pastoring role is articulated in Contextual Family Theory as "multidirected partiality." It means to show "understanding and crediting all relational parties for the different concerns, efforts and impacts for what people have done in relationships and what has been done to them."[2] In other words, counselors are to take sides, to mentor, to stand with and to identify. However, the idea of multidirected partiality is that the counselor shows partiality or preference to one spouse, and then focuses empathically toward the other. Both spouses are to experience the support and solidarity of the counselor even while they stand in opposition against each other.

There is a powerful message implied in the demonstration of multidirected partiality. Often there is a less-than-subtle message from both conflicting spouses that their intent is to recruit the counselor to join forces and "defeat the common enemy." In that effort both will present evidence to shore up their argument that it is the other person that is unreasonable, inconsiderate, disrespectful and/or downright mean. However, by demonstrating partiality—first to one, then to the other— the counselor is making a bold declaration: "I know of the faults, inadequacies, violations and mistakes that both of you are guilty of committing, but I stand with you in your effort to mature, grow and change as a person, spouse and parent." A second message is, "If I can like you, and like your spouse simultaneously, then you can too."

Multidirected partiality implies an important subtext. Caregivers must be careful of the trap of overempathizing with the injured spouse. As we will see in chapter eleven, this is particularly challenging when there is an identified wrongdoer—such as in marital infidelity. A crucial goal is to assist the couple in establishing mature boundaries that balance the power between the two. By overidentification with one partner, the counselor can accidentally reinforce power imbalances.

Separating the factors of conflict. Frequently in supervision, marital counselors say, "There was so many issues, so many fights, so many acts of disregard, it's hard to know where to start. And as soon as we start on one, we get yanked into talking about another." It is essential that the counselor separate the different factors in every conflict by distinguishing their presence in the relationship, and attend to each of them, one at a time. The counselor must be disciplined to maintain focus on the problem, respecting the fact that there will be a natural pull from both spouses to divert from the single purpose toward paying attention to multiple issues.

When the couple gains a "buy in" to the distinct presence of the present, historical and family-of-origin conflicts, it becomes easier to maintain focus with them. Part of the confidence that a couple develops in their counselor is found in the counselor's ability to recognize the diverting tactics that both will employ, and gently yet firmly block them, keeping the couple attentive to one detail at a time that they have prioritized. Table 2.1 is used to identify and organize the characteristics of the three issues.

Table 2.1

Present Conflict	Relational History Conflict	Family of Origin Conflict
"What is this fight about?"	"Have you been hurt before from this same issue?"	"As a child, what role did you play in your family that is like the current situation?"
His perspective:		
Her perspective:		

MEMBERS OF ONE BODY

Just about every child who watches cartoons knows something about the feud between the Hatfields and the McCoys. It's a story that is carved into the hills of Kentucky and West Virginia. In American folklore, no family conflict is as well known as theirs. It emerged after the Civil War and continued for fifty years. In the Warner Brothers rendition of the story, the fighting between the families continued for so long that the members forgot what they were fighting about. They just fought because "that's what the Hatfields do" and "that's what the McCoys do."

We find that marital conflicts are similar—the fighting continues because "that's what we do." When negative emotions are triggered—anxieties, discouragements and fears—husbands and wives respond to control, prevent and maintain. It is usually a thoughtless argument; that is, we engage in these arguments without much thinking. But it doesn't have to be that way. Couples come to us as counselors and pastors because they hope to learn a different way of doing life together. They seek to replace the automated responses of pain reaction, defensiveness and "do unto you before you do unto me" with an intimate, compassionate understanding.

In Colossians 3, Paul writes to couples, counselors and pastors about how we can heal from the wounds of our relational pain. His instruction is quite clear that we are to rid ourselves of anger, rage, malice, slander and filthy language. We are to be characterized by truthfulness as we become renewed and reformed into the image of our Creator. The vision of who we are to be as men and women in relationship is clear, and so is the outline for how we are to form this into reality. Paul writes in Colossians 3:15: "Let the peace of Christ rule in your hearts, *since as members of one body you were called to peace*" (NIV). In conflict resolution the important phrase is "as members of one body." To amplify Paul's meaning, the peace of Christ is nurtured and fostered through the proximity of intimate relationships—that is, through our "oneness." In marriage it is our Us, which will be the focus of the next chapter. The Us is the therapeutic tool that a marital counselor will use to bring healing to the injured souls. The science of therapy has demonstrated that "it's the relationship that heals, the relationship that heals, the relationship that heals—my professional rosary."[3] But the nature of the relationship, bordered by the security of grace, justice, trust and forgiveness, provides a potential quality that only exists in Christ. It is toward that end that you as the pastor or Christian counselor can guide couples as they understand their conflicts.

NOTES

[1]Worthington, E. L., Jr. (1999). *Hope-focused marriage counseling: A guide to brief therapy*. Downers Grove, IL: InterVarsity Press, p. 20.

[2]Hargrave, T. D., & Pfitzer, F. (2003). *The new contextual therapy*. New York: Brunner Routlege, p. 100.

[3]Raley, R. K., & Bumpass, L. (2003). The topography of the divorce plateau: Levels and trends in union stability in the United States after 1980. *Demographic Research, 8*, 245-60.

3

MARRIAGE IS AN *US*

*A good coach will make players see
what they can be rather than what they are.*

ARA PARASHEGHIAN

MARRIED FOR TWENTY-SEVEN YEARS and in their mid-fifties, Bruce and Gloria played tennis as their empty-nester pastime. Nathan and Joanna were their Sunday afternoon mixed doubles competition. They were in their late twenties and engaged to be married in six months. They were at the top of their game—tan, trim and in love. In warm-ups, their coordinated Fred Perry–designed tennis apparel, their smooth strokes and their comfortable movement on the court was a declaration of competitive domination. In contrast, Bruce and Gloria were okay. Slightly weighted with middle-aged tummies and too practical to sport the latest in gear and fashion, their play had to be slow but smart. In the end it was the young athletic couple that got schooled—in both tennis and in marriage.

How could age defeat virility on the tennis court? Bruce and Gloria knew how to play doubles tennis. Nathan and Joanna were stronger and more gifted as individual players, but they did not know how to play as a team. Bruce and Gloria played as an Us—adjusting to each other's position on the court. They identified open space and anticipated where their opponent was going to hit the ball. Alteration, compliment, coordination, adjustment and accommodation were how they played the game. Conversely, Nathan and Joanna played with power and aggression. They both could hit the ball very hard, but they did not work as a team, coordinating their strategy. Their objective was to hit the ball and hit it hard. They paid insufficient attention to position and court coverage. Deferring to the other was an afterthought. The result was that they overlapped their skills, leaving open spaces for Bruce and Gloria to loft their soft and spongy returns. By the middle of the first set, Nathan and Joanna were frustrated with one another. After they lost the second set, they were outright angry and embarrassed. Their emotion became directed at their teammate. Terse words followed failures or mistakes. Forced compliments followed successes and winning shots. There was no solace in their occasional winning points. They were defeated. The "intelligent Us" won over the "athletic Me."

UNDERSTANDING THE GAME

Nathan and Joanna epitomize a common problem among couples—they don't understand the game they are playing. If the tennis court is a platform for couples to exhibit their "real in life" strengths and weaknesses, Nathan and Joanna showed how intimate partners become intimate opponents. Competition is formed between the spouses rather than an alliance to stand together against external opponents. Marriage, like mixed doubles tennis, is a team sport. It requires the two individuals to think and act as a team. Marriage demands from couples the mentality of an Us in an environment that pulls them every day to think and act as a Me.

It is on this "court" that pastors and counselors do their most important work. Couples come to you as their marital coach with protective defenses raised high and offensive triggers held tensely at the ready. They are angry that they are not winning, and they think that it's because the other person has a kink in their skills. They don't arrive as an Us; they arrive as a "him against her." Their initial request in therapy is frequently the wrong, or at least shortsighted, request. They arrive wanting "the problem" to be fixed. The problem is usually defined as the fight, the source of frustration or even the affair—it is that thing that is infuriating, frustrating or fatiguing, that event or pattern that has caused such pain. Couples come to counseling wanting the pain to stop, and they usually visualize the pain as embodied in their spouse. It is true that unless those presenting problems, the "hot spots," are extinguished, the couple's capacity to build a stable and intimate marriage is seriously reduced. However, removing the current source of fuel and heat provides success for this fire season, but does not insure against the threat of future fires. Therefore a primary task for you as their coach is to break down their game to the essential components and help them rebuild it. This means that counselors must not only help them develop effective couple skills, but they must also help them develop couple understanding. Before couples can function effectively as a team, they need to value the game in which they are competing. They must comprehend their Us.

In this chapter we have two purposes: first, to convey the importance for pastors and counselors to serve as advocates for marital integrity; and second, once you have become an advocate for the marital Us, to prepare you to instruct, model and counsel couples in being successful in this endeavor. We consider these challenges as more difficult than they may initially sound. Regarding the first purpose, we find pastors and counselors who are active in Christian ministry or professional therapy to have underdeveloped understanding of the purpose and potential of marital intimacy. Most commonly this is manifested by the argument of what constitutes a "biblical marriage," and it consistently falls into either-or categories of complementarian or egalitarian role definitions. (In fact, many pastors and counselors will peruse this book to determine whether our view of marriage is consistent or inconsistent with theirs, and set our ideas aside if indeed we do not match up with views of marriage already established.)

To be clear regarding our agenda, we hold a conservative theology of marriage that includes a respect and support for traditional marital roles. Yet we also hold to a sociology that recognizes that the abuse of power by authority within the church and the home has led to a severe limitation of the utilization of gifts given by God to both men and women. Ultimately, we seek to bring the argument of what constitutes a biblical marriage beyond its definition of "who does what" to the qualities of Christian maturity and integrity.

BECOMING *US* IN A CULTURE OF *ME*

There is no topic that carries more confusion in the twenty-first century than that of marriage, and more challenge for the pastoral counselor or Christian professional counselor. It should be of no surprise that couples are frequently in conflict, for indeed our culture at large is in a severe conflict over defining, expressing and functioning in marriage. Cohabitation, civil unions, same-sex marriage and single parenthood have increased in frequency and acceptance within the culture as alternative relational structures that individuals select to meet their sexual and intimacy needs. The issues regarding how to be effective in a relationship can become lost by both counselor and couple because of this cultural ambiguity about what a relationship is. Confusion exists as to whether marriage is worth it in light of other options available to men and women in our culture.

In our consideration of marriage, we find that prevailing cultural attitude undermines the ability of couples to succeed in it. But to you as a pastor or marital counselor, this is not new information. The challenge for you is to be an effective change agent in encouraging a culture of marriage. We suggest that the place to start is to engage couples in conversation about the depth, width and breadth of their marriage. It is important to examine with them the assumptions and ground rules that they employ—often without forethought—in their day-to-day existence of marriage. David Blankenhorn suggests that this examination begins with consideration as to the significance of their marital vows. He notes that the meaning of marriage hinges on the couple's capacity to understand the vow. He argues that most couples in the United States see themselves as a couple prior to the vow. Marriage is not an external institution by which they are united; rather, they see themselves as "already together" as evidenced by their emotional bonds, shared domestic tasks, common interests and goals, current living arrangements, and sexual involvement. Marriage for most couples is based on the attachments formed by feelings and experiences. The vow of marriage is a public confirmation of that love affection and future intention of commitment. Whether stated or implied, these marriages are defined by the emotion of love and are held together "as long as our love shall last."[1]

An alternative is for couples to consider themselves an Us, beginning at the point of their vow. That is, when they take the oath of marriage, they move from the vantage point of Me to the perspective of Us. Clearly, couples exist through their emotional attachments and relational bonds prior to the wedding ceremony. Because of the preexisting relationship, it is easy to assume that a vow changes nothing. But for couples who understand the significance of the institution of marriage and the value of Us, the vow is what creates the couple and gives it membership in an institution, a tradition, a system and an entirely different way of being. Blankenhorn writes, "In a sense, the vow helps to create the couple. On their wedding day, couples become accountable to an ideal of marriage that is outside of them and bigger than they are."[2]

THE IDENTITY OF US

Constitutions define nations. They put forth a set of guiding principles and ideals that grant freedoms by defining restrictions. A law is some restriction on our behavior in order to protect those who do not have the power to protect themselves. In the same way, every couple operates with a "constitution." That is to say, there is a set of rules that define their Us. This identity is rarely discussed, and it is even more unusual for a couple to ever attempt to write it out. Though the Us identity is seldom articulated, however, it is always in operation.

The Bible informs us about the importance of Us. Adam and Eve were described as being "one flesh" in Genesis 2:24. Then both Jesus and Paul used the same phrase to describe marriage (Mk 10:8; 1 Cor 6:16; Eph 5:31). In the Adam and Eve story, one flesh was a literal phenomenon. But in the New Testament, and in our marriages, the concept of one flesh is a spiritual, psychological, emotional and relational truth. In healthy marriages the couple is knit together emotionally, psychologically, materially and spiritually. They are an Us. Relational researchers have identified this occurrence in couples. Social scientists call it "cognitive interdependence." Dutch scientists Johan Karremans and Paul Van Lange state that "previous research has shown that couples who perceive a relatively strong overlap between the self and the other are happier partners than those who perceive themselves as two separate persons. Moreover, there is research to show that the sense of 'we-ness' may promote various forms of pro-social behavior toward an interaction partner."[3] In fact, they found that couples who described themselves more frequently with the pronouns *us* and *we* would more likely be able to forgive and to experience relational closeness compared to couples who commonly used the pronouns *I, me* or *you* when talking about their relationship. Understanding the Us and building a mentality of one flesh is crucial in assisting couples in the management of their conflicts.

In the simplest way, we can think of an Us like the "apart" necklaces that lovers often wear as tokens of affection. A medallion representing the whole of the relationship is broken in two parts. With a jagged edge that corresponds only to the other, the two pieces are worn by lovers as a symbol of their Us—together in spite of the distance. A truer picture of real relationship is that both spouses enter marriage broken, and the breaks do not correspond to one another. Yet a couple matures by learning the nuances of each other's cracks and crevices. Throughout this book the Us will be visualized as a circle, consisting of two halves that correspond. In reality, the correspondence is not the perfect fit. But it is one that can be worn into fitting as time permits opportunity for growth and accommodation.

Figure 3.1. The Us: Two broken pieces forming a whole

ADDRESSING THE INTERNAL VALUES

Pastor Kevin understands the importance of Us, so he asks Mike and Nancy a peculiar set of questions. First, he asks, "Is your bucket big enough?" Then, "Does it leak?" Finally, he asks, "Are you sloppy?" They respond with a bewildered stare. He smiles and tells a story.

"Imagine the two of you are backpacking. Your campsite is on a hill. You must share the task of hauling water from a mountain creek up the path to your campsite. You have a five-gallon bucket that weighs about forty pounds when it's full. It is a difficult walk. There are a few places where the path is steep and that require extra care. You have learned that the most efficient way to get water up the hill is to carry the bucket together. As you are carrying the water, you notice that there is a slight crack in the bottom and the water is leaking. So you walk faster, spilling more of the water. When you reach the top of the hill, you discover that half of the water was lost. You both realize that you will need to work harder to get the water to the camp more quickly. But every time you use the bucket, the tear gets a little bit worse. And when you try to run up the hill, you are prone to slip and spill more of the water. Exhausted, frustrated and without good remedies, you both become critical of one another, prone now to arguing, bickering and blaming. This only compounds your anger. Isn't camping fun?"

Pastor Kevin continues, "Consider the bucket as the tool that holds the values, principles and priorities that define you two as a couple and as a family. The first was, How big is your bucket? The second question was, Does it leak? And the third was, Are you sloppy? I am talking in riddle and metaphor, so I need to be clear about what I mean. If you think of the bucket as the thing that contains the values, principles and priorities that guide your lives as persons and as a couple, you can ask, Is it big enough? Or, are you clear about your values and priorities, and have you made commitments as a couple that will carry you through the challenges you face in your circumstances?

"Second, if we have a bucket that is big enough but it leaks, it does us little good. So, if you have identified a set of rules but don't follow them, then your principles do you little good. It will be important to assess how you are doing at pursuing the essential principles that you hold as a couple.

"Finally, in carrying your bucket, each of you have slipped or stumbled. This means that you, by accident or by intention, have acted in ways that have caused you to spill some of the water needed for survival. So, it's important to consider how you are carrying the bucket as a team. Are you working together, or yanking on the handle trying to go in different directions, maybe even acting in ways that cause you to drop the precious, life-giving water?

"All three of these conditions—having a bucket that is too small, having a bucket that leaks, and being sloppy or careless—will leave you thirsty. Before we go forward, we all need to be clear about how you are able to work together in carrying your bucket up the hill."

Using this metaphor, Pastor Kevin teaches Mike and Nancy about how to identify the characteristics of marriage, their Us. Later it will be essential to unwrap the specific events that have caused each of them pain, all of the frustrations, conflicts and tensions that brought them in to see Pastor Kevin in the first place. Effective marital counseling needs to address the external problems and the internal values simultaneously. Our biblical text gives us a clear mandate as to how couples can best experience life: they are to become an "Us." The social science literature has uncovered how this Us—or, using their terminology, this cognitive interdependence—is nurtured and fostered in couples.

COMPONENTS OF A HEALTHY US

We recognize that probably all who are reading this chapter know on an intellectual level the magnitude of Us. We assume that you understand the importance of Us as the foundation for successful marriage. It is acutely obvious to everyone that relationships cannot be sustained in an environment of gluttonous selfishness. What is lacking among marital counselors, however, is the curriculum of value and practice to help couples elevate their Us to the place where they can administer healing to their marriage.

An Us consists of two components: the "Me" (individual identity) and the "You and Me Together" (relational identity). Both marital partners will have perspectives or mental frames to understand each of these components. We believe there are specific attributes and skills associated with the mentality of a healthy and mature Me and the mentality of a healthy and mature You and Me Together. When these mental frames held by the husband and wife are joined, they have an Us. The quality of the Us can be defined by the degree of maturity that each spouse possesses regarding their individual identity and their relational identity. Regarding these two parts, Terry Hargrave, author of *The Essential Humility of Marriage,* writes:

> "Us-ness" is the relationship. It transcends each person in the relationship, but depends on the individuals to keep it alive. It is the "us" that is the essential element in keeping marriage together, because, in fact, it is the only part of the spouses that is together. In family therapy theory we are taught a useful concept of individuation. Essential in this concept of individuation is the ability of a person to balance the drive between individuality and relationship, or individuation means that a person is able to be in a relationship and at the same time is secure in knowing that he or she is an individual.[4]

We will examine these two components—the individual identity and the relational identity—in greater detail. We will also provide ideas for how you as the counselor can enhance the Us by building up both the individual and the relational identity.

The individual identity. Clearly and correctly, the emphasis within the Christian tradition is to encourage the denial of self for the fulfillment of the Us. But this emphasis can be easily misconstrued to wrongly suggest that our individuality in marriage is usurped or erased. Frequently in the Christian subculture we espouse an ideal of selfless marriage. This is well-intentioned in that it seeks to place value on the importance of sacrifice and giving to the other, yet in so doing, we can unintentionally negate an essential component of relational intimacy. We argue here that when the Me, the individual identity, is not effectively regarded, the capacity to serve the Us becomes undermined.

The biblical instruction is to love your spouse as more than yourself (Eph 5:21-30; Phil 2:3-4). This means that one's partner is to be so cherished that one is to serve the other above serving oneself. If this is true, then both selves carry value and are worthy of elevation. And if both selves are worthy of elevation, it is essential that both selves are able to understand their needs and communicate them to the other person so that the other can fulfill their mission of service.

Now consider the potential illogic of the ideal of selfless marriage. If individuals in the marriage are not able to understand, communicate and recognize the unique identities of each member and direct their self-denial toward enhancing the individuality of the other, then efforts at self-denial will likely be misunderstood as self-enhancement under the guise of sacrificial love. If one cannot or does not express will, opinion, interests, wants and values to the other, then the other is left to determine what those needs and wants are and make decisions accordingly. In essence, one is loving the other as one would want to be loved, not loving the other as the other would want.

To illustrate this idea, let's imagine that a wife wants to do something special for her husband. She purchases very expensive tickets to an event and gives them to her husband as a surprise. But the concert is jazz fusion—and he has absolutely no interest in that style. The sacrificial act of purchasing the tickets would not build the strength of the Us because it would not enhance the individual identity of the other. If the husband doesn't like jazz, it's hardly a selfless act to offer that gift— even if the tickets were $125 apiece. Each person must be able to know their own musical tastes, communicate what those tastes are and recognize the communicated tastes that the partner has articulated. At some point, the husband must recognize and communicate with his wife that he likes bluegrass and that he would like to attend bluegrass performances. This is not an act of selfishness; it is an act of self-awareness, and that awareness is communicated to one's lifetime lover so that he or she could demonstrate selflessness by attending to the needs and wants that are identified and expressed. A healthy Us is dependent upon individuals who possess insight into their own character and can communicate that insight so that the other may serve them sacrificially.

Selflessness or valuing the other as more important than yourself must be preceded by a knowledge of the other's individuality and their knowledge of yours. Couples must know the structures of individual character, personality strengths, history, defenses, motivations, coping patterns and life goals so as to be sacrificial in the right direction. This means that at the core of Us is a mutual understanding of both persons.

The knowledge of self as the basis for Us is an entirely biblical theme. Throughout the Old and New Testaments, the biblical characters are encouraged to "examine themselves" (Lam 3:40; 2 Cor 13:5). The danger of self-assessment is that it can lead to self-worship. Instead, self-knowledge is for the purpose of effective service, or in the case of a marital relationship, being able to communicate how another might exercise his or her gifts of service in an effective manner. The give and take of relationship requires that each self be known so that the loving life partner might be knowledgeably informed as to how he or she can exercise love.

Building individual identity. Individual identity is something that must be accepted for what it is and simultaneously encouraged to grow, mature and develop. We have found that identity can be examined and supported as well as nurtured to grow by using a technique drawn from Objection Relations Family Therapy (ORFT) called "projective identification." ORFT is a psychodynamic approach asserting that the core search in our individuality is to seek validation through our relationships by our actions. This means that individuals act in the relationship in ways that are designed to evoke the kind of messages needed to confirm worth and legitimacy. If the actions don't produce the desired or needed result, confusion, tension and conflict will follow.

The intervention consists of three parts. The first is to identify how the individual defines his or her identity through projections. This means that the counselor listens to the person's explanation of need. While listening, the counselor is asking, "What is the response that this person is evoking from me and from others?" Second, once the projection is identified, the counselor can provide whatever is being sought by the individual—encouragement, discipline, affirmation or empathy, for example. Third, after the projection is supported, the counselor is in a position to describe the projection that the person is requesting and inquire as to the limitations and frustrations that are experienced when the projection is achieved. The intervention assumes that the response being sought is both essential and insufficient to meet the emotional needs of the individual. With this realization the individual can work with the counselor and the Us to build individuation strengths.

This individualization intervention can be seen in Dr. Tom's work with Toni and Mark, who have been married for thirty years. Their two children are adults, married and launched into their life trajectory. Now it's just Toni and Mark. They are happy to be together. Their life as a couple has been relationally rich. But they find themselves confused about who they are and what they are to do. This is especially true for Toni.

"I just don't know what to do with myself," she tells the counselor with her husband present. "I have worked all of my life, and I continue to do so, but clearly my life wasn't about work. That was just to help pay the bills. When my daughter got married sixteen months ago I thought, Okay Toni, for twenty-six years you have been a mom—that was your main thing. And I still am a mom and now a grandma, but I am not needed in the same way. . . . So I guess I don't really know who I am anymore."

Mark joins in by saying, "Toni is the person who would never do anything for herself but would live sacrificially for me and our kids. But not just our kids—for our kids' friends and for anyone they would bring in the door. She is the kind of person that when the kids would buy her a Mother's Day gift that was too small or too large, she would return it to the store and buy a new pair of shoes or a new coat . . . for one of the kids. She would say that she has plenty and that someone else needs this or that more. I think that when the kids left, a major mission in her life ended. Me, I know it's different, but I just don't think about it as much as she does. So when there is just me in the house, it produces a pretty big empty space for her."

Imbedded in these words, and in the words of every couple seen by a marital counselor or pastor, are the words of individual identity. In defining how an individual defines his or her identity, it becomes obvious how the counselor and the Us can work to build individual identity. Consider how Dr. Tom responds:

"Mark and Toni, I hear important expressions from both of you as to how you have adjusted to the change in your home. Toni, your identity, the way that God made you to confirm your importance is to give to others. You have a legacy of giving selflessly to your husband, your children, and it sounds like to almost anything that breathes."

Toni responds, "We haven't even begun to share the stories of homeless cats, birds with broken wings . . . but I do have my limits—I hate bugs! But it's true, I do take great joy in giving to others."

Dr. Tom continues, "Toni, it is obvious to you and Mark, and now to me as you tell me your story, that you ache from not having others to whom you can demonstrate your capacity to love. The simple solution that I say with tongue in cheek is to get a puppy, or teach a children's Sunday school class, or find others who will need you. But I think that you know how to do that already, and that you and Mark are seeking things beyond the band-aid solutions. And Mark, I hear in your story the complement to Toni's. Just as she wears her heart on her sleeve—showing her loss to all who care to see—you are able to not be affected by these losses in the same way. You can turn off that switch and just stay focused on the immediate. In this case it is to still get up every morning and go to work. Come home every night and take care of all of your 'got to's.' You know, got to pay the bills, got to take out the trash, got to clean the rain gutters."

Mark smiles. "That sums it up pretty close. It's true that I don't get caught in thinking too much about my kids and the empty house. It's there, it is pretty quiet. I just try to stay busy."

In this conversation, Dr. Tom works with both Toni and Mark to identify their projections—each are inducing their counselor and everyone else with whom they might converse to support their strengths. For Toni it is, "Affirm me as a caregiver." For Mark it is, "Affirm me for my resilience." To both, Dr. Tom fulfills the implied request—to affirm their needs. But he also describes that type of affirmation that they are seeking. Next he will shift to understand the limitation that each of them experiences through their current identities, and then utilize the power of familial community to build the identity of each.

Dr. Tom continues, "Toni and Mark, I wonder if with all of the benefits and strengths that each of your abilities offer—Toni, you as the caregiver; Mark, you as the stalwart supporter—if there are not some difficulties, challenges or limitations that come with who you are. I mean to say because you are good at doing one thing, it leaves you not as good at doing something else."

Mark jumps in first. "I see that with me. I really love my kids. And I really miss them. But my relationship with them is different than Toni's. I am who they call when they have a question about buying new tires or whether it's time to ask their boss for a raise. I am not the one that they call just to say what is going on, like hey, what's up? I see Toni being able to do that and she is really good at it. I am not as good. If they did call I would probably just say something stupid like, Oh, not much . . ."

"Toni, what about you?"

"I think mine is pretty obvious. I mean, it's what we came here to talk about. I am so invested in others that I don't know who I really am, I guess, as a person. I think I am a good wife, a good parent and mother-in-law, a good neighbor, worker and friend. But all of those things are things that I do for other people. I don't really know what I want, even though I am pretty good at helping people understand what *they* want."

The essence of individual identity development is to build the Us by encouraging maturation in the two intimate life partners. In this case, Dr. Tom is seeking to grow a dimension of each personality by recognizing their strengths, identifying the complement of that strength, and offering it back to them in the form of a new opportunity for growth. In this case, both Toni and Mark are in a position to develop new vistas in their Us as they grow in their individual identities. Mark and Toni can now use their Us to help him become more able to be an emotional caregiver, beyond his effective problem-solver identity; and to help her become more able to define herself beyond the successful "nurse, teacher and den-mother" identity that she has developed up until now. They are in a position to utilize the power of their familial community to further enhance their individual identities.

The relational identity. A great paradox is central to marital health— spouses are whole beings while at the same time a component of a greater whole. Though cultures vary in the emphasis and value placed on the individual versus the group, the fact remains that in all cultures intimate life partners are both independent individuals and dependent family members at the same time. An essential Us skill is the capacity to be communally connected, to be a part of something greater than oneself. When there is a relational mentality, the "ME" is reduced to a "me." It isn't suppressed, squelched or disregarded. It is voluntarily placed aside in order to participate in a greater good. The couple with a relational mentality thinks and behaves like a member of a drama troupe or athletic team in which there are no small parts or bit players. Everyone plays a differing role. A person with honed relational skills is capable of setting aside his or her own interests and pursuing the interests of another.

Many scientific studies have addressed where relationships are centered, or the qualities around which people in marriage relate. Some of the most common conclusions are lifetime commitments, loyalty to one another, shared moral values, respect and friendship of spouse, sexual faithfulness, shared parental commitment, shared faith in God, mindset toward seeking forgiveness and being forgiven.[5]

Rosen-Granden, Myers and Hattie[6] offer a valuable contribution to our understanding of marital satisfaction. Using an advanced statistical tool called "structural equation modeling," they surveyed nearly one thousand marital partners. They found, as would be expected, that qualities such as respect, forgiveness, romance, support and sensitivity were essential components to a marriage characterized by couples as being loving. However, it appeared that just being successful in those categories was not sufficient. They found that all of the "Loving Variables" had to pass through another set of qualities, which they labeled "Loyalty Variables." They found that

> relationships in which loyalty relationships is important are those in which devotion to one's spouse is viewed as a priority regardless of sexual activity and despite possible disagreements about the expression of affection. It is interesting that the most important characteristics of what we have called loyal relationships . . . were: lifetime commitment to marriage, loyalty to one's spouse and strong moral values.

Furthermore, these researchers found that it doesn't appear to mat-

ter about the style or the roles that are characterized by the relationship—traditional or nontraditional. Rather, they found that when a
couple was satisfied with the degree of loyalty or commitment in the
relationship, the couple would likely be satisfied. This characteristic of
relationship is more important than whether the couple performs their
roles "right"; it's more important than if the wife is a stay-at-home
mom, totally dedicated to the family's success; it's more important
than measuring a marriage by great sex, great incomes, great vacations
or a great house. Great relationships are best predicted by great loyalty
and great commitment.

Building relational identity. Relational people are dependent and
needy. Many may cringe at the thought because it runs contrary to our
culture-laden values such as independence, freedom and self-sufficiency.
People don't usually seek to be needy; we seek to become needless. How
often are these words spoken by those in the advanced stages of life: "I
just don't want to be a burden on anyone"? But marriage is a declaration
of need. To be married is to acknowledge that one has psychological,
emotional, material, spiritual, social and existential needs that are in
part fulfilled through the formation of intimacy in lifelong partnership.
To be married is to exercise the give and take of being sufficient for
another and permitting another to be sufficient for you.

When we consider what can aid couples in building their relational
identity, we come full circle to the core of orthodox Christian theology—sin and redemption. The faith system of those who follow after
Jesus is centered on need and dependence. The condition of sinfulness
and the impossibility of its eradication by any good work make Christians dependent on God. In the same way, the cultures that have a high
regard of relationship are also the cultures that have been shaped by the
high need for interdependence and interreliance. John Newton's testi-
mony "I am a great sinner. Christ is a great Savior," and Paul's confession "It is a trustworthy statement, deserving full acceptance, that
Christ Jesus came into the world to save sinners, among whom I am
foremost of all" (1 Tim 1:15 NASB) are the theological parallels to the
marital demand of being humbly dependent and serving as agents of
grace to one another. We want to emphasize that we find a parallel

between our dependence on Christ for salvation and our dependence on our spouses to manifest grace within the marital Us. Marriage does not save us; rather, the attitude and action of being dependent on God and receiving his grace is similar to the attitude and action required of couples who seek to establish and nurture their intimate Us.

Peter was smart, talented, respected and needless. A gifted musician, he wrote and performed songs that are heard daily on every country music station. In music he had flair, style, intellect and depth. He had everything except a successful marriage. Peter was married to Cyndi, whom he met and married after college. Two children joined the family, three and five years into their relationship. They moved to Nashville, a requirement for any country music star, but to do so they had to separate from all that had centered them—their home, neighborhood, church, friends, small group and extended family, which consisted of both parents and six sets of aunts, uncles and cousins.

As expected, the move was great for Peter's career but devastating for the family. Untied from the relationships that anchored their lives as a married couple, Cyndi and Peter soon found that they were lost—not geographically, but relationally. The high-speed Nashville culture wanted Peter and Cyndi for the notoriety they could achieve by being around the rich and famous. Peter called a counselor whom he and Cyndi had worked with earlier in their marriage. He asked Dr. Chris, "We know you and respect you. Can we fly up to see you every couple of months for an extended session? If we can't come, I don't think our marriage will make it." Dr. Chris agreed, and they scheduled the first session. During that four-hour marathon meeting on a Saturday afternoon, two things became obvious to Dr. Chris. First, Peter and Cyndi were extremely lonely and longed for intimate connection. They were like a boat bouncing in rough waters looking for a safe harbor and a sturdy dock to tie up to. Second, they were failing at being needy to and for one another. Cyndi was able to articulate her feelings most clearly:

"I have lost two things in this move. First, I lost connection with the people who know me and sustained me daily. Second, and most importantly, I have lost you. You intend to do right, but I think that you are overwhelmed with the pressures of your career. You can't be there for me. I think that you have nothing left. What hurts or scares me the most is I don't see you being able to use me. I know that you love me—like, you have a lot of affection—but I don't see you able to be loved by me, to have emotional needs that I can care for. We are just doing our duties—you with your work, me with the girls. We are cordial, cooperative and nice. But we don't soothe one another. We aren't that close anymore."

Cyndi's appeal and confession set the tone for the extended session. The working task became, "How do we build the relationship to include our respective neediness?" Knowing that Peter grew up in a family of alcoholics and that he watched both the devastation and the reconciliation of family, Dr. Chris asked him about the parallels between his family story and his current story.

> Dr. Chris: Peter, do you remember the first step in the AA Twelve Step program?
>
> Peter: I know it like the alphabet. Step 1—We admitted we were powerless over alcohol—that our lives had become unmanageable.
>
> Dr. Chris: Is there a common thread between all that is happening in your family now, and what your parents learned about themselves when they went into recovery?
>
> Peter: *Recovery.* There is a word that I hadn't thought about in terms of me. It was always about them. Well, if you mean, "Do I have the attributes of a 'dry-drunk'?" I guess that I would have to say I do. If I bury myself in my work—the work of being creative—then maybe I wouldn't have to remember or feel or face stuff.
>
> Dr. Chris: You guys are on your way to learning something, and if you get it, it doesn't matter if you live in Nashville, Hollywood, Nairobi or Springfield. The reason I bring up the AA model is first, you are familiar with it. Second, it is similar to a need that both of you exhibit. When substance abusers come to AA, they are at the end of their rope. They have tried everything they could to cope with life evasively, dishonestly, indirectly or with avoidance . . . and have failed. When they realize that they are stuck, they must become honest with themselves,

even brutally honest in a way that causes pain, in order to become healed, restored and whole.

Peter: I think I have made a few connections. Cyndi, in the last six months I have lost focus on the Us—particularly I have not attended to letting you care for me. I have let the cancer of the "Big Time" steal away being with you. I want to do better . . . no, I want to do different.

Cyndi and Peter were back on track. They renewed their focus in being relationally oriented. They finished the session discussing the metaphor "Who's got your back?" meaning, each talked about the threats and fears that they each possessed and what the other could do to bring empathy, aid and assistance.

THE US: IN CONCLUSION AND INAUGURATION

In this case, the conclusion is the beginning. In a very simplistic sense, we see the process of counseling as starting with insight into how a problem will be solved rather than how a problem has begun. We suggest that you don't start with the conflict, but focus on the resources contained in their Us. We want couples to possess an image of relationship, of intimacy and of marriage at the "ideal" level because that is the target toward which we want couples to take aim. We as marital counselors serve as target coaches, helping marital teams reach their goals through understanding the nature of conflict that impedes or interferes with what they are trying to become. It will be through the focus on the target, the Us, that the challenges faced by intimate teams can be addressed. The Us is the working agent. It is not through you as the counselor or pastor that the restoring work of God in the lives of the couple is accomplished; it is through their Us. Counselors help couples position themselves and help them determine how to go through the steps to enhance individual identity and build a relational mentality. But the couples do work and reap the benefit.

NOTES

[1]Blankenhorn, D. (2007). *The future of marriage.* New York: Encounter Books, pp. 18-19.
[2]Ibid., p. 18.

[3]Karremans, J. C., Van Lange, P. A. M., Ouwerkerk, J. W., & Kluwer, E.S. (2003) When forgiving enhances psychological wellbeing: The role of interpersonal commitment. *Journal of Personality and Social Psychology, 84*, 1011.

[4]Hargrave, T. D. (2000). *The essential humility of marriage: Honoring the third identity in couples therapy.* Phoenix: Zeig, Tucker & Theisen, p. 7.

[5]See, for example, Baumeister, R. F., & Leary, M. R. (1995). The need to belong: Desire for interpersonal attachment as a fundamental human motivation. *Psychological Bulletin, 117*, 497-529; McCullough, M. E., Worthington, E. L., Jr., & Rachal, K. C. (1997). Interpersonal forgiving in close relationships. *Journal of Personality and Social Psychology, 73*, 321-36; and Myers, D. G. (2000). The funds, friends, and faith of happy people. *American Psychologist, 55*, 56-67.

[6]Rosen-Granden, J. R., Myers, J. E., & Hattie, J. A. (2004). The relationship between marital characteristics, marital interaction processes, and marital satisfaction. *Journal of Counseling and Development, 82*, 58-68.

4

PASTORAL AND COUNSELING BOUNDARIES

INVESTED BUT NOT OVERINVOLVED

This is what marriage really means:
helping one another to reach the full status of being persons,
responsible beings who do not run away from life.

PAUL TOURNIER

GERALD IS ON THE PASTORAL STAFF of a church that has grown tremendously in the past four years. He is involved in a lot of event planning, as well as curriculum development for Christian education programs. Gerald also provides a lot of pastoral counsel. In fact, when he recalls the last six couples he's met with, he knows two couples from his previous small group, one couple from his current small group, and three couples in which he knows either the husband or wife from various ministries or retreats, such as the parking crew, ushering ministry and fall men's retreat.

Recently he has worked with a couple that is struggling in their marriage. Gerald and his wife have known them for many years, as this couple had been a part of the small group they led earlier. Although they have not done a lot with them socially, they definitely know each other, have prayed for each other and have a good, friendly relationship.

The wife in the couple reminds Gerald of his sister, and some of the concerns she has raised about her husband's work schedule are reminiscent of what his sister has said to him about her husband. But Gerald also feels somewhat protective of the husband in the marriage. He knows that the man works at a demanding job for a difficult boss. He puts in long days, week after week, and that can be a grind for anyone in that situation, especially if there doesn't seem to be much appreciation for what he does.

When Gerald meets with the couple, both the husband and the wife make their case.

"He's up and out the door by 7 in the morning. And he's not home until 7 at night. I understand that," says Carla. "He's got to do his work. But on the weekend that's another thing. He has no reason to get together with the boys every Friday. Those days are done. We're married, and I don't know where he got the idea that he was going to keep that up. I know you're home on the weekends, Pastor. I talked to your wife just a week ago, and she said you guys set aside time as a couple, take your 'date night' and all of that. So you can understand what I'm saying."

Antonio jumps in. "Wait a minute. What are you saying? I can't get together with the guys anymore? I know I didn't sign up for that. We are just talking about blowing off steam at the end of a long week. You said it yourself—I've got to do my work, and I work a long day. The last thing we are going to start talking about is how I need to sit home and watch TV if I'd rather watch the game with the guys. Besides, you never said anything when we were dating. Why is it such a big deal now that we're married?" Antonio looks to Gerald. "You know what I'm saying, right?"

The discussion continues for almost ninety minutes. Carla looks at her watch and says, "We have got to get home. My mother can only watch the kids until dinner, and she's got other plans tonight." She turns to Gerald. "Gerry, let your wife know I am going to give her a call. I've missed talking to her, and it is time we caught up anyway. We should get together with you guys, too. Maybe the four of us can go out to dinner—sound good?"

Antonio stands up and shakes Gerald's hand. "Thanks, man. I appreciate it. Maybe we should catch a game some night, too. You're not a Celtics fan, are you? Just kidding. We'll do something fun."

One of the most important lessons pastors and counselors can learn is where couples end and where the counselor begins. We are talking in this chapter about the role, responsibility and boundaries of pastors and counselors working with couples.

How is this pastoral counseling role different from professional counseling? We believe that the boundaries in pastoral care and lay counseling relationships tend to get blurry. Furthermore, pastoral counselors are more likely than professional counselors to have multiple relationships and to relate with couples on multiple levels even outside of their counseling role. Of course, by saying this, we also think there is a greater risk for burnout than with the more rigid boundaries found in professional counseling relationships.

Is it wrong to have more blurred boundaries when providing pastoral care? Is it wrong to be in the multiple relationships that so often characterize pastoral care and lay counseling in the church? We say, No, it isn't wrong; in fact, it may be beneficial to the couples to whom you provide care. But the potential benefits come with an understanding of the unique opportunities in pastoral care, as well as an awareness of how to achieve balance in setting and maintaining more flexible boundaries.

So we turn our attention to the symbolic boundaries that often define a professional relationship and how those might be different for the pastoral care provider or lay counselor. By symbolic boundaries we are referring to limits placed on the relationship that make it a helping relationship (professional or pastoral) and not a friendship. This will bring up a discussion of the unique opportunities in pastoral care. We will then shift our attention to how to manage boundaries around couples' conflicts.

PROFESSIONAL VERSUS PASTORAL BOUNDARIES

It may be helpful to reflect on specific boundaries and symbols of boundaries.[1] What we mean by symbols of boundaries is that pastoral care, lay counseling and professional counseling possess significant differences in the boundary around the helping relationship. There are benefits with each approach, depending on the context of the couple.

For example, a professional counselor typically meets with a couple at an office, and so *location* becomes an important symbolic boundary of the professional relationship. They don't typically meet in someone's home or other settings, although there are exceptions to this of course. In contrast, a pastoral counselor or lay counselor may meet with someone from the congregation with whom they have an ongoing relationship. They are more likely to see people in other settings, such as visiting with a couple in the ICU or visiting someone in jail. House visits are also not uncommon for many pastors.

Think about your own practice of pastoral care or lay counseling. If the normal routine and expectation is to meet in a church office, then departures from the normal routine should be looked at so that the normal boundary remains in effect.

The *role* is also different between the pastoral and professional counselor. Professional counselors will provide help for about twelve sessions, over an average span of three months; pastors may have a couple for three years, or five years, or ten years or more. Those in the ministerial role will have a much more significant impact with a couple over time. Professional counseling may provide the much-needed input, structure or program, but it is worked out by the couple in their lives, versus being part of their lives over time. With Christian counseling, these lines can become blurred—"Is it professional, is it pastoral?" One has to ask whether what they are doing is what a professional counselor does, because a professional counselor has a more prescribed role in the life of that couple. So when professional counselors are asked to go out for coffee, they decline. When they are asked to help a couple move, they decline. When they are asked to attend a graduation or a funeral, they usually decline.

While the role of the professional counselor may be more prescribed, the role of the pastoral counselor or lay counselor can be much broader, as your lives intersect with the couples you know over the course of your lives together in Christian community. This can be tremendously helpful for a couple you get to know well, but it can also be emotionally draining over time.

A similar boundary is that of *time*. In the professional counselor role, there is a standard time for beginning and ending the counseling session. Professional counselors limit themselves to the time that is standard for other counselors—typically a fifty-minute session, weekly. This is a boundary. When they go over that time, the decision to extend beyond the normal boundary provides an opportunity for reflection and scrutiny.

Some pastoral and lay counselors practice within a similar, established routine. It becomes their professional boundary, and when they go beyond that, they evaluate the decision to do so.

Related to length of counseling or pastoral care is the *times of day* that care is provided, including the use of late-hour times. Professional counselors are to scrutinize the use of late-hour times to be sure that they are not placing themselves or their clients in a vulnerable spot. Pastoral counselors and lay counselors can ask a similar question, as this is yet another symbolic boundary. At the same time, there is often greater variability in pastoral care.

Do you receive any remuneration for your pastoral care or lay counseling? For professional counselors, money defines the nature of the professional relationship. It can be quite different with pastoral care and lay counseling. Do people provide a donation? Is it free? *Money and gifts* are another form of a boundary. If you normally receive some remuneration but in one case you waive it, you have an opportunity to reflect on why in this case you are making an exception. Some people offer gifts to a lay counselor or pastor. How will you respond to this? Do you receive gifts? If you've been invited to a baby shower or a wedding of someone you provide care to, do you send them a card or a gift? Do you attend?

In general, it is much more likely for the pastoral care provider or lay counselor to attend these kinds of life events, such as a baby shower or wedding, and to send cards or gifts, although it depends largely on the pastoral care setting and expectations in that context.

Clothing or other things you might wear is also a boundary. This is especially true for the professional counselor who wants to convey a certain kind of professionalism in his or her choice of clothing.

Dressing too casually could convey a different kind of relationship or familiarity. Dressing inappropriately or too seductively is also sending the wrong message. Pastoral care and lay counselors can similarly reflect on clothing as a boundary, although they are more likely to "be themselves" throughout their relationships with couples in the church over time.

Another symbolic boundary is *language*, particularly that of names or designations. How do you have people refer to you in your role as a pastoral counselor or lay counselor? Many professional counselors prefer a more formal designation, as it conveys a boundary and the nature of the professional relationship.

How about you? Do you prefer to use your first name? Many pastoral and lay counselors have this preference. It can be more intimate and informal. The potential downside is that people may slip into the perception that it is more of a social relationship. In these cases, it is important to attend to the other boundary symbols. Others might use "Pastor Gerald" as their designation. This can help with the boundary but can be experienced by the couple as more formal or distant.

Self-disclosure is another boundary. Some professional counselors illustrate a point by talking about themselves, but they are generally trained to refrain from doing so, or to do it only under certain circumstances, recognizing that it is a boundary. If they are married, they might share an anecdote from their marriage to help a couple. Self-disclosure, though, is an act of intimacy that can lead to professional counseling being more about the counselor and what you have to share than about the couple and what they are working on together.

Pastoral care and lay counseling are more likely to employ self-disclosure almost by default. As you spend time with couples in church, as you and your own family are known by those in your church community, they will observe your interactions and draw conclusions. These conclusions may or may not come up in pastoral care or lay counseling sessions, but you will want to be aware of the challenges of living in a "glass bubble," if you will.

The last symbolic boundary is that of *physical contact*. When professional counselors receive their training, they are taught that it is wise to reflect on or scrutinize any physical contact beyond that of a hand-shake. Even hugs can mean one thing to the person giving the hug and another thing to the person receiving the hug.

Pastoral care and lay counselors are more likely to have opportunities for physical contact such as hugs. These can also be scrutinized, as a hug can be interpreted differently by the giver and receiver, just as in a professional relationship. But because of the differences we've already cited—differences in location and role, for instance—there may be occasions in which a supportive hug is appropriate.

UNIQUE OPPORTUNITIES IN PASTORAL CARE

We can see from the previous section that there are a number of aspects to pastoral care and lay counseling that may not be typical of professional counseling. What unique opportunities does this present in pastoral care that make it a different experience from what we see in professional counseling?

Pastoral care offers the opportunity to see facets of a couple that may not be seen by a professional counselor. You see, a professional counselor is limited in practice to a fifty-minute hour once a week. As we said in the previous section, that is their role. But the pastoral role may extend far beyond that, and we think that can be healthy for the couple. Pastors have the opportunity to be truly steeped in their lives. They may provide premarital services like a professional counselor, but then actually attend their wedding as a member of the community. A pastor may meet with a couple as they transition to having children, just like a professional counselor, but then might actually attend or participate in their child's baptism or dedication ceremony. A pastor could work with a couple with teens just like a professional counselor, but might also have his or her kids in youth group with the couple's kids, and may officiate or be witness to their confirmation or adult baptism. Pastors and lay counselors are steeped in the life of the couple in ways that professional counselors are not.

Pastors have the advantage of seeing facets of a couple over time. Of course, a pastor or lay counselor may function much like a professional counselor in his or her role, and we understand there is a great deal of diversity in how pastoral care providers and lay counselors function in their communities. Let's examine two different approaches.

Pastoral care/lay counselor A. This counselor meets with couples in her office at the church. She meets on the hour for about forty-five to fifty minutes. There is a nominal fee associated with the counseling services, and couples pay when they first come in for a session. This counselor goes by her last name, so she is referred to as Mrs. Jefferson. She keeps session notes in a locked file cabinet and meets regularly with a licensed counselor for supervision. She has a therapist disclosure form that all couples read, introducing them to her approach to counseling, her fee structure, cancellation policy and her policy regarding confidentiality. She addresses with the couple how they would like to handle times when they might see each other at church or in the community—do they want her to acknowledge them or would they prefer not to have any contact? Church policy limits them to eight sessions together, which could be extended by written request if necessary. They each sign informed consent forms and release of information forms so that information obtained in their individual meetings can be discussed freely. She informs them that due to the nature of the counseling relationship, they would not be in a small group together—that she does not see people who are in her small group and that she asks those she meets with in counseling to participate in other small groups.

Pastoral care/lay counselor B. This counselor meets with couples in their homes or at the church. He has also been known to meet with couples at the hospital in emergencies or to visit a couple during times of serious illness. He has met with couples from the small group he is in, and he has had couples he's met with previously join the small group he's been in for years. When he meets with a couple, he talks about their concerns but is able to place them in the context of the relationship he's had with them and their extended family for years now. He has seen their children baptized and has served on the parking lot ministry team with the husband. His wife knows the wife in the marriage and has been on a couple of women's retreats with her. When he meets with couples, he goes by his first name and lets them know that his door is "always open," in the sense that they do not have to set weekly sessions that begin and end in a time-limited format. Rather, he is available to them at this time, which can be more formal, but he is also a part of their lives—he has been and will continue to be far beyond the present issues that bring them in for a more focused pastoral discussion.

These are two ways in which pastoral care or lay counselors might relate to a couple. They are more at the extremes of emulating professional boundaries versus expanding those boundaries for more of a life course in ongoing pastoral relevance. By sharing these two cases, we want to illustrate the idea that care providers will each approach their role quite differently. Some require more professional boundaries, while other circumstances will lend themselves to a more expanded role that is characterized by more diffused boundaries and multiple roles.

We turn our attention now to the boundaries in relationships that often characterize professional counseling. We discuss the boundaries that can be identified for professional roles as well as ways in which they can be adapted for pastoral care and lay counseling under certain circumstances.

UNIQUE RELATIONAL BOUNDARY CONCERNS IN PASTORAL CARE

There are many ways in which pastoral care and lay counselors can be in multiple roles with the people under their care. We've mentioned being in a small group together, participating in church retreats, attending specific men's or women's gatherings, serving together in another ministry such as ushering, traffic and Christian education, as well as having their children go through classes or events together with the children of other couples in the church.

We want to recognize that there are risks when forming multiple relationships. Some people cross the line and can do harm to those under their care. It is possible not to be sufficiently trained as a pastoral care or lay counselor to navigate the boundaries we have been discussing. This is also a process. We learn over time how to do some of this. So sometimes people who are new to the role may not yet have a clear pastoral or lay counseling identity, may not have received sufficient training in this area, or may not have had good models of how to navigate boundaries.

Probably the greatest risk concerns not having good personal boundaries. This can come from a number of sources, and it is something that every pastoral counselor or lay counselor should consider. The danger here is that personal boundaries become diffused especially when counseling couples with psychological stress or low levels of maturity, and these are often the people who come to the pastor or counselor for assistance. When the counselor's boundaries are vague, he or she fails to model mature distinction of responsibility. Instead, the counselor gets pulled into the problem rather than acting as an objective source for insight out of the problem.

On the other hand, it is also possible to have good personal boundaries while providing ministry to couples who do not have clear boundaries. Sometimes poor boundaries are a result of their own history. Maybe you are working with a couple in which one spouse has suffered from a history of boundary violations. When early needs go unmet, it is possible for one or both partners to look to a pastor or lay counselor to meet those needs.

The important thing here is to set limits and to do so constructively. The way to do this is to distinguish between *what they need* and *what they are asking for*—these are often not the same thing.

For example, a couple with young children may need help with childcare while they both work or travel. But if they ask for you to take their kids to school and pick them up each day for the next two weeks, this may be beyond your role and what is best for them in terms of taking responsibility for their circumstances and the needs of their family.

There is also just the reality of being in relationship with those to whom you provide care or counsel. This is something that professional counselors avoid, but it may be much more difficult for the pastor or lay counselor. Indeed, there may be untapped elements of healing and restoration to be found in these relationships if they are navigated properly.

When is a friendship appropriate? It is important to reflect on the level of influence in the relationship, as well as the length of time in counseling or care. By virtue of providing pastoral care or lay counseling, there is a difference in influence from that of a professional relationship. The pastoral care was not provided to impact you, even if you have grown and changed as a result. Rather, the pastoral care had an impact on the couple, and so there is a sense in which that power or that influence needs to be respected before transitioning to another kind of relationship.

In addition to the question of influence is the question of time spent in formal pastoral care or lay counseling. It is one thing to meet with a couple three to four times, providing them with information and coaching them in communication, for example. But it is another thing to have an ongoing set of meetings for many months over a more intense topic that is emotionally charged for them as a couple.

The possibility of shifting into another type of relationship is something you can discuss with the couple. Most pastoral care providers and lay counselors want to retain the capacity to meet with the couple again should they desire it. So you want to be careful about switching into another role if doing so makes it less likely or impossible to revert back to a pastoral care or lay counseling role.

It is wise to avoid getting into a business relationship with one member of the couple. It might also be wise not to hire one or the other spouse as an employee of the church, even though you may be in the position of providing counseling services to existing employees. There is no need to add additional layers to the existing pastoral care or lay counseling relationship if it is avoidable.

You will probably most often work with those you know well or fairly well, as well as those they refer to you, who are likely to be their friends or family. So good boundaries also involve remembering when and how you came to know information about a couple.

Part of recognizing where a couple ends and you begin is recognizing and establishing boundaries. The specific boundaries that we've discussed are symbolic, and they are reminders to you and to the couple of your role in their lives.

CONFLICT AS A BENEFICIAL SOURCE OF INFORMATION

An important idea to remember is that conflict—the emotional tension between two people—is not the enemy. The actions that produce the tension are the real focus of change. Conflict in marriage provides the counselor with valuable information. Therefore, counselors should not be too quick to suppress, control and eradicate the tension, for it often highlights essential details of how a couple engages with one another.

Sometimes couples respond to one another like they respond to themselves. If there is something in themselves that they don't like, and then they see that quality in their spouse, they are likely to be critical of it. The fact that they like it or don't like it may have as much to do with their own upbringing and what was valued in their home growing up. Conversely, if there is something in themselves that they like or value, and they see that quality in their partner, they will respond very well to it. This is all thought to happen at an unconscious level. The couple may engage in this "dance" around what is valued and what is not valued, none of which is understood very well by the couple.

Couples typically "invite" their pastoral care provider into this dance. If the counselor is not careful or is unaware of the dance, he or she is likely to be drawn into the scene. In order to establish boundaries in this area, the counselor must keep an eye out for the dance that is occurring between the spouses.

One way for a counselor to gauge this is to pay attention to his or her emotional experience of the couple. What is felt when attending to them? What are the emotional responses experienced? Is there a pull or a tug that draws the counselor into the fray? This pulling sensation is what we, and others, refer to as "counter transference." To be aware of counter transference is to be cognizant of the counselor's visceral responses in the counseling relationship—it is to use one's emotions as a relational barometer. Cashdan[2] suggests that the counselor's use of self is the most important tool in helping people change. Awareness of the counselor's emotional responses creates opportunity to craft a response that can be intentional and corrective. This is why self-awareness is critical for navigating marital conflicts. Counselors must be able to experience the couple's conflict and to assess the emotional pull, so that he or she can make good choices about how to respond in a manner that does not repeat the common or typical reaction.

If we return to the case[3] of Antonio and Carla, let's say that Antonio is largely unaware of his own impulses toward anger and inner hostility. His behavior—working late and spending time with the guys—ends up provoking Carla to criticism, anger and resentment. He may apologize initially and try to work things out with Carla, but he may be managing his own impulses by inducing her to react the way she is reacting, which is by being angry with him. Rather than be pulled into the dance or sorting out a schedule for mutually agreed-upon time with friends, and so on, it may be more helpful for the counselor to explore the ways in which they are responding to one another and what is going on just beneath the surface.

Pastoral care providers and lay counselors can do this by connecting with the couple. We do this when we show an interest in their lives by being engaged as they talk to us about their interests and the challenges they face. What is recommended at this point is "emotional linking," or linking emotions to experience. You might say, "You seem frustrated when the topic of finances comes up" or "You're really upset when we are talking about family devotionals."

A good response to the pull is to be able to talk to the couple about the experience. This is the beginning of an interpretation. The counselor's experience of the couple gives him or her important data for understanding them. This helps form a hypothesis. "Do they draw out of me a tendency to want to protect one or both of them?" "Do they draw out of me a feeling of anxiety or irritation?" "Do I feel responsible for them?" The pull to be responsible for them is something like a "messiah complex" or "superman complex." It refers to the tendency to jump in and try to save the couple—to take responsibility for the outcome. Part of having good boundaries is letting them take responsibility for their decisions while also reflecting on what is being pulled at inside of you through the dance that they do with one another.

Another way to work with the dance between the couple is to help them become aware of their emotional reactions. This begins with marital conflict. The conflict typically elicits negative emotions, such as frustration or anger. One important gauge is to determine whether their emotional response is commensurate to the event. Are they responding at the appropriate level of anger given the offense? In many cases, one spouse will overreact to the offense, showing significantly more anger than is warranted.

Some conflict creates dialogue on the qualities or characteristics one sees in the spouse. It might be helpful for you to see if this quality exists in the spouse who is raising the complaint, and how this quality has been discussed or addressed with the partner who is complaining.

Other conflicts reflect on unmet needs from earlier in life. When this happens, you as a pastoral care provider have a great opportunity to sit with them in their emotion and to ask them what they were expecting from their spouse. Their expectation—what they wanted but did not get from their spouse—tells you a lot about their emotional needs. These needs can be named. These needs can also be bridged back to earlier experiences when they were first felt and were not addressed adequately.

This is not a time for problem solving per se. Rather, what you are doing as a pastor or lay counselor is giving them the room to sit with what they experience. Sitting with their emotions and learning more about what is at the root of those emotions can be tremendously helpful and healing.

Helpful questions to ask include the following:

- What were you feeling just now?
- When have you felt that feeling before?
- Tell me about the first time you felt that feeling—what was happening?

The emphasis, then, is not actually on solving the problem itself. This isn't about who does the dishes or takes out the garbage; it isn't about spending habits or saving for retirement. Rather, it is about what is underneath those exchanges. What's underneath those exchanges is an important part of each spouse's personal story, and it is getting played out in the drama of their marriage, though often neither spouse is aware of it.

In terms of pastoral boundaries, it can be helpful to see this exchange, to gain a perspective on it. This makes all the difference. It distinguishes those who get pulled into a couple's conflict and those who can stay on the outside of that conflict and help the couple come to a better understanding of it.

CONCLUSION

We have seen a number of ways we can discuss boundaries in pastoral care and lay counseling. We began with a discussion of some of the ways in which certain boundaries are symbolic of a professional relationship and how pastoral care and lay counseling may expand these boundaries due to the unique nature of these helping relationships. We also discussed ways to keep from being drawn into a couple's conflicts. This involves identifying the emotional dance that is going on before you and using your own response as a gauge for interpreting the data.

In keeping with this approach, it is also helpful to talk to the couple about their Us, about viewing their marriage as the thing to which you are providing care. As you lead by example in this mentality, they can begin to see their marriage as the thing they are trying to care for.

NOTES

[1]Portions of this list are from Gutheil, T. G., & Gabbard, G. O. (2003). The concept of boundaries in clinical practice: Theoretical and risk-management dimensions. In D. N. Bersoff (Ed.), *Ethical Conflicts in Psychology* (3rd ed., pp. 214-21). Washington, DC: American Psychological Association.

[2]Cashdan, S. (1988). *Object Relations Therapy.* New York: Norton.

[3]This discussion is adapted from ibid.

Part Two

THE PROCESS
OF CONFLICT AND
RESTORATION

OUR INTENTION IN WRITING PART ONE of this book was to establish the preconditions that contribute to successful counseling experiences with couples. Now we turn to the centerpiece of the book—working with couples who are stuck in a self-perpetuating cycle of conflict. Our approach is based on a model that contains pathways. One path focuses on addressing individual protection from pain. While at times essential, the long-term outcome of this tendency for self-protection results in misunderstanding and miscommunication between marital partners. A cycle of defense and injury is created that, if left unattended, becomes a self-perpetuating pattern. However we believe that there can be an alternative path accessible to couples.

The second pathway focuses on many of the great themes of the Christian faith, such as grace, justice and trust. These themes must be translated from theological ideals to specific behaviors that enhance the relational experience. Central to our model is helping couples put into practice the values they hold as Christians. A side note: when counselors are working with couples outside of the Christian faith, the content is perfectly appropriate, though the counselor may need to communicate the nuanced meaning of some words. *Grace*, for example, often is not part of the common language used by people outside the Christian tradition. However, the principle of offering oneself in service without precondition or expectation of response can be widely understood. Though the model emerges from our understanding of the Christian faith, it is not exclusive to the people of that same faith.

Looking at the full model may be daunting. Yes, there are many components to the process. Being able to cognitively digest the whole model could be likened to swallowing a whole meal in one bite. We have separated the model into bite-size chapters and will present the components sequentially.

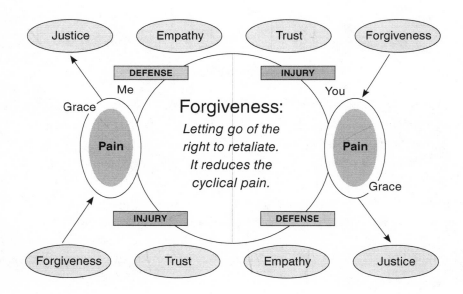

5

PAIN AND DEFENSE

It is not true that suffering ennobles the character;
happiness does that sometimes,
but suffering, for the most part makes us petty and vindictive.

WILLIAM SOMERSET MAUGHAM,
THE MOON AND SIXPENCE

A man in armor is his armor's slave.

ROBERT BROWNING, "HERAKLES"

IN ORDER TO EFFECTIVELY ASSIST couples in the process of restoration, counselors must teach them the patterns or cycles that destroy most relationships. Furthermore, counselors must learn from them the unique components and characteristics within their marriage and translate that awareness back to them so that they can implement changes. While there are many explanations as to what goes wrong in marriages, a common denominator is the experience and response to pain demonstrated by the couple over time. The mismanagement of pain, through the use of archaic defenses, places the couple in a cycle that destroys their Us. In this chapter we will consider these two crucial components that form the basis for most conflict: pain and the corresponding defenses.

MATT AND LAURIE: A CASE STUDY IN RELATIONAL PAIN

Nothing destroys a good relationship like pain. It happened to Laurie and Matt; it has happened to most couples who come to see a counselor. Pain killed their marriage like it kills many others. Marriages are not destroyed by events such as acts of infidelity, neglect or disrespect; marriages are destroyed by the pain produced by these events, and the disregard for the pain that husbands and wives carry. It's not the fire that kills, it's the smoke. The failures to understand, respect and heal Matt's and Laurie's pain destroyed their Us. The noxious gas seeped through the cracks of their relationship. It poisoned the life of their Us, choking out their capacity for honest, trusting intimacy. They both could smell the smoke, and both were aware of the potential destructiveness that could come. They both knew they were suffocating in their relationship. They could feel it coming on slowly, but they didn't make the right decisions to provide themselves with oxygen.

This is not to say that they ignored their problems. On the contrary, both were active in trying to save their marriage—they fought fire with fire. The harder they "worked," the more intense was the heat and thick the smoke. They went to a counselor. They learned to fight fairly in the counselor's office and to reflect and to paraphrase communication. These were superficial solutions. It was like the bucket brigade tossing pails of water, one at a time, on an engulfed home. They never accomplished the most fundamental need: to soothe each other's suffering. When you can't breathe, not much else matters. During this time their perceptions of one another shifted. Rather than seeing each other as "I got your back" partners, they saw one another as the one responsible for the arson. Instead of seeing their lifelong lover as the one who could be a source of oxygen, each maintained the mindset that the other was the fire-starter—the one to blame. The intimate lovers became intimate enemies.

Eventually, Matt and Laurie determined that divorce was their only option for survival—like a fire sale. The body—the Us—had turned against itself: "The structure is destroyed. Maybe we can salvage a few remnants, settle with the insurance company, then go our separate ways." How did it happen that a couple once so vibrantly in love, consumed with the optimism of life, could become such bitter enemies?

In a word, pain. Any couple who fails to manage pain will find themselves eventually on the verge of divorce. This is not to say that any couple who has pain will divorce. All couples, all people have pain. Job wrote, "Yet man is born to trouble as surely as sparks fly upward" (Job 5:7). It is avoiding the pain, mismanaging the pain and misdirecting one's resources to clear the pain that will cause the toxic gases to build.

As pastoral, lay and professional counselors, it is imperative that we understand the role of pain and how it shapes the relational processes occurring in marriage. Furthermore, it is essential that we are able to translate that understanding of pain into a language that conveys empathy for the unique process that has brought the couple to the counselor's office. Current circumstances, repeated disappointments and family injuries bring the couple to the office. In essence, pain brings them to us.

To further understand the destructive effects of pain mismanagement, let's return to Matt and Laurie and hear their story. We have chosen to be detailed in the elaboration of their story to show how the seemingly insignificant events have an effect in greater magnitude long after their actual occurrences.

They began, like all of us, as individuals, entering the world in December 1967 and June 1969. From the beginning each of them exercised effort to manage their circumstances. Utterly helpless at first, yet over time both learned to interpret events occurring around them and to act in ways that seemed at the time to be in their best interest—that is, in the interest of reducing pain and maximizing their respective needs for safety, significance and acceptance. Their parents were like most: wanting to provide for their children, to nurture them into adulthood, to teach them how to manage the complexities of life, and to help them become mature, kind, responsible people. At the same time, their parents had to manage their own pain emanating from the pressures and demands of their own lives.

Laurie was the youngest child in her family. Her two older half brothers were in late elementary school when Laurie was born. For her, childhood was hard. She was raised in a small town in the central plains. Money was scarce. Work was hard and long. Life provided few pleasures. Her father had alcohol as his buddy to comfort him and soothe the pain that emerged from daily living. Her brothers had each other. Her mother had Laurie. Laurie never really "had" anyone or anything. Rather, Laurie's job from early in life was to make Mother happy. At first she was successful at this. Her mother could make her cute. Laurie was dressed with ribbons in her hair, pretty shoes, and gloves and a hat. Laurie was her mother's human doll. As she grew older Laurie continued to perceive her worth through her body. Baby Dress-Up grew into an adult Barbie. During adolescence her emotional needs and her sense of security, safety and significance were met through friends— usually male and usually physical. Breaking away from her mother as an adolescent was seen as rebellion, and some of it truly was. Her mother tried to cling to and control her daughter—especially when Laurie began making decisions that did not fit with the role she was designed to play. She was supposed to be cute, not sexual. Shirley Temple was supposed to remain a child. Her mother's honest efforts to guide were mixed with the selfish motive of gaining her own worth vicariously through her daughter. When mixed, they couldn't be distinguished, so Laurie rejected them all. Immediately after high school Laurie moved to Los Angeles in hopes of stardom as an actress. She only had a few bit roles in inconsequential productions. She waited tables at a restaurant in Malibu at night, and auditioned and honed her acting and image skills during the day. Even if her hope of stardom didn't materialize, at least she was on her own.

The years allowed the development of her maturity. She rekindled her interest and involvement in church. She gained control of her sexuality—seeking a truer form of intimacy. The conflict with her family was never really resolved, but it was neutralized. Her mother learned that she had to let go of her daughter; Laurie learned that she couldn't remain resentful forever. She would go home for Christmas and stay for a week. Hugs and kisses were present at the airport. Gifts were exchanged at midpoint, but there was never a direct address of their lives. Tensions were always there underneath the hug or behind the Christmas sweater. The family found that the tensions could easily surface, so all parties tried pretty hard to keep things gentle and calm.

Back in L.A., church became Laurie's place of center and grounding. She joined a musical group that performed every Sunday. She wrote and performed with the church drama troupe. She had friends. Waiting tables was hard work, but lucrative. Life was pretty good when she met Matt at church. He was recently located to the community. He was handsome, educated and self-assured. In fact, she thought he was just about everything that she wasn't.

Matt grew up in the Southern California beach culture. His father was an attorney. His mother worked in her family's furniture business. Matt was the oldest of three boys. Most would perceive a Midas-like childhood, adolescence and early adulthood: whatever he touched was golden. He received good grades in school. He was athletic—not spectacular but entirely competent in most sports. As a high school senior he was elected student body president. He had his father's articulation and his mother's ability to organize. Matt always did it correctly. He seemed almost sinless. However, underneath his external compliance was the presence of an individual who never was given the freedom to fail or to break away from expectations. He was diplomatic in just about every aspect of his life—meaning, he was a polite liar. He followed his family's prescription for image. Never would he challenge his parents' authority. He was the prodigal's brother—the one who stayed home and "managed the family farm" while the younger sibling blew the family's resources on having a good time.

Laurie and Matt were a natural couple: he was stable like a brick; she was spontaneous like a butterfly. They were each what the other needed. Butterflies need safe and secure places to land; bricks are safe. They wear well but are not usually associated with a good time. In the same way, butterflies have no pattern or consistency—decisions are made in the moment and determined by the direction of the wind. They are free to do what they want. Matt and Laurie each felt somewhat secure in their roles and in what they received from the role of the other. They made a connection. Each offered promise to soothe the internal wounds caused by previous experiences, and the external wounds of circumstances and situations yet to come. These were promises made with every intention of fulfillment. But they were unprepared to manage the challenges before them.

It was not long after their marriage that the effects of their individual pain began to corrode the tentative Us that they had begun to build. This is common. The anesthesia of romance and sexuality, along with the hopes for the relationship, can carry a couple a few months into the marriage. Sometimes even a few years. Then the honeymoon drug wears off; the pain of life returns. Matt longed for a freedom within his soul. Duty and expectation had robbed him of life's joy. It continued to pick his pockets. Laurie retained a longing to be loved with a security she had never known. "I will love you if . . ." had been her experience before marriage. The pain from tentative, insecure love left her searching again, as before.

The pain became unmanageable about the time they bought their first home. The mortgage debt would have been fine, except that not long after, Matt's company downsized. He was retained by the business, but with less responsibility and less pay. Matt had failed. As the pain of Matt's failure permeated his being, he began to exercise control (the term he preferred was "fiscal responsibility"). Matt didn't engage in conversation with his intimate partner about his pain residing in the form of anger, fear and shame. Rather, he focused on the solution—*his* solution—of simply cutting back on purchases—and he meant cutting *way* back. Matt didn't share life with Laurie. He decided for her. He justified his actions defensively: "Somebody has to be the responsible one here, and it's not going to be Laurie. It has to be me." Their Us was absent from his thoughts. There was Me and there was Her, colliding at the point of pain—failure over their finances.

Laurie likewise was experiencing pain. Debt meant sacrifices. They could no longer afford many of the external pleasures that Laurie had been dependent upon to escape from her internal pain. They cut back on dates, travel, fine dining and clothes. They didn't even have enough to furnish and decorate the house as she had hoped. As a single adult Laurie had significant freedom—and sufficient money to enjoy it. Now there was restriction. Matt no longer represented the safe, secure man that she had come to expect. He was usually distant now, and his presence was experienced as another form of an old enemy—someone trying to dictate or control her. Laurie had the thought, *Oh, no! I married my mother!* Laurie began to act out against the onslaught of pain—reverting back to activities that had previously brought her escape, diversion and fun. She stayed out late with friends. At first it was female friends, then male and female friends, and eventually just male friends. She never actually had an affair, but she was investing her emotional energy, the core of her soul, in relationships with others. Her lack of extramarital sex gave her ammunition against Matt when he tried to "reign her in." She was, after all, "not doing anything wrong." She believed that he couldn't accept the fact that she could not be controlled in every aspect of their life. The Us for Laurie was just nonexistent. To be with someone was to be controlled by them.

After six years they gave up. Each other had become the embodiment of pain rather than its comforting balm. Over the course of their marriage, their understanding of culpability changed: each turned to see the other as the one responsible for the pain. It is always easier to manage your pain when it has a face, and when the face is readily accessible.

Their Us is over now. They are over each other but not over their pain. Each has moved on to manage pain alone. Their story is a sad one. It did not end well. And the ending keeps on hurting. True, they no longer hurt from each other—in that sense, they have relief.

After the fact, postrelationship and divorce, they both have perspective on their lives when they were married. Matt confided that he just couldn't hear her. His hurt from the injuries of life and from the wounds of relationship was so intense that there was no capacity to receive her. There was no space for Us. The swelling from his own emotional contusions left no room to consider, let alone seek to ameliorate, the suffering of his wife. Pain does that—it produces such high-decibel emotional static that we often can hear no other voice—especially the voice of reason, but also the voice of care and empathy. In the same way, Laurie has been healed by time. And the years have brought insight into their life as a couple and the effect of their personal pain that never was acknowledged or addressed within the relationship.

THE FUNCTION OF PAIN

Pain is the experience of aversive stimuli—both physical, as in that throbbing sensation that is felt when the nightstand is kicked with a bare toe; and psychological, as in the anxiety or depression experienced when one anticipates or reacts to tragedies in life. Pain's primary purpose is to alert the body that something is wrong. It is a warning device—as irritating as a car alarm cutting the midnight silence and disturbing us from our sleep. When pain is present it becomes the brain's priority. It is difficult to even think about other things. Pain rearranges our values and demands that we attend to it first, before anything else. It cuts in the front of the line and declares, "Me first!" Pain does not wait; it just demands. But as in any alarm system, it cannot discern friend from foe, real danger or real threat from the accident or the innocent. It delivers its warnings to the brain like a trained sentry would notify the military leadership in the presence of suspicion. The sentry does not think—that's not his job. The sentry's existence is to stand watch and to fire off a warning at the slightest hint of danger.

Unfortunately for most couples, pain is not usually respected as the important signal that something is wrong. Instead it is treated as the problem. The headache, which compels us to anesthetize, is relieved, but the presence of tension or stress between people, which prompted the signal of pain, remains. It is easier to gag and tie pain than it is to attend to its source. Likewise, the painful emotion—depression, anxiety, shame or rage—becomes the focus of the attention instead of the issue which provoked the pain. Defending against pain is a primary pursuit of life. For most, *happiness*, *contentment* and *joy* are simplistically defined as being free from pain.

This defense against pain is the beginning of the cycle of conflict. We consider pain as the place where otherwise good marriages break down. Misunderstanding and misinterpretation is regularly the result of pain disregard, mismanagement or miscommunication. It is followed by a series of self-reinforcing events that perpetuate misunderstanding. The failure to recognize pain as an important indicator of imbalance in the relationship, the need for personal attention to some undefined factor, or the call to adjust pace, cadence, or focus of life leads one to shoot the messenger, rather than to attend to the message.

For the pastor or counselor, work with couples begins with pain and requires the counselor's ability to recognize it and remain comfortable in its presence. The essence of marital work is in helping couples in healing two manifestations of pain. The first is *the pain within*—that psychological state of residual pain from our childhoods that holds captive the individual. This pain stunts the person's maturation, steals their joy and decimates hope. The second pain that counselors must address is *the pain between*—the community pain that exists between spouses or resides within families. It is the pain from failure of the family or marital system to operate with a balance of the giving and receiving of love and trust. We recognize that many couples come to counseling with the need to address specific issues and develop concrete solutions. In these contexts a problem-centered, solution-focused approach is excellent. However, in such cases where behavioral directives are insufficient, in situations of persistent and long-standing conflict, we find it prudent for counselors to see their responsibility as assisting couples to identify, verbalize, and attend to the individual and shared pain within the system.

The pain within. Rudyard Kipling wrote in the poem "The Rabbi's Song" that "the arrows of our anguish fly farther than we guess." Neither Laurie nor Matt made a full accounting of their individual suffering. Though their bodies were strong, toned and beautiful, and their minds were intelligent, capable and insightful, below the layer of the public and observable characteristics grew a cancer. Each demonstrated significant need and expectation that remained unarticulated and unmet. Their story lines were common. The characters and details can change, but the fundamental plot is the same for us all: we struggle with the existential threat of becoming known, to ourselves and to others. To be known is to be vulnerable—open and indefensible against potential onslaughts of pain. Throughout the ages, spanning time and culture, we have tried to label and define this internal fight. Augustine saw it as the unrest of the heart; Kierkegaard called it dread; Heidegger referred to the idea that we are not at home; and Freud called it anxiety. These, and others, commonly identify something that is gnawing at us, or better said, in our Us.

Skilled counselors offer to couples a precious gift in assisting the couple in understanding how the pain experienced by both spouses affects the quality of their intimacy. The counselor is in a unique position to use the power of Us to help both partners reconcile themselves with their pain.

From birth we carried the pain within—it was experienced every time our body had need. It was an internal message that something was wrong, out of place or insufficient. Harville Hendrix describes the source and nature of this pain in his book *Getting the Love You Want.* He says, "When we were babies, we didn't smile sweetly at our mothers to get them to take care of us. . . . We simply opened our mouths and screamed. And it didn't take long."[1]

Psychologists have labeled this condition as a state of psychological disequilibrium. During infancy the pangs of hunger or the chill from cold are aversive signals that prompt us to cry out in helpless hope that someone will come to our aid. As babies our need and the pain signaling the existence of that need is rudimentary—we cry. Most can identify the empathic reaction to the crying infant. The sound compels us to intervene. The infant cry is a call to response. It is a helpless declaration of need that must be heeded by another with greater capacity. Babies have only one way to declare their distress. Very soon, however, we learn different cries that reflect variations in our pain. A perceptive parent knows the meaning of the distinct cries. The cry of hunger is different from the cry of a pinched finger or the cry of loneliness.

As the human brain develops it continues to regulate physiological equilibrium through the senses of touch, taste, smell, sight and hearing. The brain also begins to regulate through the formation of the will. We not only can perceive and respond to pain but we can anticipate comfort. For example, sitting in a La-Z-Boy recliner would be more comfortable (or less painful) than sitting on a milk stool. We grow in our ability to anticipate and direct circumstances that will reduce our pain and increase our pleasure. The management of pain and pleasure becomes a primary function of our brain—it is always thinking about how to prevent or reduce pain. Our brains think about this task in the presence of many other brains that are pursuing the same goal. In a sense, we are in a competition with everyone else over how to beat others in the race to the pain-free finish line.

James writes of this same idea when he asks, "What causes fights and quarrels among you? Don't they come from your desires that battle within you?" (Jas 4:1 NIV). He suggests that the prime force behind conflicts is not the external circumstances; rather, fights and quarrels are driven by internal forces. In this specific passage the force he is emphasizing is our depraved envy and selfishness.

The pain between. In the play *No Exit* by Jean Paul Sartre, the hero, Gracin, describes the pain of relationship. "So, this is Hell. I'd never have believed it. You remember all we were told about the torture chambers, the fire and brimstone, the 'burning marl.' Old wives' tales! There is not need for red-hot pokers. Hell is other people." "Hell as other people" is his processing of multiple experiences of pain, loss, disappointment, frustration and failure occurring in relationship with others. The internal suffering could not be alleviated in relationship with others, so they became the embodiment of that pain. The internal message sounds something like this: "Because you could not ultimately soothe the pain within, a new injury emerges between me and you. The new pain is because of you." This pain now has a face.

Indeed it is easier to project responsibility for our pain onto others. Scapegoats are in constant demand. Our need to be shielded from insecurity, insignificance and abandonment prompts us to look for some external cause for our pain. If we could isolate the pathogen as having an external source, then we have less accommodation. "If the source of my pain can be found to reside in someone else's childhood, the injury from a previous relationship or my spouse, then I am not responsible to change." The pain between becomes the pain of blame. Ultimately, responsibility lies with the other. If fault lies with our spouses then it is our moral duty to inform them of their gross deficiency and urge them to initiate the necessary changes immediately so as to no longer cause a continuation of our suffering.

Couples usually seek a counselor while in distress because of their pain between. They have come to the point of exasperation in managing their respective suffering. Almost inevitably, however, the intervention of therapy is an examination of the interaction between the pain between—stated as the specific marital conflict—and the unarticulated pain within.

THE FAILURE OF THE MARRIAGE TO ATTEND TO PAIN

The effort of each partner in the marriage to quench their thirst for security, significance and acceptance is present throughout the relationship. Everyone longs to feel secure within themselves, to possess a perspective that they have value, worth, and purpose, and to experience that security and significance through relationship—to be accepted by others, but especially by the one they have chosen to marry. We all remain like little children with outstretched arms and a facial expression that pleads to be held. Robert Browning wrote in "Two in the Campagna" that

> Only I discern
> Infinite passion, and the pain
> Of finite hearts that yearn.

We seek relationships that offer promise to meet the need within. A yearning exists to have connection with another as a means of comprehending and healing the pain within. So we select partners who we believe are the best "fit" for us, and we for them. Other books on marriage address this topic much more extensively than I do in this chapter. Hendrix's[2] *Getting the Love You Want* and Jacobson and Christianson's[3] *Reconcilable Differences* both offer excellent explanations for unconscious and behavioral motivations in mate selection. But suffice it to say that spouses are chosen because somewhere in the center of our being, we believed that this partner could help soothe an internal pain. Sometimes this belief is articulated in the most mundane language: "We were in love. I have never been as happy as I was when I was with him. It's as though all of the other things didn't matter. We had each other."

Inevitably, we fail. The expectation that our partner can "save us from ourselves" is an impossible challenge. Hope and expectation that our spouse can, by their continual devotion to meeting our needs, satisfy the pain within, is beyond the capacity of any human relationship. Psychologist Larry Crabb describes this expectation and failure:

> A marriage bound together by commitments to exploit the other for filling one's own needs (and I fear that most marriages are built on such a basis) can legitimately be described as a "tick on a dog" relationship. Just as a hungry tick clamps on to a nourishing host in anticipation of a meal, so each partner unites with the other in the expectation of finding what his or her personal nature demands. The rather frustrating dilemma, of course, is that in such a marriage there are two ticks and no dog![4]

Our pain within naturally bends us toward an expectation of relief, first from our parents and those in our life responsible for our care. As we age and mature, the source of solace for our pain broadens to include friends and other sources of meaning like work and play. Eventually, the marital union becomes the intended relief for our hurt. But when it's not there, or when its presence feels unbalanced, the pain within moves beyond the borders of our soul and occupies the space between our injured soul and our intimate partner.

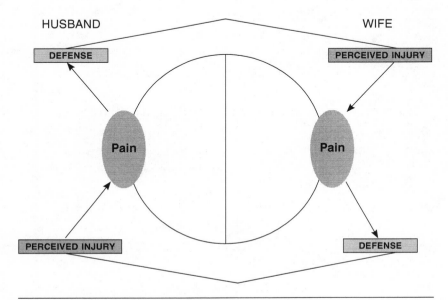

Figure 5.1. Pain-defense-injury

ENSLAVED TO OUR OWN ARMOR:
UNDERSTANDING OUR DEFENSES

The primary products of pain in any relationship are protective behaviors, attitudes, thoughts and emotions that are designed to keep the person safe while in the presence of others who may cause hurt or harm or expose the person's wrongdoing, which illicits shame, disrespect, embarrassment or other pain-producing emotions. Defenses are essential, and counselors should always treat the layers of protection with respect. We find that education level is an apt metaphor for how we are to respect the protective defenses of others. Counselors offer dignity to everyone regardless of their training or knowledge, subtly encouraging others to learn, grow and discover. In the same way, they can respect the defenses of others while assisting couples in developing a wider array of protection. Let's take a look at Mike and Barbara to see these protective defenses played out in relationship.

"There you go again. You're being defensive." The veins were already bulging in Mike's neck as he spoke these words. His fists were clenched, his breathing shallow and rapid. Every fiber of his being was on high alert—called to duty from the central command center deep within his brain. He was fighting in a war of words. Barbara, his wife (the "enemy"), was on an equally high-alert status. She paused no more than a nanosecond before retaliating with her response: "I am not! You're the one who is defensive." Words were volleyed back and forth as both sought a strategic advantage.

But there was little value in the bilateral attacks. Both Barbara and Mike were maneuvering to find weak spots in the other's defense. At the same time both wanted to shore up their defenses—trying to be impervious to the accusations and attacks of their "lover." This argument was going nowhere. It was unproductive, circular and sometimes mean. However, one useful thing did emerge. They provided accurate labels for each other—defensive. Both of them had their protective shields raised and locked in place. And they should have. To be defensive in the presence of a threatening spouse is pretty intelligent. Who wouldn't want to be guarded and protected in the middle of such an attack?

Yet in marriage, we usually consider defensiveness to be a grievous mistake. Somewhere we formed the idea that we are not supposed to be defensive, and when we are, it implies that something is wrong with us. Or more accurately, wrong with our spouse. We usually accept our own defenses but find our spouse's defenses offensive. It is somewhat like the fox being insulted that the hen house is locked. The audacity that our spouse would take measures of self-protection when in a fight often feels like an insult to our integrity. Once a husband was screaming at me in the presence of his wife, "You know what the problem is? It's that she doesn't trust me! Plain and simple! My wife doesn't trust her husband!" My reaction probably paralleled his wife's. It's hard to trust a person who is screaming at you, veins popping out of his neck and a pointed finger invading your space of safety. To the husband, his wife's lack of trust was an insult; to the observer, it was a chainlink fence erected to keep out carnivores.

Defenses say a lot about both spouses. We all have them, use them and can learn from them. We can learn how we manage our pain and how we can assist our lifetime lover in managing theirs . . . if we want to. Or we can be like Mike and Barbara—mean, frustrated and stuck. When we understand our defenses we can better understand our injuries and the nature of our maturity. How adept am I at managing my pain and minimizing the relational damage as a result of this pain?

DEFENSES DEFINED

Defenses are what we use to prevent relational pain and injury and to soothe our hurt when we suffer. Defenses are our unique set of coping styles for anything that is uncomfortable. Defenses are as important and natural as breathing, eating and sleeping. But the challenge with breathing, eating, sleeping and defending is how you do it. Breathe too rapidly and you will hyperventilate. Eat only saltine crackers and eventually you will become malnourished. Deny yourself sleep and your mind and body become exhausted. React to painful realities with a limited set of roles and styles, and you will be left inadequately protected from the harshness of life, and more importantly, unable to distinguish your friends from your enemies.

Defenses are a set of skills that we employ to navigate our way through life. We learn them progressively as we emerge through childhood into adulthood. As we grow, our defenses increase in both number and complexity. One way to understand the word *maturity* is to understand the many ways a person can manage their pain effectively. To be mature is to know what to do when faced with pain and when to do it, to be able to use the right amount of the right defense at the right moment to resolve our challenge.

Defenses are our psychological tools to manage problems. We never know what lies ahead. So the more defenses we possess, and the more skilled we are at using them, the more likely we will be able to manage the obstacles, hazards and dangers that may lie in our path. Defenses are our coping styles. They are the ways that we manage painful situations.

Defenses need to be distinguished from defense mechanisms. *Defense mechanism* is a term that Freud used to explain our unconscious reactions to experiences in order to control and prevent anxiety. Words like *repression* and *reaction formation* are technical examples of defense mechanisms. Most defense mechanisms are signs of immature coping. Our use of the word *defenses* has some similarities, but it is not the same. Defenses are the ways that we choose to interpret and respond to challenging, stressful, difficult and painful events in life. Sometimes these choices are deliberate behavioral paths; most of the time they are reactions that are almost automatic because we have habituated them into our lifestyle.

Barbara Kranser and Austin Joyce, two marriage counselors, have written about the need for protection in the face of the reality of life. "Initially impelled by fear of pain, given or received, people actively opt, by omission and commission, for hurt withdrawal, imposition, and other well-entrenched barriers and dismissive defenses of monologue."[5] They say that if we have hurt, we defend ourselves—and that the defenses we regularly employ make us safe by making us alone. *Defenses of monologue* is their revealing description of the effect of defenses—they create protective isolation. Monologue, distinct from dialogue, is a conversation of one. It is safe. It does not need to exercise the effort of understanding another, but neither can it experience the support and strength from others. Defenses misapplied create monologue.

COMMON DEFENSIVE REACTIONS

People have unique patterns or response styles to challenges, difficulties and pain. We want to avoid reducing the description of defenses to simple categories. It is restrictive to identify five, fifteen or even fifty ways that people defend themselves from pain. Our protective styles are as unique as our individual personalities. Such patterns are the unique constellation of personality, genetic endowment, and childhood, adolescent and adult experiences and personal choices. There is limited predictive power in describing how couples will manage pain, both as two individuals and as a team. But even as snowflakes are each individual and unique, it is possible to describe snow in patterns that most people can identify—powdery, wet and heavy, sleety, and so on. Similarly, there are some characteristics and patterns in defenses that can be described. Consider the four common defenses discussed below not as an exhaustive list but as examples. To know defenses is to know oneself. Defenses are a customized integration of personality acting in unique circumstances. For counselors, to understand defenses is the first step in creating intervention. These defenses cannot be eradicated, as they serve the necessary function of maintaining safety. Rather, counselors should think of defenses as protections that can be substituted with more efficient and appropriate protective tools. The four defenses that we have chosen to elaborate on are anger, depression, intellectualization and avoidance.

Anger. Anger seems to have two purposes. First, anger is our emotional SOS. It is a loud message clearly stating that there is a problem. It is a psychological flare gun that informs those nearby that something is wrong, out of balance or unjust. Anger as a defense declares that something needs to be straightened, fixed or even destroyed.

Anger usually is not very intelligent, just loud. Anger cannot think; it can only declare the perceived emergency. In our community, we have a tornado warning siren. When a tornado is sighted, the alarm sounds. Throughout our region everyone is to take cover. It is not a time for specific information about the tornado; it is a time for immediate action. And so it goes with anger. Anger usually doesn't identify exactly what is wrong—only that something out there is a threat.

The second function of anger is best depicted in the cartoon character Yosemite Sam. The short, mustached figure in an oversized hat with pistols in both hands would say, "Back off, varmint!" That's what anger does—it drives people away. It broadcasts the message: "Stay away or you might get hurt!" Anger as a defense creates distance. It is the human equivalent of the snake's rattle, the hairs on the back of the grizzly's neck or the shark shaking its head side to side. Anger declares the presence of a disturbance and the need for space to protect oneself.

Anger heightens our body's impulse to act. It shifts us into an oppositional mode of thinking, sort of a "them or me in a fight to the finish" mentality. Anger is wonderfully useful as a protective device. It prompts action. It is usually extremely effective at reducing immediate pain. Anger is not supposed to be quiet or passive; rather, it is an emotional bugle call to "battle stations." The downside of anger is that it does not prompt us to think as a team. It does not promote collaboration. The anger defense is effective in creating distance

It is easy to mix up anger with aggression. They are not the same and should not be confused. Anger is an emotion, a normal defensive reaction to pain. Aggression is an action of control. Often people who do acts of violence do so in a state of anger. Therefore, it is easy to associate the toaster thrown through the window with anger. It is not. Anger and aggression are as different in relationships as stress and cheating are different in school. We all have stress (the emotion) usually experienced as anxiety right before a test. But we don't all cheat.

Depression. Like anger, depression warns us of the presence of pain and is an effective defense. But depression has the opposite mechanism of anger. Instead of encouraging us to act out against others, depression as a defense says, "I give up. I have no ambition to fight on. My cause is hopeless. I can't win. I am powerless." Albert Camus, the French existential philosopher, caught the essence of this defense in his work *The Plague:*

> They forced themselves to never think, to cease looking to the future, and always to keep, so to speak, their eyes fixed on the ground at their feet. But naturally enough, this prudence, this habit of feinting with their predicament and refusing to put up a fight, was ill rewarded. For,

while averting that which they found so unbearable, they also deprived themselves of redeeming moments, frequent enough when all is told. Thus, in a middle course between heights and depths, they drifted through life rather than lived, the prey of aimless days and sterile memories, like wandering shadows that could have acquired substance only by consenting to root themselves in the solid earth of their distress.

Depression is a numbing defense. The body anesthetizes itself against outside pain. Years ago psychologists learned a great deal about pain and depression by administering small levels of electrical currents to animals. They would put circuits in different sections of the floor of the animal cages. Then they would turn the current on and off in different sections of the cage. The scientists found that an animal will seek to avoid the current by trying to anticipate and understand the pattern of pain. If the floor had an electrical current that moved in a clockwise direction, the animals would move clockwise just ahead of the current. Reverse the direction of current and the animals would adapt and move in the other direction. They would learn from the pain and implement a defense: escape. But if the scientists put the current in a random pattern, one that the animals could not understand, the animals would just take it. They would become passive, sit and endure the shocks. They become depressed.

We can respond to pain in the same way. If you or I do not possess the resources needed to manage our pain, if we are powerless to defend ourselves with any active tool, then our only option is passivity. We will give up. Defenselessness becomes our defense.

The effect of depression on a relationship is usually futile support. It creates inequality in the marital dyad. To use a metaphor of a rowing team, depression declares, "It's hopeless for me to row. You can row if you want, but I will not." For a while our partner will row for both of us—until they get tired. Then he or she will implement their own defense because of their pain from the unfairness and imbalance in the relationship. Often, depression is met with anger; it tends to illicit anger in others. Passivity encourages activity.

Intellectualization. We humans can't run fast enough to flee danger. We have no poisonous fangs to render our attackers helpless. Our skin is not tough like leather. We have very limited physical defenses. But we can think and solve problems. In the presence of crisis, a valid defense is our brain. We can intellectualize.

Intellectualization should not be confused with using our intelligence. People with high IQs are not prone to more intellectualization. Intellectualization is the protective device against feeling anything. We don't experience pain, we *observe* pain in ourselves or others. Intellectualization keeps pain from getting too close to our souls. We intellectualize by converting emotional experiences into rational, cognitive problems. This has a disengaging effect. We cease to be in the problem. We step out of it and examine it, put it under a microscope. We need this defense to think clearly in times of emergency or threat. It requires us to be able to separate ourselves from the emotional and painful realities, to disengage from the real hurt that is around us and remain focused on a solution. To solve any problem, a type of intellectualization must occur. This is the defense that allows us to contain our emotions, whether they be frustration, sadness or fear, in order to think through our problem.

Pain kills creativity. Intellectualization allows us to put the pain in a box by disengaging from it and analyzing the problem. When preschool children are at the height of their frustration—when the shoelaces won't tie correctly, or the ball doesn't bounce straight, or the soup keeps slipping off the spoon and they are on the verge of a tantrum—adults are often telling them to focus, use self-control and think. We all must identify our feelings and then solve problems. Intellectualization keeps us sane as we work closely with the difficulties of life.

Every intellectualizer will be overwhelmed with pain at times. This defense is very useful, but it is limited. When we intellectualize our pain, we place it in an emotional holding tank that, when full, will spill out in many types of destructive ways. When we reach our capacity, we lose our ability to tolerate new sources of pain and stress. If we can't intellectualize we must use another defense strategy. Alcohol, substance abuse, violent outbursts, withdrawal, depression and sexualization are a few options that people often use when they can't think through the pain and don't know how to let others help.

Avoidance. Avoidance is to delay attending to or addressing a pain-producing concern. It is grounded in a very wise reality. Some problems are indeed best resolved if one just leaves them alone. When individuals ponder an issue, consider their best options and deliberate maturely, they are not avoiding; they are taking time to consider a problem wisely. However, people who employ avoidance often report that they are so overwhelmed with the difficulty of a circumstance that they do not know how best to address it. They become frozen in their decision making. In pushing the problem aside, the hope is that external events will occur to resolve the concern or that with time they will receive clarity in choosing the best option. Avoidance is passive problem solving.

When the discomfort of confrontation, incompetence or another threat emerges, the response is to not act assertively to solve the problem immediately. The first reaction is to stall. Frequently, the reasoning is, "Maybe the problem will fix itself, and I will not have to deal with it." Unfortunately, sometimes that works, which encourages the management of future stressors in the same way. Most of the time, however, it makes the problems more complicated. The dental checkup delayed becomes the root canal, the car maintenance put off becomes the engine overhaul, the minor misunderstanding with one's spouse becomes a major fight.

Fear. In the first chapter of Joshua, God charges him at least six times to "be strong and courageous." Over and over is that declaration made. It seems that the reason God so much wanted to impress upon Joshua the need for strength and courage is that Joshua wasn't strong and wasn't courageous; he was weak and fearful. There would be no reason to reiterate it. It is doubtful that Jesus ever needed to tell Peter to speak up! He already would do that.

Fast-forward two thousand years to Poland when Pope John Paul II stood before a million Polish Catholics who had gathered to hear him say Mass. He declared, "Do not be afraid . . ." to the Polish faithful as they were considering the overthrow of the communist government that had suppressed them for decades. They had reason to be afraid, reason to hide, reason to be consumed with anxiety about the future.

Fear causes us to freeze from motion. Lest we take a wrong step, we

become like we are paralyzed and take no step at all. Instead, we ruminate, reconsider, look for signs and direction—we do anything but
commit to action. Frequently fear prompts others to act, prompting an
acceptance of passivity or a subsequent anger toward the other who
acted for us and anger at ourselves for "cowardice."

THE COUNSELING PRACTICE: USING PAIN AND DEFENSE

Through this chapter we have conveyed the cycle of pain and defense
as the common and natural process through which marital conflict *is*
conceived, incubated and launched into the world to multiply. Typically
a couple comes to therapy ready to talk about how they have been hurt
by the other person. They need little prompting to get them to talk about
their hurt. Each person *is* usually quite willing to cast light on his or her
spouse's actions that have brought them to this point.

Nevertheless, there can be a crucial shift that occurs during the initial sessions *once* pain and defense are defined and understood. At this
point, you create the environment for growth and change. There is an
assumption among individual partners at the onset of marital counseling that "I am suffering more than you." But the counseling experience
must begin with declaring the obvious: naming what is the *common*
experience. So a crucial task in counseling is to affirm the important
first part of the assumption that "I am suffering," while simultaneously
assisting the couple in rejecting the second part of the assumption, the
"more than you."

While each individual expresses his or her pain in the presence of
the other, the other is able to acknowledge, affirm and identify with
that pain, which sets up the sequence for change. *Realizing that both
spouses are injured and both can play a shared role in the healing process places
the couple on a path toward change.* This will be addressed fully in chapter
seven, but first we must attend to an important sidebar—confronting
people who can be mean, nasty and vindictive.

NOTES
[1]Hendrix, H. (1988). *Getting the love you want.* New York: Henry Holt, p. 78.
[2]Ibid.

[3]Jacobson, N., & Christiansen, A. (2000). *Reconcilable differences.* New York: Guilford.

[4]Crabb, L. J., Jr. (1992). *The marriage builder: A blueprint for couples and counselors.* Grand Rapids, MI: Zondervan, p. 32.

[5]Krasner, B. R., & Joyce, A. J. (1995). *Truth, trust, and relationships: healing interventions in contextual therapy.* New York: Brunner/Mazel, p. 4.

6

OFFENSE AND INJURY

Where I grew up, there weren't many trees
Where there was we'd tear them down, And use them on our enemies
They say that what you mock, Will surely overtake you
And you become a monster, So the monster does not break you

U2, "PEACE ON EARTH"

YOU KNOW THE CHILDHOOD RHYME: "All the king's horses and all the king's men couldn't put Humpty together again." The egg just fell and cracked. No criminal investigation, no bad guy. Eggs break. But what if Humpty Dumpty was pushed?

Up to this point, the marital conflict model has been described as a large, significant and somewhat innocent misunderstanding. In couples who come to counseling, conflict is generated by the misuse of pain and defenses, and by the misunderstanding of family-of-origin injury, historical conflicts and the current conflict theme. The origination of conflict typically begins by the normal process of misreading the compass points, then embarking in a direction that eventually leads to becoming bogged down in a swamp of anger, resentment and despair.

In the last chapter, we stated that defenses are usually not interpreted as they are intended; that is, for self-protection and survival. Rather, it is common for one's spouse to interpret the other's defenses as an effort to injure. We have described this defense-to-injury process like a serious misunderstanding. But at other times, marital conflict does not occur accidently. Sometimes partners push. Intimate partners know of each other's vulnerabilities and can pounce on one another like carnivores on wounded prey. At crucial moments, in efforts to control, to win, or to manipulate, spouses will make a cutting comment, articulate a weakness, or recall a previous failure with the intended purpose of *causing injury*. When this happens, those who pledged life-long commitment to protect the holy and sacred Us are forced into full retreat. Each must abandon the ideals of relational intimacy and must seek fortified protection against the threat of further injury. Intimate allies become intimate enemies. It is now "him against her" in the fight to the finish. When intimate partners become provokers of pain and injury, neither can risk thinking about Us—only about Self, and how to survive this battle with self intact. Because Humpty Dumpty fears being pushed, maybe he or she should push first. After all, if someone's egg is going to be cracked, it might as well be the other person's.

THE CASE OF SAM AND JULIE:
"CAN YOU PLEASE FIX OUR PARENTS?"

Sam and Julie are an example of how a couple intentionally inflicts harm. They had been married for eighteen years and had four children. Their kids brought them into therapy—not that they ever suggested their parents should go to marital counseling, but through their actions the elder two adolescents made it clear that their parents needed help. The daughter, seventeen, was a senior in high school. She had always been a pretty good student. She played in the band and was a member of the scholastic club. She didn't even listen to music with offensive lyrics! Yet in the past two quarters, she did not receive any grades above a C. She had quit the activities that previously had provided pleasure. In the minds of most adults who knew her, she was spiraling downward. Likewise, her younger brother, a freshman, was picked up by the police for loitering in front of a convenience store—at 2:00 in the morning. He had crawled out of a bedroom window after all had gone to sleep. It was not a single occasion, but part of a growing sense that the parents were losing control of the family. So they made an appointment for the sake of the kids.

The family session revealed the utter incapacity of the parents to work together at nurturing and directing their children. While the parents fought, Diane, the counselor, felt that the kids were looking at her and asking silently, *Could you please do something with these incorrigible adults?* It became obvious that the best way to help the family was to help the parents, and they agreed and established an appointment as a couple.

Julie was overweight and depressed. She saw herself as powerless, ashamed and, in her words, "fat," which to her meant something ugly and unchangeable. She didn't just have excess fat—in her mind, she was *fat*. It wasn't just a condition, it was a trait. Her body was a metaphor for her life: heavy, inert and hopeless. Much of her time was spent lying on the sofa, unable to muster the strength to face the tasks of the day. The laundry was piled in the middle of the living room—there was a clean pile and a dirty pile. It never seemed to get to drawers, closets or shelves. Likewise, the kitchen was a disaster. The cupboards were usually empty. Dishes and food from the last meal, the last day, week or even month were scattered on the counters and table. The total disarray of the home would send Julie back to the couch.

Sam, on the other hand, was fit and disciplined regarding his eating and exercise. In fact, he was somewhat of a fitness and health fanatic. Tablets of alfalfa and ginseng sat on his desk. He ran in the morning, swam and lifted weights in the afternoon. It's only fitting that he was a banker—controlled, reasonable, logical, merciless. Sam saw the world through the lens of order, discipline and strength. He had little understanding of and empathy toward failure. When he encountered it, as in the example of his marriage and his children, he attributed responsibility to others. He had done all that he could. They had to bear the weight and responsibility for the relationship as well, and they were to bear the failure part. He would maintain responsibility for the successful part.

But before you award Sam a gold medal and create an exercise and diet plan for Julie, think about pain and coping with pain defensively. Very early in life, Julie learned to cope with pain through the presentation of helplessness. That is to say, as she faced difficulty, she shifted into passiveness: "When life gets tough, shut down—someone is sure to rescue you." Likewise, Sam learned to cope with pain by being self-sufficient. He could not be hurt because he would manage everything. There would be no room for mistake, failure or error because he would be ever present, ever watchful, ever controlling. In the beginning their marriage made sense, and actually it still does. Julie desperately needed a rescuer, and Sam desperately needed to be a rescuer. Julie's narcissism prevented her from seeing herself as responsible to care for another even as she was cared for.

Likewise, Sam's narcissism deluded his perception of himself. He believed that he was a self-sufficient individual. He could help others balance their accounts, with his always in perfect order. He was available to help others, but he himself would remain needless.

When Sam or Julie exhibited their defenses to ward off daily pain, the other was injured. They did not do it with the other in mind, but each was injured daily by the failure of the other. Julie consistently failed at demonstrating strength. Her actions demanded that Sam and others take care of her. Sam consistently demonstrated needlessness. His actions demanded that no one aid him in life's challenges.

However, their "natural" defenses masked a malicious quality to their actions. Their exhibition of meanness was not a frontal attack—there were no open wounds or visible bruises. But there was a deliberate and calculated malice demonstrated by both. A recent fight can serve as a case in point. Sam and Julie had an appointment with their youngest son's teacher. The conference was scheduled for 7:00 p.m. Sam's schedule was sharpened with minute-to-minute efficiency. He planned to leave work at 4:00, arrive at the gym at 4:30 and work out until 6:00. He would arrive home at 6:15, eat dinner with the family until 6:45, then leave with Julie for the appointment—a ten-minute drive. Life was as efficient as a Swiss watch. You set it, wind it and then watch it tick.

Except when he arrived home, dinner was not ready. This was not in his plan. Sam became angry at Julie's failure to keep to the schedule. In fact, he exploded, calling Julie a "fat lazy blob!" (To Diane he confessed that he really regretted losing his self-control and yelling like that. He did not show remorse for causing harm, for losing the containment of self. He said with pride, "Talking like that is not who I am.") He left the house, bought a low-fat sub sandwich at a fast-food restaurant and went to the conference alone. The conference with the teacher focused on the problems that their son was having because of the challenges he faces at home with a mother who is so inept and incapacitated. Sam soothed his wounds by expressing a willingness to help his son and help the teacher—he would dedicate increased time in the evenings to help with homework.

Julie knew of the appointment. She knew that Sam and the kids needed dinner. She watched the minutes pass in the late afternoon and couldn't get herself moving. She did go into the kitchen. It was such a mess! She got discouraged and went outside to water the plants. Many were dead. Others were waiting to die but needed just a little more time. The plants were a metaphor of life and meaninglessness. She thought about ordering a pizza—but she didn't have enough cash, and her husband didn't trust her with credit cards. She returned to the sofa and watched TV—she hated Judge Judy, but she watched anyway.

When Sam came home and they had their fight, Julie didn't really yell back. She knew he was right. He was always right about everything—just ask him, he would tell you so. She walked into the bedroom and went to bed. She heard the tires squeal, knowing that Sam had left. The kids found food for dinner—something like chocolate and potato chips—and ate in front of the TV. She was grateful that her antidepressant medication helped her sleep. She never heard Sam come in after the conference.

The Nobel Prize–winning poet Juan Ramon Jimenez wrote that "our hearts were bleeding to death. And perhaps we wept without the other seeing the tears."[1] Julie and Sam were hemorrhaging. The wound to their Us was self-inflicted—that is, both individuals were acting in a destructive way. Let's reconstruct the important aspects of this fight and look at the mutual maliciousness that is corroding the core foundations of this home. Both Julie and Sam have pain—a lot of pain. Both have employed individual strategies to manage it. Both have come to see the other as a major source of pain and not as a source of relief. Because both perceive each other as likely contributors to their own pain, they don't need to wait until they are hurt to use their defenses. They already are! The rules of engagement have shifted from "fire if fired upon" to "shoot on sight." They each are proactive in their defensive strategy. In the name of self-protection, they are fighting with their gloves off. It's as if they have received a "fire at will" order from the military high command. They are free to be offensive. They can justify their offensive actions on the previous injuries they have received and because they each are under threat of further injury.

Both Julie and Sam entered the day's interaction with the intent of escalating their conflict, not reducing it. They both anticipated how, when and why they would experience pain, and they colluded to create the situation that would exacerbate the problem. Like two wounded animals retaliating for their injury, Sam and Julie sought to hurt the other. After all, the other deserved it.

Sam knew that Julie would be late with dinner. He was fully aware that the expectations he had of himself could not be applied to Julie with the same standard. She could not keep up. But he did it anyway. When he entered the house he was anticipating that she was not going to be ready and that she probably couldn't keep the appointment with the teacher. This is not baseless conjecture—the information was revealed by Sam with just a few questions from their counselor, Diane.

Diane: Sam, on most nights, what is it like when you come home?

Sam: Well, it's total chaos. I usually find Julie on the sofa, not moving. Dinner typically is nonexistent. Sometimes the kids are watching television, but often they are still out—God knows where and with whom. Nobody is in charge.

Diane: So when you came home that night, were you expecting things to be different?

Sam: Oh, no, I knew they would be the same. I knew that she would have done nothing. And I knew she was going to make us late for the appointment.

Diane: Given what you knew, did you do anything to help this situation be different?

Sam: That's not my job. She is an adult. She needs to be responsible to manage the little that she has. She won't even do that.

Sam entered the house injured. He was free and justified to act in ways that produced more injury because of the past and because of anticipated hurt. Rather than trying to work with Julie on a solution, he acted on his sense of entitlement—he felt he had the right to be angry, aggressive and demanding because of the continual injury and disappointment that he had experienced with her. He was mean because she deserved it.

Julie also exhibited the same type of aggressiveness, only she acted out her aggression and anger in a quieter way.

Diane: Julie, as you contemplated your afternoon and evening, were you aware of the plan for dinner and the meeting with the teacher?

Julie: Oh, yes, I was aware of it, and I knew how upset he would be if I didn't have everything perfect as he wanted it right on his schedule.

Diane: So, you knew that your husband was not going to be able to contain himself when he came home and found dinner not according to his plan.

Julie: He is like that every day. If it's not according to his way, look out, heads will roll.

Diane: You knew exactly how to make him angry that evening—that by not preparing for dinner, you were going to set him up for a tantrum.

Julie: Are you saying that I did it on purpose?

Diane: If you say that you didn't do it intentionally, then I believe you. I am saying that you knew how to prevent the escalation of the conflict and chose, for whatever reason, not to do it.

Julie: I guess I could have prevented it, but I couldn't. You have no idea how hard it is to get moving. I look at myself and I am a complete and utter failure in every way. And he just makes me feel worse.

Diane: I have some idea of your pain. I can imagine. I also can imagine that because of the ways that he has hurt you in the past, that the most effective way to hurt him back is to do nothing. I wonder if doing nothing is the most effective way at getting back.

Though their pain might differ in depth and degree, all couples are similar to Sam and Julie. Each has encountered injury from friends, families and marital partners. To be in relationship is to be injured. The act of injury is often the result of the other's normal defenses that we take personally. But, many acts of injury are not so innocent. Many are "offensive." They are part of a plan to hurt one's spouse before one's self is hurt again. "Do unto others before they do unto you."

Julie and Sam resented each other—they resented each other's lifestyle and they resented the undercurrent of emotional need daily manifested by passivity and activity. Each had wounds. Each saw the other as responsible. And each believed that they were entitled to retaliate—not only entitled but that they were morally justified as a way to ward off future attacks.

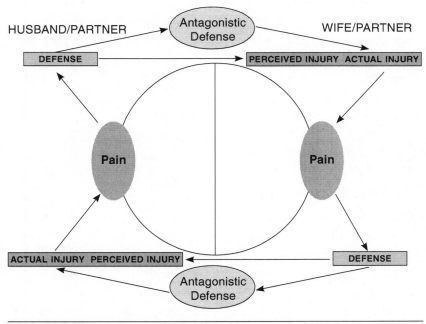

Figure 6.1. Actual injury as an antagonistic defense

MARITAL INJURY, DEPRAVITY AND THE POWER OF COUNSELING

Marriage reveals our dark side. To outsiders, our marriage may come off as a beautiful garden bursting with a profusion of color and symmetry. But we are not deluded. We know that the manicured gardens are the result of daily weeding and regular pruning. If our garden is left unattended, weeds will overtake and destroy all that is lovely. For underneath the beauty of every marriage, far away from the romance, there lurks the ever-present possibility of selfishness, deception, malice, rage and brutality.

We usually live in a quiet state of denial about the evil that exists within, and that which we create between us. It exists in every relationship, even though we would like to think of it applying to only a select few—those in abusive relationships, for example. Reserving judgment for the selectively labeled allows us to protect ourselves from a stark reality. That reality is that we—you, me, all of us, regardless of race, sex, wealth, education, religious values or any other variable—can be, and are, mean. Aleksandr Solzhenitsyn, the Nobel Prize–winning novelist, wrote, "If only there were evil people somewhere insidiously committing evil deeds, and it were necessary to separate them from the rest of us and destroy them. But the line dividing good and evil cuts through the heart of every human being. And who is willing to destroy a piece of their own heart?"[2]

The phrase used in historical Christianity, currently out of vogue, is *depraved*. This means that our being is affected by a polluting influence. To prevent the tendency to dilute the meaning of the idea, Christian leaders during the Reformation, such as John Calvin, used the adjective *total* whenever they referred to depravity. "Total depravity" means that all of us are corrupted down to the core of our being. And if left unrestrained, our depravity will lead to self-destruction and the destruction of Us. Left unattended, all gardens are weed patches. We like C. S. Lewis's depiction of depravity in his science fiction classic, *Perelandra*. The residents of the Red planet, Mars, referred to humans as the "bent ones."[3] We are not upright, but exist with varying degrees of misalignment. We are crooked.

There is tremendous delusional relief in believing, assuming and wishing that we are not as bent as another. We are always looking for ways to soften or mask ourselves from the reality of who we are. We do not exhibit our dark side all the time. But it is always there. A common expression for cowboys wearing their Sunday best is, "he washes up pretty good." The meaning is, he can be clean for a moment, but don't be fooled by the temporary shine. We try to put on this shine through contrary acts, such as kindness to stray cats, buying a burned cookie and a cup of lemonade from a child at a sidewalk stand—even though you don't want the cookie or don't like warm lemonade—or giving your seat to an older person on a crowded bus. We are a people veneered to look good, act good and sound good. But at our core, we all have the ability to inflict tremendous harm.

A brief reminder is appropriate concerning the pastoral and professional counselor's response to spouse-to-spouse spitefulness. Merely knowing the ease by which couples can injure does little good by itself. Telling individuals that they are depraved, that they have caused harm, or that they can be ruthlessly mean (1) is usually no surprise to anyone; (2) is usually met with resistance and denial, in spite of the fact that it is no surprise; and (3) usually has no effect on instigating change. But knowing of the cruel or callous ways that spouses treat one another is a central component of the beautiful dance of marital counseling. James writes at the close of his epistle about the one who brings others back after they have wandered from the truth. We see this mission consistent with that of the pastoral or professional marital counselor. There is a rescuing that occurs in the process of marital restoration. Couples have wandered off into waste-deep muck of conflict, sin and selfish protection. We find that it is the power of the counseling relationship with both husband and wife that permits you to look courageously at how each is guilty of inflicting harm. Such honest assessments of malice, spite and self-centeredness can only be beneficial if conducted within the walls of safety and trust. If no such environment exists, then either partner will employ their defenses to thwart any process that suggests exposure to risk or vulnerability. That such vulnerability was not shown between the two by themselves suggests that there is not sufficient safety or control to permit it. That they can't do it by themselves suggests that they need a third party to act as a reconciler—one who is trusted by both to send, deliver and interpret messages, and who can protect each by enforcing boundaries and helping them contain their defenses and emotional reactivity. We believe that the pastoral and professional role of restoration is more powerful than a couple's capacity to be mean to each other. While either spouse may refuse to engage relationally in the process, if they do choose to respond to the counselor's invitation for a healing relationship evidenced by the personhood of the counselor through the presence of integrity, grace, maturity and fairness, then, we believe, any couple can improve.

We liken the role of a pastoral or professional counselor to that of a parent of twin infants being taught how to eat. The babies will throw food, steal from each other's bowls and pout when they don't get their way. The parent with his or her children and the counselor with his or her couple, do not become offended by their misdeeds, are not pulled into the food fight with them, and are not provoked into utilizing defenses. Rather, the parent/counselor uses gentle control, removing and supplying resources, guarding each from the other, and ensuring that each receives nutrition, attention, and safety. In the process, a civility is instructed, modeled and internalized. Just as the children learn to behave with manners as their parent has instructed them, so the couple learns to behave with the manners that have been modeled by the counselor.

THE COUPLE'S "RIGHT" TO DESTROY

The destructive ways that both Sam and Julie behaved toward each other would be recognizable by the youngest grade-school child. Every first-grader knows the basic rules of community living, whether that community is a school or a home: "Don't be mean and do hurtful things." Kids understand this basic dictum and have no trouble identifying when they or others break the rule. So what is wrong with Sam and Julie? How is it that they can teach their children the basic components of life together but can't follow it themselves? And, they are intimate partners! Why is it that they probably have greater tolerance and cooperation with strangers or friends than they do with each other as intimates?

The answer, we believe, is that they feel entitled to act mean. They see it as their necessary right and responsibility. While they may act mean with some regret, they see it as an essential act required for survival. The term *destructive entitlement* has been described by many authors who write about family relationships. The term was developed by Ivan Boszormenyi-Nagy, a Hungarian-born psychiatrist who works extensively with families and couples in conflict. In popular language, the expression "cut off your nose to spite your face" explains the meaning of destructive entitlement.

> Through being victimized, a person can also earn the "right" to be destructive. This right is not essentially psychological either in attitude or content. Nor is it faulty learning, "basic fault," displacement, or projection. Destructive entitlement is a consequence of reality or the unfortunate vicissitudes of injustice.[4]

Destructive entitlements have their origin in childhood. We marry as damaged goods. Our childhood experiences were not able to provide all that we needed in terms of our thirst for significance, security and acceptance. Even the best parents are incapable of providing the perfect environment for human development. While the environment does affect the degree of "bentness," no one emerges upright. Even the best parents produce depraved children. It is who we are. This depravity is not because of our parents; it exists within. Therefore, they and we, even with our best intentions, are not capable of preventing it. Then we grow up and find that our marriages can be a safe environment to express our rage, disappointment and discouragement with the lack of justice and the imbalance experienced in childhood. Marriage can be the source of the balm that soothes the wounded soul, brings healing and provides the next generation with a new legacy. Or marriage can be a place where words are laced with venom, love and trust are trashed in favor of deception, and the legacy that transcends the generations is this: that no one should be trusted, especially your family.

Most people possess an innate sense that life should be just, balanced and fair. But it is not. Therefore, we look for ways to make it so. The great philosopher Francis Bacon referred to this as a "wild justice" in his work titled *On Revenge*.[5] It is our effort to establish balance after we have lost all hope and trust in the system—be it society, family or Us—to act fairly in our interests.

To Sam and Julie and to every other couple that engages in conflict, life isn't fair, and we deserve better. Because we believe that the scales of relational justice are off-balance in favor of our spouse, we decide to act unilaterally in "correcting" them. However, any correction will be perceived by the other as further evidence that their destructive entitlement is valid. "The underlying problem is that both sides may honestly feel that they are being cheated in the flow of family transactions. If both believe they are already paying more than they should be, it is difficult to alter the terms without perpetuating more injustice. At the same time, since both are already emotionally close, they know the other's weaknesses, and have acquired great skill at neatly hurting the other."[6]

The more troubled and injured the relationship, the more likely the marriage will operate under the axiom "the best defense is a good offense." Inflicting injury before the spouse has opportunity to injure is the more basic and destructive interactional pattern. Humorously, history has recorded the communication across the battle lines between British Lord Charles Hay and French Comte d'Auteroches at the Battle of Fontenoy in 1745. Hay is believed to have said, "Gentlemen of the French Guard, fire first." To which the French officer replied, "Sir, we never fire first, please fire yourselves."[7] Oh, that spouses could demonstrate such civility in their conflict, restrained by a moral imperative greater than themselves!

THE MOTIVATION FOR DESTRUCTION

So, why do they act this way? How can couples who start off in a white dress and a black tux, with all of the dreams and aspirations of relational bliss, end up as marital pugilists rather than marital partners? In talking with couples about their fights, we have observed two main motivations that reinforce the pattern of relational destruction: (1) it's necessary and (2) it's fair—they deserve it!

Necessary right to harm. Preemptive strikes are viewed as necessary to prevent further harm. In our irrational minds, it's part of the defense. This reason is logical, sensible, understandable and corrupt. Though we say it is corrupt, however, we can't say it is always wrong. Preemptive strikes may indeed be necessary to prevent further harm to oneself. In this case the goals of the relationship, the Us, are superceded by the needed protection of the individual. Its corruption is found in that while it offers temporary protection, it extends the tit for tat process that ultimately escalates the conflict. It is like Milton's perspective on revenge: "At first though sweet, Bitter ere long back on itself recoils."[8]

The internal message often sounds something like, "If I cause hurt, and cause this hurt to a significant degree, then he/she will realize that I am being hurt! And it will stop." A kick in the groin (literal or figurative) does provide a temporary respite to the person who kicked. It provides safety only for the time that the partner is consumed with his or her own wounds. Then there is retaliation—either active or passive. Gandhi said such a victory, attained by literal or emotional violence, "is tantamount to defeat, for it is momentary."[9] After recovery, the wounded one must think of ways to keep the partner from hurting him or her in the future, and must consider ways to balance the books, or even the score. Bono's words cited at the beginning of the chapter have clear resonance: "And you become a monster, so the monster does not break you."

Justified to harm. Every parent and every marital counselor have been placed in the position to hear children and couples insist, "But he/she did it first!" The offensive actions are justified because of a preceding injury. This motivation has nothing to do with self-protection; it is retaliation. It is rationalized as a fair administration of justice, but it is really marital injustice. It says, "Because of what the spouse has done, he or she deserved the harm that I have inflicted." It is the balancing of the scales by tipping them to the opposite extreme. Lauren reveals this justification in her explanation of throwing a coffeepot (hot coffee included) at her husband as he delivered cruel words amidst a corrosive fight.

> No, I am not proud of what I have done. I am especially sad that the kids saw me in that rage, but would I do it again? Absolutely, I would! I think I would change the time and place, but after what he did to me, he completely deserved it. I don't care if it put him in the hospital, I don't care that I got in trouble with the police and went to jail over this. He deserved it. Maybe he'll think twice about how he treats me.

Probably Lauren's husband will think twice—but not as she hopes. His second thoughts will not likely be how he can exercise fairness in light of his mean-spirited attack upon her. Rather, they will more likely be, "The last time I was in this situation she threw the coffeepot at me. So this time I am going to throw the toaster at her before she gets the chance. That will teach her a lesson." Our justifications to harm become futile efforts to "instruct," when neither partner is receptive to learning.

People report that these preemptive strikes produce a vigilante feeling. Underneath, there is a rationalization process built around the belief that the partner is going to get away with something, and you must prevent it from happening. Initially, individuals have some awareness of the immorality of their acts. However, we can easily drive through this ethical stop sign with delusional self-talk, which declares that justice or fairness is served if the partner suffers as we ourselves have suffered. Eventually, this rationalization becomes patterned and normalized as standard behavior so that there is no recognition of a moral hesitation.

ATTENDING TO OFFENSE AND INJURY AS PART OF MARITAL COUNSELING

There is no session as significant or powerful as when a pastor or professional counselor demonstrates that he or she is both stronger and gentler than either individual or the couple combined. The pattern of conflict created by couples that becomes a cyclical trap indicates that by themselves, they are unable to stop the process. Though they can see its corrosive effects, they feel themselves to be unable to stop it individually. Often, because both spouses want so much to have a successful marriage, yet they consistently fail, they assume that the responsibility for the problem must therefore lie with the other. The logic goes something like: "After all, look how hard I am trying, and it's still not working. It must be his/her fault." Left to fester, conflict and thoughts of blame become carcinogens. It is at this point in the model where the counselor can employ direct and specific confrontations to stop destructive, entitled behavior that is justified because of ongoing frustration in the marriage.

It is obvious to everyone that the first step in getting out of a hole is to stop digging. Because the counselor has successfully engaged the couple by understanding the pain and defense process, the right to challenge destructive practices by both partners has been earned. There are specific steps to help ensure a positive outcome for the confrontation of destructive marital processes.

First, the counselor must do the first thing first—build the trustworthy counselor relationship. The counselor has established crucial rapport. The Us has been fixed in the couple's minds as the relational goal of a healthy marriage, and the characteristics of their Us have been declared by the couple. They each know and understand what they are in counseling to accomplish, and that goal is not to defeat or control the other, nor convince the counselor that his or her marital partner is the embodiment of evil and not worthy of respect, regard or rapport.

Second, the counselor has established the ground rules for the session—the counselor can set the agenda, can serve as the protectorate of the vulnerable, and can bring under control either partner when he or she becomes harsh, aggressive or manipulative.

Third, the counselor will use the discussion of the typical process of pain-defense-injury to discuss the atypical and immoral process of destructive entitlements. To understand this, let's consider the work of the counselor, Diane, as she worked with Sam and Julie.

> You both have given me a full picture of how the mess between you grows. I can't help but notice that it starts out with some kind of disappointment or sorrow about the circumstances in your lives of which both of you feel powerless to change. Julie, I hear the sadness that you feel about the relationships that you do not have with your teenage children, the sadness you feel in your marriage by not being heard or believed to be capable. Likewise, Sam, it is clear that you feel most secure when there is predictability, efficiency and order, and that life in your home is stressful to you. You both have shared of your common reactions to pain events—what you do to manage circumstances to minimize discomfort, and how both of you react to the presence of the management efforts of your spouse.
>
> Now, I want you to assess yourselves on a different dimension. We

can call it the "my capacity to be mean" dimension. It is not the spontaneous reaction to painful circumstances. It is the clear, intentional decision that you know will produce pain, injury or difficulty for the other,
but you do it anyway, clearly justified for some reason, but still intentional and destructive. And as an aside, I am not going to let you tell me
what the other person has done to you. I want to hear what you see
yourself doing that contributes to this problem in your marriage.

Take note of how Diane identified with both of them using supportive
language, then in almost the same breath demanded from them that
they come clean about their destructive behaviors.

CONCLUSION: *DE CAPO AL FINE* . . . WITH *FINE* BEING GRACE

In a musical score we find the Italian phrase *De capo al fine*. It means to
go back to the beginning and play it over until you come to the word
fine. With marital conflicts, the cycle of pain, defense, offense, injury
and back to pain is repeated over and over again. Tragically, it can be
the song that never ends, unless a couple makes specific and intentional
decisions to stop.

In the next chapters we will consider a different cycle. It is one that
redirects pain toward grace rather than defense. It is a cycle that leads
away from destructive patterns and implements relational skills that
lead to intimacy.

NOTES

[1]Jimenez, J. R. (1957). *The selective writings of Juan Ramon Jimenez*. Toronto: Ambas-
sador Books.

[2]Solzhenitsyn, Aleksandr. (1973). *The Gulag Archipelago, 1918-1956, Vol. 1-2*, trans.
Thomas P. Whitney. New York: Harper & Row, p. 168.

[3]Lewis, C. S. (1972). *Perelandra*. New York: Scribner's.

[4]Boszormenyi-Nagy, I. (1986). *Between give and take*. New York: Brunner/Mazel,
p. 110.

[5]Bacon, Francis. (1625). "On Revenge." In *Essays on Counsels, Civil and Moral.*

[6]Stuart, R. B. (1980). *Helping couples change*. New York: Guilford.

[7]Bartlett, John. (1944). *Familiar Quotations*. Garden City, N.Y.: Little, Brown, p.
941.

[8]Milton, J. (2007). *Paradise Lost*. New York: Random House, book 9, line 44.

[9]Gandhi, M. K. "Satyagraha Leaflet, No. 13," May 3, 1919. <www.quotationspage
.com/quote/3246.html>.

7

GRACE AND JUSTICE

Mercy, detached from Justice, grows unmerciful.

C. S. LEWIS, THE HUMANITARIAN
THEORY OF PUNISHMENT

HERE IS A TWO-PART STATEMENT that we believe can be made
unconditionally: (1) No one can achieve mature, contented, successful
existence unless someone has extended to that person sacrificial, unmerited love or *grace*; furthermore, (2) no one can achieve mature, contented, successful existence unless he or she returns that grace to others
with a commitment to fairness, which we refer to as *justice*. Grace and
justice, love and fairness—marriages cannot thrive without them.
Grace and justice are the two components required for couples to offset
the caustic effects of pain, defense and destructive entitlements. But
grace and justice, left to our own devices, would be rare occurrences if
it were not for admonishing, teaching, modeling and encouraging them
into being. Gardens don't naturally grow in the aftermath of a fire;
weeds do. Gardens are planned. Gardeners are selective as to the particular foliage that is cultivated and will be permitted to flower. Grace
and justice are the plants to be grown to replace the use of defenses in
the presence of pain. Counselors don't just put out fires, they teach
couples how to grow gardens.

In the counseling profession, no phrase is as sacred as *therapeutic relationship*. Lambert and Barley summarized the articles that described

what makes counseling work. They found "that the development and maintenance of the therapeutic relationship is a primary curative component of therapy and that the relationship provides the context in which specific techniques exert their influence."[1] Their conclusion was not that the counselor-client relationships cause healing; rather, it is the relationships that permit the specific intervention to be received and implemented into the lives of the clients.

Their conclusion calls for an important question: What type of relationship is necessary in order for marital counseling to work? It is our opinion that a therapeutic relationship is characterized by the same qualities that are required in a successful marriage. Counseling researchers call this a "parallel process." It is when pastors and counselors demonstrate in the real relationship with couples what they wish the couples to demonstrate to each other. Counselors that model, exemplify, and administer grace and justice in their dealings with couples, we believe, create a counseling climate that diffuses the need for defenses and permits pain existing within and between intimate partners to be soothed. In the presence of grace and justice, clients are free to lower their defenses.

To us, this chapter is crucial for being an effective marital counselor. First, it will focus on explaining who couples are to be to each other—gracious and just—in their efforts to store and restore intimacy. Second, it will focus on explaining who counselors are to be, in order to help the couples who come seeking marital reconciliation.

RELATIONAL GRACE

Grace is one of those magnificent words that have been so normalized over generations, such that its power and significance is often misunderstood. Most think of grace superficially, as a prayer before a meal, or an Audrey Hepburn demeanor or style. Christians are more familiar with God's grace through the work of Christ on the cross because it is an essential component of theology for all Christians. Our use of *grace* is a human application of the ideas represented in divine grace set to marriage and family contexts. In simple terms, grace means to receive a good thing that is unmerited. We did not deserve the gift of salvation; we accept it as an act of faith or trust in God's goodness given to us.

Similarly, relational grace is a gift offered without precondition. It is the most powerful force in human relationships. The offering of goodness, kindness, gentleness or patience when the circumstance calls for self-protection, isolation, control or demand is the single most transformational power in human-to-human relationships. To show grace in marriage is the most delicate of arts.

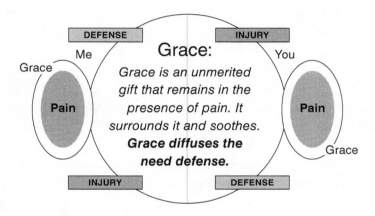

Figure 7.1

The case of Robert and Marti: Becoming gracious partners. Robert and Marti were artists. They were newly married when they came to therapy. Both were fifty-seven years old. They came because they were afraid. So much was new and different, they wanted to enlist professional services from the beginning. They grew up together in a small industrial city in southern Indiana. In high school they dated some. Marti really wasn't interested; Robert wasn't very cool back then. Forty years separated them after high school. Marti married a farmer from a neighboring community. The marriage started off well, but financial difficulty—a string of failed farms—was a burden too great for them to shoulder together. She was widowed as a young woman in her early thirties with four children when her husband died in a single-car accident. He was intoxicated. She raised her children as a single mom, staying in the same small town and working in a drugstore, and later as a schoolteacher. In that community there was ample support for the challenges of raising her children. Life was rough financially, but she succeeded. She never really considered marriage again—she had more important things to accomplish. She would say with a sad humor, "I have four children; I don't need a fifth." After she finished her job, she found herself alone, living in a small town, able to allow love to return.

Robert had never married. He was successful starting and developing a business in Chicago. Romance did not seem to work out in his life. His employees became his family. He often said that he had ten wives, ten husbands and about thirty children—but none of them were his. He had given up hope for personal intimacy years ago but exhibited a quality of goodness through the way that he gave to others. He was a George Bailey type, rich with friends. His introverted personality allowed him to be comfortable with times alone. He loved to read. He served on a number of charitable boards. However, at age fifty-seven, he did not have many other challenges ahead of him. He was successful professionally, but he often ate microwaved meals alone in his home. He never really got depressed from this aloneness—he could stay busy—but he was becoming more and more saddened by the prospect of retirement. Retire to what? He found that his business was losing some of its challenge. To maintain the competitive edge required his full attention and all of his energy, but he didn't feel that he had it any longer. He knew that the business should be sold, but it was his life.

Robert returned to his hometown in tragedy after being away for twenty-five years. He went to bury his mother. His father was buried there, having died when Robert was a young man. It was his first time to return to the southern Indiana town as an adult. There he met Marti through a mutual friend, and it was good. They began corresponding, visiting, and then they decided to marry.

The relational grace between Robert and Marti was a gift of acceptance without the demand for being somebody different. Robert and Marti knew they faced challenges in being able to experience and demonstrate love. For many years they fortified themselves against the pain of isolation—each found ways to give care and affection to others, and managed to receive love and trust. Both spent their lives primarily being faithful providers for others; now grace would call them to be faithful receivers—to allow them to trust in each other. They started seeing a counselor before they were married, which continued after the wedding. They wanted help in learning to be both graceful and fair.

The counseling experience started slowly, because there was no pressing issue, no crisis, no threat. If there was intensity in this process, it was intense politeness. Robert and Marti were very polite to each other and to the counselor. The conversation was kind and gentle, but relatively motionless—counseling wasn't going anywhere. Holding fast to the idea of parallel process, the counselor told them, "I thoroughly love being with you in these hour sessions. You show to me and to each other love and respect that is not often observed. But I am aware of an absence. I think that it is the absence of vulnerability. In the commitment to be kind to each other, I wonder if we have sacrificed some level of honesty and openness. I wonder if your kindness is a defense to guard against being close and being known."

The counselor identified the defense being used in the room and offered it back to them as a gift. The operating idea is that defenses in "real life" are going to be exhibited in "therapy life"—so what a counselor receives in the counseling office is likely very similar to how the couple conducts their relationship with one another. The counselor found Marti and Robert to be unusually kind, at the expense of speaking of their respective disappointments and difficulties. The gift given to the couple was the counselor's willingness to accept their defenses, should they need to retain them, and simultaneously offering to the couple the freedom to live beyond them by taking risks toward grace with one another.

Marti caught on first, choosing to challenge Robert's tendency toward isolation. The intensity of grace could be seen as Marti held Robert's face in her hands, gently caressing his cheeks. She boldly challenged his fear, which was evidenced by the defenses of isolation and escape. "Robert, I am strong enough to be close to you. It hurts me when you keep me from you—not when you just want to be alone, but when you are trying to protect yourself. Not hurt me like you're trying to be mean, but hurt me as I see your wounds, and your pain becomes my pain."

Marti had many reasons to respond to Robert's fear using her own defenses. Her fear likely matched his, and her experience gave legitimacy for self-protection. Instead, she courageously offered relational grace. Marti's actions raise a crucial question: "Who should show grace first?" Our response is, "It doesn't matter." When grace is initiated, equal reciprocation must occur or protective defenses will have to be reinstated.

Robert's eyes darted back and forth. He struggled to stay with her words. Crawling under the sofa would have been much safer, but he remained. Receiving grace requires courage. Though it is a gift without conditions, it is a demanding gift. To receive grace you must remain in relationship when every part of your defensive, protective being calls for you to run. To receive grace requires you to trust.

Marriage that is graceful—literally full of grace—is truly radiant. It is that radiant grace that is obscured when pain provokes our defenses. Defended couples cannot shine. So they come to us for help in achieving the glow, the brilliance and the joy. Marti and Robert chose to learn the conduct of grace with the aid of a marital counselor. They understood that new mental structures needed to be created for both of them to adjust from their position of single adult to their desired position within an intimate Us. They didn't know that they were seeking to become gracious partners. They didn't have the words, but they knew the idea, and that a marital counselor could help them get there.

Grace as a component of marital therapy. In our view, it is relational grace that is transmitted in successful Christian marital counseling. It is the pastor or counselor who models it, creates a therapeutic curriculum for its transmission, then coaches couples in its delicate administration. Pastors and marriage counselors too frequently move to justice through admonition, confrontation and solution finding. If such endeavors occur prematurely, the defenses are raised, passive or active resistance is encountered, and change, growth, and maturation are thwarted. But by initially modeling grace and then teaching it, the counselor can help couples contain their pain and create an alternative to their defensiveness.

Return to the cycle of conflict. We have argued that conflict begins with the presence of pain and that pain's existence demands that each of us act in its defense. The self-protection that pain provokes is usually constructed to limit access to all who might draw close and exacerbate our vulnerability. Pain and its defenses put into motion a chain of responses and interpretations that perpetuate a cycle of injuries and subsequent defenses. The result is that we build emotional barriers with those whom we share intimate commitments. We hurt and distance those with whom we are closest and with whom we have covenanted to manage the challenges of life together.

Grace envelopes pain at the time when the person is most vulnerable. Grace surrounds it and contains it. Marital grace draws near to the pain of another when all signals scream, "Run away!" It is not easy to walk closely with your partner as they fight depression or grief or bitterness or a host of other painful issues. Paul Tournier, the eminent Swiss physician who wrote extensively about courageous living, explained how difficult grace is: "We need to see that universal sickness, that innumerable throng of men and women laden down with their secrets, laden down with their fears, their sufferings, their sorrows, their disappointments, and their guilt. We need to understand how tragically alone they find themselves. . . . Yet what eats away at them from within is that they may live years without finding anyone in whom they have enough confidence to unburden themselves."[2] Grace is that process of being "unburdened."

We have found that it is easy to teach *about* grace from the pulpit or from the classroom, but it is more difficult to exemplify and model grace to couples in the counseling room. We have found that grace as a focus of instruction is not a skill that can be observed and practiced, then copied. Teaching grace to conflicted couples is similar to teaching angry children to be nice. It is possible to demand niceness, but what you get is external compliance and suppression of angry emotion. Instead, grace (and niceness) is taught through the experience of reciprocating acts of grace, initiated by the counselor to each of the conflicted partners in the presence of the other. In essence, the counselor says by his or her actions, "I will love each of you simultaneously, while understanding that each carries resentment and hurt caused by the other. If I can possess the knowledge that each of you can cause injury and hurt, and nevertheless maintain a sincere understanding of you and affection toward you, then each of you can learn to offer the same gift to one another."

This principle of teaching grace is drawn from Contextual Family Therapy and the theory of Ivan Boszormenyi-Nagy. Boszormenyi-Nagy developed a graceful intervention that he labeled "multi-directed partiality."[3] In essence, it is a therapeutic gift that says, "I will be partial to you (client A) and receive your life hurts. And I will hold that pain for you." Then turning to the spouse, "And I will be partial to you (client B) and receive your life hurts as well. And I will hold yours (client B) while at the same time holding yours (client A). My gift to both of you is that I can be partial to each at the same time." Hargrave and Pfitzer described multi-directed partiality as first an attitude held by the therapist, and second as a technique used in therapy.[4] As per the attitude, they write "that the psychotherapist is aware and accountable to all people in the relationships who may be potentially affected by interventions."[5] In regard to their methods, they write that "it is a technique of understanding and crediting all relational parties for the different concerns, efforts and impacts of what people have done in relationships and what has been done to them."[6]

It also can be seen within the biblical frame. Colossians 4:6 admonishes the believer to use words that are full of grace. Literally, this means to "make your words into unmerited gifts." Likewise, Paul prepares both Timothy and Titus to occupy their role as pastor with terms such as *exhort, give recognition, teach, encourage* and *exemplify goodness* (2 Tim 3:10-17; Tit 2:1-10). These pastoral gifts given to those whom the counselor serves are the essence of counseling. They are words of healing, hope and encouragement.

JUSTICE

Grace in relationship is elegant. But grace cannot dance alone. While the application of grace has a transforming capacity, we find that it cannot be sustained by itself. Grace must be partnered with justice. Grace is fragile, and it lacks endurance. The fragility of grace occurs because partners must offer a gift of vulnerability—specifically, the lowering of self-protective defenses. In the demonstration of grace one becomes open to being hurt by the manipulator. Unless grace is matched by justice, a pervading bilateral commitment to mutual fairness, grace will be retracted. The gift giver will stop giving if it's not safe.

In the opposite way, justice is robust, tough and enduring. But justice can be seen as insensitive and unkind. Apart from grace, justice can appear like the seven-hundred-pound gorilla—self-centered, dominating and, at times, merciless. Though it is usually conducted out of a need to

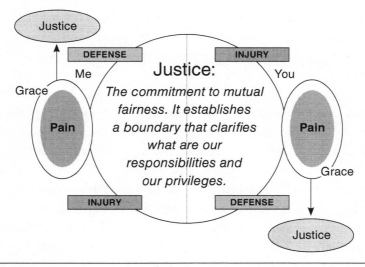

Figure 7.2

make previous wrongs right, attempts at justice outside of the buffering effects of grace raise suspicion that the actor is acting out of self-interest, not out of an Us interest. But in the presence of a gracious, consistent, mutual investment in the relationship, justice stabilizes relationships. The repeated demonstration of fairness and mutual decisions that lead to mutual benefit creates a stability and security in your partner. It suggests that he or she will be present when grace is required by the other. While grace is the loving, unmerited gift to another, it must be replenished or it will die. Justice is the exhibition of earned rights.

If you conducted a free association with the word *justice*, ideas such as civil rights, protest marches and challenging oppression likely come to mind. Not marriage, and not counseling. But the big social issues related to justice between races, economic classes, nations and the sexes are the same issues that must be confronted by couples seeking to build successful marriages in counseling. Ultimately, justice is about a fair distribution of power so that both individuals and couples can fulfill God's purposes. Intrinsic to marriage is justice, fairness and well-being.

Justice is a set of values, disciplines and behaviors that reflect decision making by both marital partners. It is the way that a couple decides together everything from career, children and church to the color of the bathroom wallpaper and whether to have cloth or leather seats in the new car. The nature of just decisions made by a couple reflects the value they place on Us, and their individual perspectives on entitlement and rights. Justice is the declaration that the boundary between people will be fair.

Justice is mutually limiting and mutually enhancing. Justice is limiting in that individuals surrender some rights in order to benefit the Us. For example, if sexual fidelity, honesty and personal disclosure are chosen, then limits on sexual expression, self-interest and self-protectiveness are established. This justice is voluntarily self-imposed. If a spouse is stating, "The only reason I am not having multiple sexual relationships is that my husband or wife won't let me," then it would be easy to see how that marriage would quickly become imbalanced and nonfunctional. That justice is limiting means that there are restrictions, rules or principles that both individuals accept in order to enhance the space between each partner. This mutual limitation enhances the Us.

That justice is mutually enhancing means that decisions made must be good for one spouse at times, then good for the other spouse at times. And that process of being good for one, then good for the other— literally the process of give and take—must be balanced over time.

Successful couples make decisions using a variety of models. For many, one of the most contentious areas of decision making is financial. Money is power. The one who controls the money controls the relationship—or at least a major part of it. Margery and Stan were a couple that made judgments and established fairness by creating a system of separation. They both worked and both deposited their paychecks into individual accounts. Both paid mutual and personal expenses from these accounts. Over time, their debts were managed and they both reported a high degree of satisfaction over how they exercised judgment regarding their financial resources.

In contrast, Deanna and Drew were a single-career couple. Drew provided the income while Deanna worked with their young children at home. Drew's paychecks were automatically deposited. Deanna was responsible for paying the bills and making the majority of purchases. Together they considered investment decisions and attended seminars on retirement and money management. Theirs was a judgment of mutual responsibility.

The specifics of what couples decide is far less important than how they decide. Justice is the process that, when it is well served, will always result in a product of fairness—an internal perspective of balance between what is given and what is received.

The case of Ron and Shirley: A need for justice. Ron and Shirley recognized the need for grace and judgment. They were both strong and competent people. Shirley was an elementary school principal. Ron was a human resources consultant. They reflected individual competence and maturity. In therapy they had learned the cycle of their pain. They were able to connect with empathy to present, historical and familial injury. They understood each other, and were able to speak directly about their individual needs, and how their Us can comfort each person from the harshness of life. They could be gracious, but not for very long. They also needed justice to refuel their grace.

Their conflicts were usually generated from the contrary demands of work and family. Ron's work took him out of town frequently. Shirley's work often included evening meetings at the school. They both needed the other to exhibit grace—as both frequently needed the assistance and accommodation of the other to manage the care of their three children, ages ten, seven and five. But when situations demanded compliance, resentment followed. Their sacrifices to one another were not gifts of grace; they were manipulative. Listen to their story:

Ron: We seem to continually be offended by each other's work demands.

I got a call from Shirley while I was in a meeting. She said that she had a crisis at school with a parent and had to have a meeting late at the district office. I had to rearrange my schedule to pick the kids up at the babysitter's on time and get them dinner. It meant canceling some appointments that I had and rescheduling them for another time. I was glad to do it, I want to help, but then when I need her to cover for me, I don't feel the same level of support. I feel as if I am making most of the career sacrifices, and it doesn't feel *fair* sometimes.

Shirley: I know why you feel that, Ron, when you are in town. But you are gone sometimes two days and nights out of every week, other weeks more. Then it's just me alone, managing the kids' soccer, piano, gymnastics, homework, baths and everything else. I do feel *entitled* to lean on you, and I am less inclined to bend on other days when you are in town. I feel that I bend with your travel, and I need you to bend for me now. It's my *turn*.

Ron and Shirley use some key words that reflect the need for justice within their relationship. We italicized them: *fair, entitled* and *turn*. Both are acting sacrificially, both are treating the other and the Us with priority commitments. Both are doing their jobs as loving spouses. And both feel the imbalance created when sacrifices are made. Justice will produce fairness and allow for the expression of mutual entitlements that are constructive to the relationship.

The justice that sustains grace can recognize and declare right from wrong, "your turn then my turn then your turn again," my entitlement to take, and my responsibility to reinvest that which I withdraw. To uphold justice is to continually weigh the relational scales and maintain equilibrium of fairness to her, fairness to him, and honor to Us. Justice, in the presence of grace, leads to establishing a safety in relationships.

Yet justice is hard because it includes the display and division of power. It becomes particularly precarious within marriage because both of the "judges" have a vested interest in self-service. This interest cannot be denied, for each individual has need to draw from the Us the necessary physical and emotional sustenance to retain vibrant life. Yet when this becomes the only goal— self-service above service to the other—the Us will suffer and possibly die. A healthy, mature marital court, consisting of two judges who are committed to upholding their constitution (their Us), can avoid this travesty of justice. However, it remains a very difficult task. It requires judges who are secure within their relationship and able to graciously accept human limitations but still be fervently committed to justice. The Spanish word for commitment is similar to the English word *compromise—compromiso*. In this case the commitment of marital judgment demands a mutual compromise.

Justice as a component of marital therapy. If one were to consider the existing individual, marital and family therapies, there is an absence of attention to justice as an aspect of counseling. Overall, justice as a component of therapy is nonexistent in all theories except for one: Contextual Family Therapy. Boszormenyi-Nagy viewed justice through the metaphor of a ledger book. The accounts between partners must balance overall for the relationship to be sustaining. If one side is more frequently giving or one side is more frequently taking, an attitude of destructive entitlement will be present. This perspective of fairness is essential in maintaining relationships. Writing of this idea, Hargrave and Pfitzer state:

> As we interact, we possess an innate sense of justice that demands that as we give our interactions to the other in relationships, we are entitled to receive something from the interactions of the other. This process describes justice at its most essential form. When we balance what we are entitled to receive from relationships and what we are obligated to give in order to maintain relational existence, we have satisfied our innate drive toward justice.[7]

Counselors must exercise great care in contemplating their role in helping couples establish justice and fairness. Because counselors can perceive marital conflicts from the outside, with greater objectivity, it is easy to impose justice rather than to let the couple balance the relational ledgers themselves. If such an imposition occurs, the counselor could accidently form an alliance with one spouse against the other and actually be undermining the goal of relational restoration. Rather, most of the time justice is formed when the counselor aids each partner in understanding and being understood. Hargrave and Pfitzer encourage the use of a ledger in which the entitlements and obligations for both spouses are delineated. Here couples identify specific needs held by each, and how such needs will be addressed by the other. By identifying needs, we are not addressing tasks such as doing the dishes or mowing the lawn; we are referring to essential needs in the relationship such as respect, intimacy, safety, companionship and love.

Teaching justice. Teaching justice is not as difficult as one might think. For most, acting justly is a skill learned early, then developed in growing capacities throughout life. Children have an early sense of justice. Indeed, the phrase, "That's not fair!" has been declared by every four-year-old child. As we age, our sense of justice matures with us. The key developmental skill that comes after childhood is the ability to delay gratification; that is, to allow for just decisions to be applied to others knowing that yours will come subsequently. In essence, the formula for relational justice consists of a commitment to fairness plus a capacity for taking turns.

> Counselor: Mike and Sherry, when I hear you each argue your positions, I join you in the sense that neither of you is making any progress. Is that what it is like for you?
>
> Sherry: Yes, I mean we just seem to talk in circles.
>
> Mike: I get frustrated that the more we talk the less we accomplish. So I just figure, "What's the point?"
>
> Counselor: Sure, it would be exasperating for both of you. Here is what I see: when one is talking, the other doesn't seem to be listening; rather, I think each of you is trying to build your rebuttal. So let me ask you both, what is happening when the other person is talking? What is your brain doing?
>
> Mike: It's as you described. I wouldn't say that I am not listening, but it is true that my main purpose is to convince Sherry that I am right.
>
> Sherry: Yes, me too. When I am talking I have the sense that he is not listening to me, so I need to argue harder—that is when my volume gets louder. Then when he is talking, I am so keyed up that I am thinking about what I am going to say next because he didn't really hear what I said the first time.

Counselor: Okay, so here is the challenge: you are operating in a "me against you" style. It's a tug-of-war argument. You both yank hard enough to ensure that the other person doesn't win. Progress is thwarted. In fact to your credit, it seems to me that you are mature enough to not pull too hard. Either one of you could act in an overpowering way in order to get what you want. Remember, that is the destructive entitlement idea that we talked about earlier. Neither of you has chosen to win at all costs; but neither of you is willing to lose. So it's like you have this unwritten rule that you won't give in to the other, and you won't let the other win. So here you are, stuck. Imagine that each of you is six years old and you are playing together in the neighborhood. You have one bicycle between you. What rule will you use to make sure that both of you have fun?

Sherry: We would have to take turns.

Counselor: What you learned in first grade is what you will have to do here. Now, I'd like to hear you hammer out the rules that will allow you both to stop tugging at the rope, but rather pull together.

In this vignette the counselor brought the issue of justice, fairness or balance back to the couple, working with them in a way that kept their defenses in check. The counselor facilitated the commitment to acting justly toward one another by not taking sides. This begs the question, Isn't there a time in which the counselor should take sides? What about when there is an egregious violation of love and trust, such as violence or infidelity? Are counselors to remain neutral even then? To which we say, competent marital counselors are never to be neutral but always objective, seeking creative ways for the couple to experience healing and restoration. Counselors should confront violence, infidelity, deception, disregard or any action that causes injury to the Us with unyielding condemnation. However, counselors need to always keep in mind that the objective is to confront behavior while seeking to restore individuals to a safe and secure intimacy.

Counselors can address such severe insults to love and trust by communicating that each partner has received injuries and hurts at the hand of the other. Each of those injury sets need to be respected and regarded for what they are. While each individual might be injured and feel justified in perpetuating the conflict by causing hurt back, the counselor's actions may not be equal in severity. As an example, I might be angry at you for breaking my kitchen window, so in retaliation, I firebomb your house. While both of the actions are criminal, they are not equal in severity. Both you and I are responsible for our actions, but the restorative path for each spouse will not be the same. We are indeed all sinners, but the consequences for individual sin and the process of restoration because of our sin will vary according to severity.

GRACE AND JUSTICE IN TANDEM

We think of grace and justice operating like a two-stage rocket. Grace, the first stage, has the capacity to lift the airship off the ground. It has enough power to provide initial lift. However, it can not carry or sustain the rocket into orbit. The second stage, justice, is able to hold the rocket and maintain its course. Justice, by itself, can evoke defenses, leading to a power struggle in which spouses are pitted against one another. Usually this leads to a stalemate in power—two entrenched opponents making little progress. Grace, on the other hand, has the capacity to diffuse situations and to encourage mutual disarmament so that justice can be rationally considered by both spouses. It is knowledge and experience in grace and justice, the very centerpiece of the Christian tradition, which contains the transformational power for individual reconciliation between person and God, as well as relational reconciliation between members who share community, especially the intimate community of marriage.

NOTES

[1]Lambert, M. J., & Barley, D. E. (2001). Research summary on the therapeutic relationship and psychotherapy outcome. *Psychotherapy: Theory, research, practice, training, 38,* 359.

[2]Tournier, P. (1967). *To understand each other.* Louisville, KY: Westminster John Knox Press, p. 49.

[3]Boszormenyi-Nagy, I., & Krasner, B. R. (1986). *Between give and take: A clinical guide to contextual therapy.* New York: Brunner/Mazel.

[4]Hargrave, T. D., & Pfitzer, F. (2003). *The new contextual therapy.* New York: Brunner Routlege.

[5]Ibid., p. 100.

[6]Ibid.

[7]Ibid., p. 72.

8

EMPATHY AND TRUST

*Trust requires the constant exercise of intelligence,
truthfulness and courage. Perhaps that is why it is so rare.*

WILLIAM LEDERER AND DON JACKSON,
THE MIRAGE OF MARRIAGE

IN THE PROCESS OF RELATIONSHIP restoration you have successfully helped a couple put out the fire. The pain and defense patterns
have been controlled. The couple no longer has to douse their domicile
with the fuel of their defensive interactions to protect themselves. The
perpetuation of destruction is contained. Furthermore, you have helped
them learn alternatives to firebombing each other in the eventuality of
future conflicts. They know that they can establish an environment of
fairness where there is a balance of giving and receiving. In essence, you
have encouraged them to build a new foundation of relational intimacy
through grace and justice. Now you need to build the house. But what
are the tools and skills that a couple must give and receive in order to
have a successful marriage? The couple now wants to rebuild and has a
vision for the new design, but the marital counselor needs to help them
with the characteristics and abilities that are essential for relational intimacy. While there are many components required for successful intimacy, the two essentials addressed in this chapter are empathy and
trust. Eckstein and Cohen found that of the twenty-one factors associated with successful relationships, three stood out as the most impor-

tant: communication, empathy and trust.[1] While communication is a well-established and articulated relational skill, we find that it is teaching the ability to connect on an emotional level (empathy) and creating an environment of vulnerability and fidelity (trust) that are most critical to the counselor's work with couples.

Empathy is a modern word that is similar to the biblical idea of compassion. Empathy declares, "I will care for you." Romans 12:10 contains this concept when Paul writes that we are to "be devoted to one another in brotherly love. Honor one another above yourselves." Later, in verses 15 and 16, Paul writes, "Rejoice with those who rejoice; mourn with those who mourn. Live in harmony with one another" (NIV). Empathy works in contrast to our defenses. While protections serve to isolate and distance ourselves from others, empathy forms emotional ties and connections. When the devotion of empathy is conducted over time, trust is the outcome. If the song of empathy is "I will care for you," the refrain of trust is, "I will care with faithfulness and consistency." Trust is the mainstay of any successful relationship. "Trust—the level of confidence that people have that another person will consistently respond to their needs and desires—is a central component of close relationships. Indeed, researchers using prototype analysis have shown that it is not uncommon for people to regard trust as the most important component of a loving relationship."[2]

It is our passion for you as marital counselors to impart empathy and trust skills as you work with couples. Couples long for more than the absence of conflict; they want the presence of intimacy. Understanding the characteristics of empathy and trust is an essential aspect of relational harmony. Most pastoral and professional counselors understand empathy as that skill that Carl Rogers identified as the core ingredient to promote change. It is through empathy that we as counselors learned the skills of listening, reflection and summarizing. The primary message was, "It's not about you, the counselor; it's about the client." Counselors in training are tasked with connecting with their clients on an emotional level. Having identified with couples' individual pain and defenses, and having established the path through grace and justice, counselors can now assist the individuals in having empathy for their lifetime lover, who at times is overwhelmed with wounds such that they act in detrimental ways—both toward themselves and toward their marriage.

EMPATHY

Because empathy is common, it is easy to see it simplistically. Most pastors and marriage counselors are no stranger to empathy as it is likely the most familiar phrase in counselor training. Often, the first lesson in "Counseling 101" includes the "big three" skills developed by Carl Rogers: genuineness, unconditional positive regard and empathy. Indeed empathy, the ability to take on the perspective of another, is one of the most basic requirements of counselors. An oft-quoted definition of empathy by Rogers is worth repeating:

> The state of empathy, or being empathic, is to perceive the internal frame of reference of another with accuracy and with the emotional components and meanings which pertain thereto as if one were the person, but without ever losing the 'as if' condition. Thus it means to sense the hurt or pleasure of another as he senses it and to perceive the causes thereof as he perceives them, but without ever losing the recognition that it is as if I were hurt or pleased or so forth.[3]

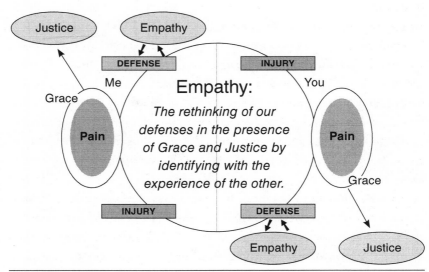

Figure 8.1

To Rogers, and to all mental health counselors, empathy is an attitude and an intervention exhibited by counselors to assist clients in promoting personal growth. The power of the professional counselor is seen in his or her ability to demonstrate care and compassion for those seeking assistance. But we see empathy not just as a counseling intervention, but as a relational skill and intimate attitude that is a contrast to the cycle of pain and defensiveness. Empathy is not just what successful counselors do; it is what successful couples do.

In our counselor training experiences, when we reflected back on the emotional expression of the classmate who was pretending to be a client, we prided ourselves on how well we were "empathic." Do you remember thinking how good you were as a counselor? Unfortunately, that exercise had very little to do with actual counseling skills, and little to do with empathy. Regarding this, Rogers later wrote, "Non-directive therapy, it was said, is the technique of reflecting a client's feelings. Or an even worse caricature is simply that, in non-directive therapy you simply repeat the last words the client has said. I was so shocked by these complete distortions of our approach that for a number of years I said nothing about empathic listening."[4]

On the surface it appears that empathy is easily mimicked. However, to be empathic is to care, to care with your whole being, and to make your care known to the other who likely feels abandoned and alone. It is this perspective that you as the counselor must model and must assist the couple in being able to demonstrate toward one another. Empathy is not sustained in the presence of self-protection and defensiveness. It comes forth when there is grace and justice, and it serves to soothe and bring healing.

There is an irony found in the importance of empathy—healthy relationships are based on the expression of a care and concern that is heartfelt, mutual and consistent. In conflicted relationships this essence is supplanted by the need for self-protection. Individuals cannot risk caring for the other; they must maintain their guard and focus on self-interest. In such conditions, relationships fail at providing essential love and affection. The continued defensive vigilance serves only to drain and exhaust. In their frustration, the couple seeks professional

assistance from a counselor or pastor. Beyond cognit.
and the formation of new behaviors, the nature of the assist.
the counselor extends a genuine, heartfelt care and concern—the u
selor offers empathy, the very ingredient that the couple had been denying one another because of their mutual need for self-protection. But
the power of empathy in couples counseling is not in showing care to
the couple, but in modeling care for the couple to emulate to one another. It is like Paul admonishing the Corinthian believers to "follow
my example as I follow the example of Christ" (1 Cor 11:1 NIV).

Empathy as a component of marital therapy. The task for marital
counselors is not just to be empathic, but to emulate empathy as an essential relational tool and intimate attitude. For healthy marriages, empathy is not a technique, it is an attitude and a value. At its core, empathy is the embodiment of Christian "other-ness"—an intentional focus
on meeting the needs of others, specifically attending to the physical,
emotional and relational needs of one's intimate life partner. Jesus described this as the life purpose for all who follow him: "Whoever wants
to be first must be slave of all" (Mk 10:44 NIV). To the Christian couple
seeking to focus on marital success, this message can be overt and specifically biblical. For the couple not coming from a Christian tradition,
your therapy will be exactly the same—to advocate a value of understanding and caregiving. For the marital counselor, empathy is the path
down which he or she leads the couple. Indeed, McCullough, Worthington and Rachal found that it is empathy that plays the mediating
role between offense and forgiveness, or between conflict and resolution.[5] Empathy lowers defenses. It gives legitimacy to the position of
the other. James Framo, one of the founding voices in family therapy,
wrote: "One of the things which seems to help marriages, as I stated
previously, is that the partners have a more empathic understanding of
each other. Having been given the opportunity to hear each other's life
history and now knowing what the spouse had to struggle with, partners find each other's behavior more understandable."[6]

Godfrey Barrett-Lennard defined empathy with greater clarity by
describing it in three phases.[7] To summarize, the first phase is when the
person gets it—that is, the person meets his or her spouse on an under-

standing level in which he or she can identify with the emotional experience of the spouse. The second phase of empathy is when the person shows that they get it, honoring the spouse's emotional experience by acknowledging its existence. The third phase is when the spouse acknowledges that empathy has been expressed, received and returned. All three components—resonation, communication and reception—are necessary for empathy expression.

We find that empathy as a relational skill and attitude can be contained in three questions:

- What does the person feel in this situation?
- What would I like the person to feel in this situation?
- If I changed by doing X, would that make a difference?

When a spouse addresses the first question, it brings them into the realm of the other. Typically, this question creates a rather cognitive reaction. It is an important first step in the path toward empathy, but usually it's a very small first step. It tends to be limited to just the naming of the feeling. The second question tends to move the couple toward the affective power of empathic identification. When the counselor confronts a partner with a question of intent—as in, "Is it your hope that your husband/wife would feel (anxious/depressed/sad/etc.) when he/she is in that situation?"—couples often make exponential growth. Two things occur here: first, spouses realize that their intimate lover is suffering and that they can join with the sufferer on an emotional level that brings some measure of relief through the intimacy of companionship; and second, spouses realize that their life partner is their attendant and sojourner through their pain, not the opponent and object of their pain. The effect of empathy is that it moves couples from the position of facing off at opposite sides of a battle line, to allies and collaborators who are facing a common enemy shoulder to shoulder and side by side.

Teaching empathy to couples. We find that empathy is not an intellectualized skill like learning to compute addition or subtraction. Though professors can teach the mechanisms of reflection, paraphrasing and summarizing of clients' emotional messages, they cannot teach *care* for clients. They can, however, demonstrate care for the student, and in doing so, show how they cared for their clients. Empathy is absorbed through the experiential pores, rather than consumed by the impersonal process of intellectual advancement. We find that couples will learn empathy in the same way that counselors are empathic. As counselors, we can follow the guidance of Paul as he teaches Titus to have an effect on those with whom he is entrusted: "In everything set them an example by doing what is good. In your teaching show integrity, seriousness and soundness of speech that cannot be condemned" (Tit 2:7-8 NIV).

Tom and Lori have walked through the marital conflict cycle. They get it—intellectually. Now their counselor, Katherine, is helping them get it empathically. Lori is explaining what happens to her when Tom is "just hanging," usually watching a basketball or football game with his friends on Sunday afternoon. Katherine will be walking Tom and Lori through the cycle that steps around defensiveness and permits them to build empathic understanding of need. Their intent is clearly on "How I can be a caregiver to you, my intimate life partner." Take note of how Lori initiates the conversation. It focuses on *her* stuff, to which Tom plays an active role in creating. This permits Tom to maintain an empathic attitude that is intent on providing aid and comfort, rather than a defensive attitude that withdraws, protects or attacks.

> Lori: I know how important those times with the guys are for you. I see how much fun you are having. I often feel hurt when you are watching the games because when you are with them, I feel . . . I feel negated.
>
> Katherine: Before you two go any further, let's recall what the goal here is.
>
> Tom: The goal is to get it. Not to get your way, but to get it. It is that I am wanting to understand Lori. And Lori is trying to understand me.
>
> Katherine: Good. Lori, any other details?
>
> Lori: Yes, that when I talk about a problem, it's not just my turn to vent and Tom's job to fix something. We both are trying to understand ourselves and the other person.
>
> Katherine: Great. Now Tom, take off. Tell Lori what you hear her saying.

Tom: I hear that something is happening when I am watching sports in the game room with friends. You are feeling devalued or something . . . which you have said before, but I don't think I really understand what is happening.

Lori: Well, I really like your friends, and I like it when you have fun with them. But on Sunday afternoons I see you treating me differently. You are coarser and less kind. I see everyone else in the house, me and the kids, more tense as you are able to relax. You know, if Nicholas has a problem with anything—say, for example, his bike needs air in the tires—asking you to pitch in and help is an insult or something.

Tom: So, when I am in my "game mode," having a good time with friends, you are feeling more on edge, and maybe abandoned or something?

Lori: That's pretty close. It's not like you are unavailable or out of reach. I'd much prefer you to be at home than at a sports bar or at one of their houses. It's more like I am an inconvenience if I need you.

Katherine: Tom, how would you phrase the "What would I want?" question?

Tom: It would be something like, "When I am watching a Final Four basketball game, what would I want Lori to be feeling?" And the answer is that I don't want her to be on edge or regretting that I have friends over. I want her to have fun. I'm relaxing and chilling. I want her to be able to relax with me.

Katherine: How do you feel now, knowing that when you are hanging out with your friends, your wife might be feeling stressed or alone?

Tom: No, that's not what I want. That is not what I want at all. If I am taking a break, then I want you to be able to take a break too.

Lori: Thanks, but sometimes that is not realistic. When you are taking a break with your friends, the phone still rings, and the dog still has to be taken outside, and the neighbor kids still ring the doorbell, and all that other stuff still happens.

Tom: Okay, I think I get it. If I am less into my stuff—still watching the game but not thinking that "this is my time," then you wouldn't feel like you were supposed to do everything else.

The effect of empathy on a marriage is incalculable. It creates a tone and tenor that enhances individual growth. This growth is the motivation needed to offer nourishment back to the marriage and the family with acts of enhancement rather that narcissistic fortifications. A main effect of empathy is that it neutralizes defensiveness. In settings of understanding and affirmation, defenses are a waste. They become like the outdated tank, plane and cannon from previous wars, now used as a city park relic for children to climb while parents walk their pets. These hostile tools are made into inert artifacts. Their violence is neutralized. Empathy is not the final product of marital intimacy; it is a principal pathway. It creates momentum for couples to trust, then trust becomes the fuel required to carry the couple toward intimacy formation.

TRUST

Michel de Montaigne describes a good marriage as "a sweet association in life: full of constancy, trust, and an infinite number of useful and solid services and mutual obligations."[8] In many ways, trust is the most fundamental of human tasks and therefore a primary component of intimacy. While empathy serves as a magnetic force that pulls people toward one another, trust is the adhesion that can keep people together. We have found that, though not an empirically based opinion, the question of trust is a better gauge of relational intimacy than the question of love. Ask most individuals whether they love their spouse, and the answer is usually an immediate, almost thoughtless yes. But ask the same person whether they trust their spouse, and there is usually a bit of hesitation in the response. "I'd have to think about that one for a bit . . ." is a more common response.

There is no concept more important, more essential and more difficult to the Christian experience than that of trust. Indeed, the organizing idea of the biblical text is to tell the story of God's dealings with humanity for the purpose that the creatures, as operators of choice, will place *trust* in the Creator. The very first lesson in *Luther's Small Catechism* says, "We should fear, love and trust in God above all things."[9] But the exercise of trusting—the relinquishing of one's will to God—has proven to be a difficult task for all from the story of the

Garden to the present story of each living person.

Trust and trustworthiness defined. Trust includes two very distinct but reciprocating roles within marriage: being trustworthy and being trusting. Being trustworthy is to be a "catcher," the one who is faithful, dependable and stalwart. It is to be reliable when another takes a risk, catching the other when they act on their courage to jump. A trustworthy mate is the "friend in foul weather." The trustworthy partner creates a security for the other to extend one's self in becoming known. Hargrave writes, "Trust serves as the basis of intimacy in that responsible and reliable behavior [i.e., *trustworthiness*] on the part of the spouses allow them to predict that the other will be committed . . . and will behave in such a way that each can fit his or her life to the other's [i.e., *trusting*]."[10] To be trustworthy, to catch a lover when he or she leaps, is creating an environment for another to trust all the more. It is to accept another and to be able to focus on their needs. A trustworthy partner is reliable, faithful and consistent. This is the "I will be there for you" trust; the "jump, I will catch you" trust. The trustworthy person is one who shows steadfastness regardless of personal circumstances. Trustworthiness "is characteristic of mature, nonexploitative relations of any kind. It helps people control their exploitative tendencies in close relationships. It serves self-interest through retaining the resource of a given relationship, and through functioning as a resource for relationship. Caring for another person's needs can enhance personal satisfaction through establishing a basis for equitable balances of imagination and love."[11]

For every act of trustworthiness, or catching, there is an act of trusting. To trust is to jump, to take risk and be vulnerable to another, believing that the other will be faithful in attending. Catching and jumping is a description of ongoing give-and-take relationships. Trusting requires that you lose control of some type of circumstance by placing yourself in a position of emotional vulnerability. To be trusting is to leap or step out in faith. Trusting is to create dependence and vulnerability. Trusting says, "I will take a risk by extending to you the vulnerabilities of my soul and the longings of my heart, believing that you will protect them as you would your own." To trust is to place oneself in a position to be hurt,

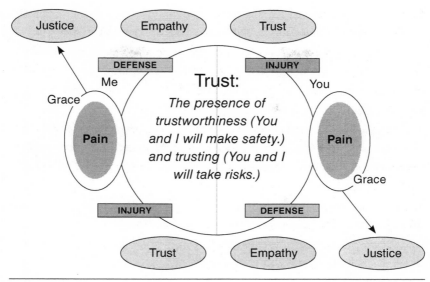

Figure 8.2

should the other prove to be unfaithful or untrusting.

Trusting is fundamental. It is among the most basic of human skills necessary for survival. It's what we learn to do first as babies and toddlers. Families teach children to trust. Erik Erikson is considered by most to be the greatest contributor to the field of developmental psychology, the branch of psychology that focuses on how people grow, change and mature throughout life. His eight stages of development are basic information in every university Psych 100 course. He describes the process of growth common to all in the human experience. His theory is based on an idea of epigenesis, which states that the first challenges in life have an effect on the later challenges. And that first task—the one upon which all others depend—is trust. To Erikson, trust is the first life skill upon which all other life skills are built.[12] Similarly, Bowlby showed that an adult's capacity to be trusting is related to the quality of his or her attachment to parents in childhood.[13] Of this, Roberts writes, "The Christian psychologist has reason to agree with Bowlby on the centrality of trust for the mature personality, and to accept the massive support he has garnered to the conclusion that trusting in mature life is deeply affected by the trustworthiness of one's early attachment figures."[14] In other words, the evidence is abundant that the ability to love with vulnerability is tied to the skill a person possesses, grown through the demonstration of secure relationship with one's parents. The sense of safety experienced from early caregivers builds the relational expectation shown in adulthood. They show us how to catch, and that assists us in our confidence to jump.

Trust as a component of marital therapy: the case of Michele and Alex.
Pastor Cameron worked with Michele and Alex as part of the church's premarital counseling program. They worked through all of the stages of the model. Trust and trustworthiness proved to be the most challenging idea for both of them. Michele, age forty-three, with two children, had married before and was not sure she could marry again. Even though she loved Alex and believed he was completely different from her first husband, she was not sure she could trust him. Alex, fifty-two, was a bachelor. Michele and Alex were family friends; they grew up in the same church. They both sang in the choir. Alex had been a consistent and faithful friend, a true gentleman in every sense of the word.

They were brought together when Alex experienced a series of Transient Ischemic Attacks (TIA)—mini-strokes—that left some minor impairment in memory. Michele was one of the people who offered to care for him in his recovery by cooking meals and helping him with the details of his work. They realized that they had a "love-improbable" growing between them. Michele vowed to never love and never marry a man again. Alex had accepted the reality of his bachelorhood, and was not thinking about marriage.

Pastor Cameron found that both were committed to a successful marriage, but they had to fight an undercurrent of mistrust. Neither had violated trust, but both carried significant fear that impeded their ability to trust.

Pastor Cameron: What is your internal reaction to the idea of trust?

Michele: It really isn't hard to trust *Alex;* it is hard to trust anybody. Trust is just really hard for me. In my first marriage, it took a lot to convince myself to marry, and it was a disaster. While there were good times, most of the time it was unfair, painful and abusive. Now, with

Alex it is like I am standing on the edge of a crevasse, contemplating the leap to the other side. I guess I am questioning my ability to make the jump, and the suitability of life on the other side. I mean, I know Alex is a great guy and the most honorable and trustworthy person that I have ever met. But still, I don't know if I can do it.

Alex: I am sorry that Michele struggles in this way. I try to do all that I can to reassure her that I am committed to her. I know she looks at me and wonders whether I am going to be like her first husband. I do all that I can to convince her that I am different. I don't raise my voice, I don't demand that I get my way. She knows who I am, and who I have been for most of my adult life. I am not going to change once we marry and become an evil man. I am who I am. I've never been married, not thinking that I would become married. But because God has brought me to this place, I have no doubt that I can be a great husband and we can have a great marriage.

Pastor Cameron: I want you both to imagine that you are hovering above the conversation between the three of us—you are watching and listening to what is going on and where the discussion is going. Michele, most of your words center around the theme "I don't know if I can do it . . . It might be a bad idea . . . My former marriage was awful . . . Do I have assurances that this one will be different . . . I am a fool for thinking of this . . . *run away!*" Does that capture the theme?

Michele: Completely. Plus the words, "I love Alex. He's a really good man. But can I do this?"

Pastor Cameron: Got it. Alex, your messages are different. You are not talking about your fear, about the challenges that are a threat to you. In fact, you probably have more adjustment, more change, and more at risk than Michele does. You have been responsible for only one person for twenty-five or thirty years. Anyone would expect you to be in severe consideration over this decision. But you are not. Instead, you are focusing on your reliability, your consistency and your faithfulness.

Alex: I don't think I really ever go there. I don't think about it. Instead, I focus on who I am supposed to be as a husband and as a stepfather.

Michele: I think that his style makes it even harder for me. He is not struggling with this decision. Maybe if I thought that it was difficult for him, than it would be easier for me. Instead, to him it looks so simple, and I question, "Is it real, can I trust it?"

Pastor Cameron: Well said. Michele, you are focusing most of your attention and your energy on whether you can trust Alex. You are not giving much thought—out loud here with me—to how you are going to *be* for Alex. You are asking, "Can I trust?" You are not asking, "Am I trustworthy?" Now Alex, you are doing the opposite. Your efforts are almost exclusively directed to convincing Michele that you are trustworthy. You say, "I will be there for you . . . Trust me . . . I am not afraid."

Alex: I don't think that I am doing it as an act or a way to convince her.

Pastor Cameron: Never would I think that of you. You words are honest and with full integrity. But with both of you, they are filtered, emphasizing one idea and not others. Let's talk about the thing that you do, and more importantly, let's talk about that which you don't do in regard to trust and being trustworthy.

Mason Cooley could have been thinking about Alex and Michele when he wrote, "Mistrust makes life difficult. Trust makes it risky."[15] Alex and Michele knew of the difficulty of mistrust. They also knew of the risks. Their fear was used to block the jump to marriage. There was too much fear, too much at stake for both of them. They found themselves stuck—not having the strength, confidence and security to trust the other, yet having too much invested in a relationship that was too good to walk away. Counseling for them was an exercise in trust building.

This story has a happy ending. It is not a "happily ever after" ending, but a "we will begin" ending. The story hasn't ended; their marriage is in process. Alex and Michele learned something about playing catch—about leaping and receiving. Pastor Cameron's work with them was ongoing. He was committed to the long haul of their relationship. He understood them, and they had an available support in their pastor. On most days they soar . . . and land safely. Some days one or the other has insufficient courage to leap or catch. At other times the emotional fog limits visibility such that it is too risky to launch—the next day might be a better day to fly.

Teaching trust. A crucial question for marital counselors is, "If trusting is tied to the fixed experience of childhood relationships with parents, is it possible to teach trust?" Can the leopard change its spots of fear, protection and self-absorption? We respond to couples who ask that question with a resounding affirmation and with a sobering explanation. Marital counselors can play a crucial role in helping couples build their capacity for trust.

Nathan, a marital counselor, describes how a client learned the capacity to trust her fiancé through the experience of counseling.

Recently I received a call from a former client. That is not unusual. Clients often call. When they do it is not usually because they are full of joy—I definitely work in a profession where the axiom "No news is good news" is true. What was significant about this client was that she was flying through Chicago on her way home in another state. She and her husband were returning from their honeymoon. She paused long enough to give me a call to say hello. And to say thanks.

I initially saw her two years earlier. We worked together for about eight months. She came to counseling because she wanted to leap but was unable to bend her knees and spring forward. She would just shake, standing at the edge. Eileen was twenty-eight. She had known William for three years, and they had been a couple about five or six times during that three-year period. She loved William. She loved his patience, his warmth, his openness and security. She felt safe with him. They would spend time together, go to dinner, see a play, have long talks on park benches, feeding ducks who had come to recognize this couple as their best source for nutrition. With him, she was in love. Away from him, she was consumed with fear. "What if it's not right? What if I love him and he turns out to be something other than what he is right now? I am not sure that I can take the risk of making a mistake." So, controlled by anxiety, she would tell him that she loved him but could not see him anymore. It wasn't fair to him. She knew that she could never allow herself to make the leap of trust.

Together we examined blocks to trust—previous injury, fear of failure, need to control for protection, perfectionism, unrealistic expectations, as well as her perception of William's ability to be trustworthy. Gradually, her anxiety softened its controlling grip, and her courage to stay in relationship grew. When we stopped therapy, she had confidence to assess and move toward intimacy or move away from it without the entanglement of controlling fear. Trust won. She learned that she could trust herself to decide, and eventually, her decision led her to be able to trust William.[16]

Krasner and Joyce suggest that trust "lies at the heart of every redemptive investment in the dialogic process and in "the sine qua non of fairness or justice *between* person and person."[17] Trust is initiated by us as marital counselors as we demonstrate the audacity to receive each wounded spouse regardless of their past, their privilege or their power. Successful trust begins, for both counselors and couples, with the capacity to be trustworthy.

Trustworthiness is a characteristic of one's being that begins and is sustained by behaviors that demonstrate an "inconvenient acceptance"— that is, the reception of another in spite of his or her limitations, flaws, inadequacies and sin. To be trustworthy is to consistently act outside of your self-interest. In the curriculum of marriage, first you teach trustworthiness, then you teach the capacity to be trusting. If individuals are secure with their lover's commitment to catch them, then they may choose the risk of leaping into their arms.

EMPATHY AND TRUST IN TANDEM

"I love you and I trust you." No two ideas, joined together, are more powerful than these. From the experience of empathy and trust emanates identity. The Us flourishes when empathy and trust are present. Individual spouses become like those in whom they place their faith, reliance and dependence. Empathy declares that "I love you for your benefit, not for my own." Then, tied to trust, it declares, "I am placing my hope in you." Marital counselors who envision the power of marriage through the Christian story from creation to the cross can emulate, model, instruct, admonish, encourage and collaborate with couples to be compassionate and trustworthy, to receive empathy and become trusting.

Because of the experience of empathy, the door of trust is opened for life mates to enter. In the presence of empathy and trust—in the very declaration of love and safety—defenses are of no use. The patterns of self-protection that emanate from our pain are recognized as useless baggage. Empathy and trust make our defenses archaic toys from our childhood immaturity.

NOTES

[1]Eckstein, D., & Cohen, L. (1998). The couple's relationship satisfaction inventory (CRSI): Twenty-one points to help enhance and build a winning relationship. *The Family Journal, 6*(2), 155-58.

[2]Miller, P., & Rempel, J. K. (2004). The development and decline of trust in close relationships. *Personality and Social Psychology Bulletin, 30,* 695.

[3]Rogers. C. R. (1959). A theory of therapy, personality and interpersonal relationships as developed in the client centered framework. In S. Koch (Ed.), *Psychology: A study of a science: Vol. 3. Formulations of the person and the social context.* New York: McGraw Hill, pp. 184-256.

[4]Rogers, C. R. (1975). "Empathic: An unappreciated way of being," La Jolla, CA: Centre for Studies of the Person, p. 1 <www.elementsuk.com/libraryofarticles/empathic.pdf>.

[5]McCullough, M. E., Worthington, E. L., Jr., & Rachal, K. C. (1997). Interpersonal forgiving in close relationships. *Journal of Personality and Social Psychology, 2,* 321-36.

[6]Green, R. J., & Framo, J. L. (Eds.). (1981). *Family therapy: Major contributions.* New York: International Universities Press, pp. 153-54.

[7]Barrett-Lennard, G. T. (1981). The empathy cycle: Refinement of a nuclear concept. *Journal of Counseling Psychology, 28,* 91-100.

[8]de Montaigne, Michel. (1588). On some verses of Virgil, *The Essays (Les Essais).* Paris: Abel Langelier, book 3, chap. 5.

[9]Luther, M. (1943). *Luther's small catechism.* St. Louis, MO: Concordia Publishing, p. 5.

[10]Hargrave, T. D. (2000). *The essential humility of marriage: Honoring the third identity in couple therapy.* Phoenix: Zeig, Tucker & Theisen, p. 107.

[11]Krasner, B. R., & Joyce, A. J. (1995). *Truth, trust, and relationships.* New York: Brunner/Mazel, p. 13.

[12]Erikson, E. (1977). *Childhood and society.* London: Paladin.

[13]Bowlby, J. (1973). *Attachment and loss: Vol. 2, Separation: anxiety and anger.* New York, Basic Books.

[14]Roberts, R. C. (1997). Attachment, Bowlby and the Bible. In R. C. Roberts & M. R. Talbot, *Limning the psyche: Explorations in Christian psychology* (p. 225). Grand Rapids, MI: Eerdmans.

[15]Cooley, M. (1992). *City aphorisms: Ninth selection.* New York: Pascal Press.

[16]"When she called, I suggested as a show of gratitude that she name her first child after me. She counter-offered with their first hamster. I agreed." From Nathan, a marriage counselor.

[17]Krasner, B. R., & Joyce, A. J. (1995). *Truth, trust, and relationships: healing interventions in contextual therapy.* New York: Brunner/Mazel, p. xi.

9

FORGIVENESS

The glory of Christianity is to conquer by forgiveness.

WILLIAM BLAKE

OUR RELATIONSHIP RESTORATION CYCLE ends with forgiveness, and it is where mature relationship begins. Unfortunately, forgiveness is misunderstood. Usually it is seen as the thing couples do to pronounce a conflict to be over. It's used to convey "kiss and make up." This is a shallow forgiveness similar to our childhood apologies. It is easy, free of vulnerable exhibitions of self and avoidant of the acceptance of the other as they really are. Recall the memory of the scolding parent, saying, "Chris, apologize to Terry, then you can join the group again." "No, Chris, not until you're sorry." "That's good, now Terry, what do you say to Chris?" "Thank you, now that wasn't so bad, was it? Go out and play, and no fighting!" Seeking forgiveness, moms and dads can feel relieved that everything is "better" now. But dear Chris and Terry were not invited to pursue justice and restoration, only avoidance. Chris and Terry learn in this instructional moment that forgiveness is what we do to placate others.

Forgiveness in this setting is the act of contrition that marks the end of a conflict, misunderstanding or argument. It is the painful step of humiliation—confessing a wrongdoing. It is the social expectation that forgiveness will mark the end of the penalty phase. If one confesses, repents and is forgiven, then one is set free from the judgment passed.

This type of forgiveness is what one has to do to avoid trouble. This forgiveness does not draw us into the depth of injury; it gets us out of situations and circumstances that we prefer to have erased.

Regarding this shallow, sentimental idea of forgiveness, L. Gregory Jones writes, "Unfortunately, the cost of forgiveness is too high for many people. Consequently, they invent and turn to cheaper versions of forgiveness, ones that will enable them to 'feel' or 'think' better about themselves—or simply to 'cope' with their situation—without having to engage in the struggles to change or transform the patterns of their relationships."[1] For most couples, forgiveness is a shallow and powerless experience.

Rather than a sentimental happy ending that is ultimately driven by avoidance and denial, we see forgiveness as a courageous beginning. Our relationship cycle does not end or culminate with forgiveness. It is the invitation to enter into a relationship of depth with another. Instead of an act of penitence, as in saying that you are sorry, we see forgiveness as characteristic of a deep relationship, a style of living, a way of being. Forgiveness is the fulfillment of being a graceful person and the manifestation of that gracefulness within the intimacy of marriage. It carries us deeper into relationship, and many times deeper into the pain experienced in life with others.

An essential element of marital counseling is to teach couples about forgiveness. Usually, this instruction is a corrective education. Couples know about simplistic forgiveness, but they may not have experienced the beauty and burden of intimate forgiveness.

UNDERSTANDING FORGIVENESS IN THE CONTEXT OF US

Joan sits in her counselor's office describing a litany of offenses that she has experienced while married to Tom. According to her, he is mean, self-centered, addicted to work, uncaring, insensitive and dominating. At the end of her extended list she concludes, "But of course I have forgiven him."

This creates intrigue. The counselor asks, "You say that you have forgiven Tom. I am curious just exactly what that is for you?"

Joan replies, "Oh, I have to forgive him. Life would be awful if I didn't. And besides, I can't just go around being angry all day long.

Tom is mean to me and mean to my kids. He's not going to change, Tom is just that way. I learned a long time ago that I had to forgive him. He's never going to back down or give in or say he's sorry. So I forgive him so I can go on. I just don't let it bother me. He has absolutely no effect on me. We are married. I suppose we will always be married—I mean I am not going to leave him or anything."

Joan's depiction of forgiveness is important and necessary for her survival. She should be commended for developing a way to make a difficult relationship tolerable, in light of the absence of other options. But we would be remiss if we let Joan's forgiveness story be the representative model of what forgiveness can be. Joan is expressing an understanding of forgiveness, but it is not forgiveness in its full form. That leaves us to the challenging task: just what *is* forgiveness?

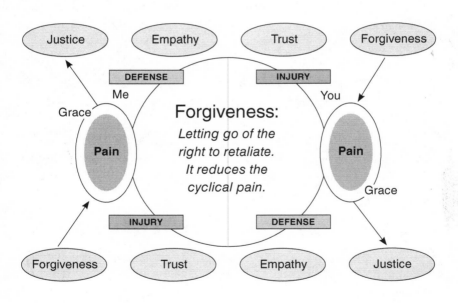

Figure 9.1

Forgiveness is deep, rich and dimensional. Single-sided explanations can create a misunderstanding of all that forgiveness includes. Our effort to define this profound idea is outlined here, then amplified in subsequent paragraphs.

1. Forgiveness is the healing experience subsequent to a violation of rights.

2. It can occur from the perspective of the one whose rights have been violated, the one who violated the rights of the other, or both.

3. Frequently, forgiveness includes both the initiator and the recipient of harm or injury.

4. Forgiveness is progressive in that it may include increasing levels of vulnerability between people.

5. Forgiveness can grow beyond a set of actions conducted by injured and injuring parties into a way of being or an outlook on life that is held by a person, and is the characteristic of the relationship between people (i.e., their Us).

6. The event around which forgiveness is needed can be a single occurrence, but most of the time it is repeated instances of injury in which both spouses are the initiator and recipient of harm.

Forgiveness as more than an apology. The variation in how prominent thinkers have defined forgiveness is indicative of the complexity and the dimensionality of the idea. The educational psychologist Robert Enright, one of the most prolific authors on the subject, describes forgiveness as when we "overcome the resentment toward the offender, not by denying our right to the resentment, but instead by trying to offer the wrongdoer compassion, benevolence and love."[2] In stark contrast, the family therapist Terry Hargrave says, "Forgiveness demands that trust be reestablished between two people after a relational hurt. Essentially, forgiving is relationship reconstruction."[3] To Hargrave, forgiveness is a part of the dialogue existing between people. While there are crucial individual decisions and commitments, he indicates that forgiveness is fundamentally a social exercise. Finally, Jones describes forgiveness from the perspective of a theologian: "forgiveness is not so much a word spoken, an action performed, or a feeling felt as it is an embodied way of life in an ever-deepening friendship with the Triune God and with others. As such, a Christian account of forgiveness ought not simply or even primarily be focused on the absolution of guilt; rather, it ought to be focused on the reconciliation of brokenness, the restoration of communion—with God, with one another and with the whole creation."[4]

Forgiveness experienced by the one whose rights have been violated. Most of the professional and popular writings on forgiveness have focused on the person who has been injured by another and whether that person should offer forgiveness to the one culpable. The moral question that is usually asked is, Should a person forgive another who has caused hurt? to which there continues to be great debate. We see the core moral question for the person who has been injured as being, What will you do with the *power* that you now possess? This question is contrary to our thinking because we typically perceive the injured as being powerless—that's how they got hurt in the first place.

The fact is that the one who has been injured is in a position of self-defense. Some form of protection must be implemented. There is nothing that the other person can do to demand, force or coerce the removal of one's protective defenses, be it anger, resentment, isolation, avoidance or any other defense. The injured person has the power to control her or his own protections, and to release the other by forgiving is to relinquish the right to retaliate and to release appropriate insulating protections that are both self-destructive and relationally suffocating.

Forgiveness experienced by one who has violated the rights of another. It is strange that for every act of forgiveness, there must be one who forgives ("the saint") and one who needs to be forgiven ("the sinner"). Almost always, people identify with the saint, the victim, the one who has been wronged. Similarly, the vast majority of both professional and popular research and self-help material in print focuses on the needs, concerns and growth processes of the saints rather than the sinners.

Forgiveness from the sinner's perspective is the role that people usually delay, deny or dilute. But the Christian faith calls us toward a different path, one that centers not on our victimization—as in "you wronged me"—but on our sinfulness and our repentance. Jesus declared, "I have not come to call the righteous, but sinners to repentance" (Luke 5:32 NIV). If marriage is to be redemptive, it must acknowledge our core sinfulness and our need for redemption as sinners, as individuals who have caused pain in the other by way of acts of selfishness that place our own immediate and long-term gain over and above the interest of the Us.

Forgiveness experienced by those who are both the initiator and the recipient of harm. We think of forgiveness as being discrete declarations after specific offenses have occurred. And that would describe a part, but only a small part of the forgiveness story. Forgiveness is the language or the dialogue between intimates. It is how good marriages thrive, often without ever using the word *forgiveness*. Rather, these couples exercise the act of forgiveness, having recognized that they each take part in the destruction and the construction of their intimacy. Both husband and wife are injuring and injured beings. Each does harm and is harmed, by both intention and by accident. It occurs daily, even hourly. To be close to another is to stand in a mixture of the depravities of both in order to render grace and seek justice. In this setting, forgiveness becomes like two beggars searching together to find bread, where both are committed to seeing that each secures enough food to survive. This forgiveness is a way of understanding the essence of intimacy: it is to place into life the admonishment that Christians should "be kind and compassionate to one another, forgiving each other, just as in Christ God forgave you" (Eph 4:32 NIV).

Forgiveness as a progression to vulnerability and intimacy. Those who reject the idea of forgiveness usually understand it in terms of dichotomous categories. It's a switch that is either on or off, yes or no, "have forgiven" or "have not forgiven." If I forgive, then I relinquish all of my individuality, rights, and privileges and place myself in position to be victimized again. If I seek forgiveness, then I acknowledge wrongdoing, error or offense to which the other may leverage in the future.

Dr. Terry Hargrave has suggested that forgiveness is something drastically different.[5] It exists in degrees or in depths. He refers to forgiveness as occurring in stations which are not rigid and linear, but exhibit individuality and complexity. Forgiveness grows in depth and vulnerability parallel to a couple's quest for intimacy. For example, the first act of forgiveness exercised by either husband or wife is to the perpetuation of injury. The ability to block the actions that have previously done harm to the couple's Us is the most fundamental act of forgiveness. This first station, which he calls *insight,* empowers the individuals to name the injuries and their sources. This is not for the purpose of blame casting but for preventing the continuation of harm. It has an eye on the ultimate motive of the love and trust of marital intimacy. In Hargrave's model, forgiveness proceeds to the station of *understanding,* in which the forces and motives which prompted the historical injury become known. After the previous patterns of injury and injustice have ceased, and the forces that led to harm are controlled, the couple can focus on *providing opportunity to trust,* safely increasing the capacity for trusting by demonstrating greater trustworthiness. Forgiveness culminates with the *overt act of forgiving,* where couples show that they are trustworthy to eradicate injustice and create paths of healing for both the injured and the injurer. This deepest forgiveness is mutual reconciliation. Both exhibit responsibility for how they have hurt the other, and practice the care of restoring and healing their Us. We see this model of forgiveness like a river. One can be in the river, whether it's ankle deep or over their head. In the same way, forgiveness exists in degrees—it is a process that increases in depth, vulnerability and intimacy.

As one offers grace, establishes justice, experiences mutual empathy, and becomes trusting and trustworthy, it becomes safer to let go of fear of injury and to be in relationship without the need of protective defenses. But in relationships that are not safe, where justice is not established, empathy is not practiced and trust has been disregarded, forgiveness is a dangerous river—it is wise and discrete to remain at the shore, maybe only getting our feet wet. This forgiveness is legitimate. It is the essential phase of early restoration. The process of grace, justice, empathy and trust/trustworthiness may allow for greater depths with time. The restoration of relationship through the dialogue of forgiveness moves slowly toward greater depth.

FORGIVENESS AS A COMPONENT OF MARITAL THERAPY: THE CASE OF MEGAN AND JOSH

Forgiveness is a painful process for couples, as is any discipline and self-sacrifice. It is humbling to face ourselves in the context of intimate relationship, to see how we have harmed our intimate partner, and to remain steadfast as our loved one confronts and addresses his or her immaturity as well. Relational forgiveness consumes great quantities of emotional energy, including grace, justice, empathy and trust. These serve as fuel to power a couple's efforts.

Megan and Josh walked that path together. Between them they carried secrets and shame. Megan was abused by her brother. She became sexually active in early adolescence, became pregnant in high school and had an abortion without telling her parents, friends or boyfriend—it was her secret, known to no one except eventually to her counselor, twenty-five years after the fact. Megan was distant, isolated, suspicious and angry. She believed that everyone was untrustworthy—her family, her husband and her friends. She lived her life with that belief as a self-fulfilling prophecy: "Because no one is trustworthy, I will trust no one." She would not be known. She was friendly, responsible, kind and well liked, but forever distant, protected and depressed. The depression was kept well hidden. She married Josh because he was convenient. He didn't make many demands on her; he seemed to be consumed with his own world. He had money, he was funny, he was active and loved to do new things. They could enjoy life together—as long as it wasn't personal.

Josh was mean. That was his self-description, and no one disagreed. He married Megan while they were in college. He was not ready for marriage—he was interested in drinking, working on his car, getting through college so that he could go to work in the family business, and hanging out at the beach. (They attended college in a Southeastern region near the Atlantic Ocean.) He was unfaithful to her for the length of their relationship. He confided that once he had sex with a friend of Megan's while Megan was preparing dinner in the kitchen. There had been hundreds of encounters over the years—prostitutes, colleagues at work, friends in the neighborhood. He had never been "caught," but he knew that Megan knew. He knew everyone knew.

Josh had the life experience of an orphaned child—not literally, but figuratively. By the age of six he was independent, or more accurately, abandoned. No one was responsible for his care; he had to fend for himself. He used his wits and sometimes his fists. He could not count on food to be in the kitchen, or anyone to be home when he got home from school. Sometimes his parents were there, sometimes they were not.

Josh and Megan's marriage reflected a philosophy that emerged from their life experiences. The meaninglessness of life was conveniently directed toward each other. Yet in it all, they wanted to change. The couple was at the crossroad of middle age—both were ripe to the idea that their Us was drastically wrong and needed radical change. Josh initiated the change by seeking therapy. He had blown up at his boss and feared that his position in his company was threatened. Looking at his individual anger in therapy was an invitation to meet Megan and to understand how the Us and the anger interacted. Eventually, the therapy turned down the road to forgiveness.

Forgiveness did not work a miracle. They did not attend a weekend seminar and suddenly change from two brutally scarred spouses into intimate lovers. It took years, but it took hold. They learned the process—grace to justice to empathy to trust to forgiveness. It was as foreign at first as any unwritten language. This new mentality or idiom of forgiveness was learned in simple phrases. Principles grow slowly. They both were attuned to their defenses and could see the effects of their mutual self-centeredness. Recognizing the presence of one condition, they could imagine its opposite. Forgiveness for each was as much about self-restoration as a focus on restoring their spouse. The insight formed was the groundwork for forgiveness. It was how each previous life experience could leak into their marriage. Their new realm of care and concern grew from a new capacity for self-control.

Forgiveness for Megan and Josh was deep in intimacy and fear, trust and threat, and security and risk. It did not occur in a single session. They did not "kiss and make up." Over a stretch of months they realized the paradox that they each were the victim and victor, the abused and abuser, the defender and attacker. They saw themselves in each other. They saw their defenses, those childish tools needed for survival when the environment is harsh and threatening. They saw how each used their defenses for protection and for injury, and that they could stop it. They also saw how their respective families had encouraged the use of the protections. Immaturity is a group activity. The powerful river changed this couple. Standing on their respective banks demanding that the other accommodate just made their throats hoarse. Then they waded in, remaining in the shallows at first, but building the capacity to swim in the depths. Over time they each relinquished their right for satisfaction for harm done to them and accepted the enormous weight from the harm done *by* them. This made them humble, broken and approachable.

To forgive and be forgiven is to live in relationship with vulnerability. Forgiveness allows spouses to have open windows into each other's soul. The tension between forgiving and being forgiven is one of power. As a husband or wife forgives their partner, each retains or loses control of self and of the other, simultaneously. When a husband or wife receives forgiveness, they are acknowledging a violation of boundaries or rights, and their need to repair the breach. Forgiving and being forgiven is the intimate give and take.

FORGIVENESS AS JUDGMENT:
THE CASE OF LLOYD AND JEANINE

The path to the river of forgiveness is uphill. Though that makes no sense geographically, as rivers always occupy the lowlands, it makes perfect sense relationally. The journey from conflict to forgiveness is one that strengthens both capacity for individual integrity and relational resilience. Forgiveness is suited for individuals who take risks, for those who perceive and act with courage because they are driven by principles greater and nobler than their own individual wants. These are people who make wise and discrete judgments, who are not prejudiced by their own fear. People who aspire to become forgiving are those who recognize wrong—both theirs and that of the one with whom they hold intimate relationship—and act to change it. This is hard because it puts at risk the very relationship that the person is trying to save. Jeanine was that type of person. Her courage saved her marriage.

Lloyd and Jeanine had been married for twenty-six years. Lloyd was a tough man. Jeanine was mousey. (That's right, the courageous one was mousey.) Originally, I was not drawn to them with affection. My initial impression contained numerous negative assumptions. First, I didn't think they were serious about addressing their problems—I thought they would likely be a "two-or three-session burnout." Second, they were chain smokers. After each session, the odor of tobacco would linger the rest of the day. They made my office smell. Third, they were both alcoholics. Jeanine had been sober for about a year; Lloyd still drank excessively. Usually, three times per week he would spend the evenings at his tavern. He would take a cab, returning home intoxicated but relatively safe. Later in our relationship, I called him "a responsible drunk." Finally, they were "uncultured." Really, what I mean is that they were from a culture different from my own. I recognize now my prejudice held during our initial meeting had an expectation that because they were from a blue-collar tradition they would not be strong candidates for marital change. But therapy means that everybody changes, especially the therapist.

Lloyd was a fighter—an active fighter—"screamer, cusser, stomp out of the house, burn rubber in the driveway, and don't come back for two days" kind of fighter. Lloyd knew the laws of the street. He knew of violence from his childhood. His father taught him the way. Hard work, hard drinking and hard living were his legacies. Lloyd once said that he learned two things from his dad: how to work hard and how not to let other people ever hurt you. Fighting was as natural as breathing, and just as essential for survival.

Jeanine was a fighter too—at least she used to be. It was not as natural as Lloyd; it was an "art" learned later in life. Alcohol helped. With a little beer she could stand toe to toe with Lloyd and match him expletive for expletive. She was as good as he was at being bad. She knew it and it shamed her—so she decided to change. Jeanine's life had been quite different from Lloyd's. Her childhood was much more like life in a zoo compared to Lloyd's life in the jungle. She was the oldest and the caretaker. Her father was disabled from injuries sustained in World War II; her mom worked nights in a factory. Jeanine was the daytime mother to her four younger siblings. She recalled her life as very modest but not poor.

Jeanine and Lloyd met in high school. They were each other's dream.

To Lloyd, Jeanine was kind, gentle, affectionate and tender. There was a gentleness to her that prompted him to want to be with her. Likewise, to Jeanine, Lloyd was strong and handsome. He had a car. He could handle himself in the world. He was not afraid to stand up to authority, or to anyone for that matter. They married at age eighteen, ready to take on the world.

Both went to work in the local factory—they lived in a small town dominated by an auto industry assembly plant. Eventually they saved enough to buy a small house. Four children were born, but the youngest died in infancy due to a genetic heart condition.

Early in their marriage, alcohol began to have its effect. Initially it was part of their social circle. All their friends drank—at the bowling alley, the tailgate parties and just to relax after a long shift at work. About ten years into their marriage they made a significant life change: Lloyd left the assembly plant and started his own business. With a partner they started an auto parts store. It was a decision that had significant impact—some good and some bad. Jeanine had quit working a number of years before, right after the death of their child, in order to care for the others. They had planned for this work change, but the death of her child provided Jeanine time to be at home to think about her life. The more she thought, the more she drank.

The new venture required Lloyd to be away often. He was well suited for self-employment—it is a hard life, requiring much time and energy. Lloyd was strong enough for the challenge. Lloyd also started drinking more often—he would stop at the bar on the way home from work. He would typically arrive home at about 9:00, slightly intoxicated, slightly exhausted and slightly angry. Then they would fight, go to sleep and start over the next day.

This pattern continued for about ten years. Jeanine's and Lloyd's personal despair manifested itself in more drinking. The drinking served both as their common solution to their individual suffering and allowed them to express their anger toward each other more freely.

Jeanine resented her husband, and she resented herself for the condition of her life and her marriage. Her resentment grew to the point of action. But her actions came from someplace down deep, from a moral place, a place that exercised judgment and courage. "I hated my husband—I hated him because I thought he was mean and small and a coward. And I hated his drinking. But what I hated in him I also hated in me." Can you hear judgment in her words as she pursued justice? She looked at her life, her husband's life, and the direction of their life together and said, "I don't want to go there. I have to do something about it!"

Jeanine's judgment prompted her to act. She didn't possess insight into how to avoid the chronic cycles of conflict, but she knew that alcohol had something to do with it. She stopped drinking. Lloyd described it this way: "One Saturday morning about a year ago, before I started drinking in the afternoon, Jeanine said to me, 'I don't like where we are going. I can't control you, but I can change some things that I do. I am giving up alcohol. I am going to go to an AA meeting this afternoon. I think that you should go too. But I am doing this for me, and for you, regardless if you do it or not.' I was just shocked! I didn't know what to say. I think I just went to the refrigerator and got a beer. I had no other response. I wasn't angry, I think because deep down I knew she was right. But I didn't want to join her. Ultimately, I was afraid."

Read the words of L. Gregory Jones and think of Jeanine:

> The judgment of grace, a judgment that enables the recovery of memory, involves moving initially from a third person stance of *holding* people (or oneself) responsible to a first person stance of *accepting* responsibility. The third person stance invites a judgmental stance that destroys others . . . and also oneself. . . . The first person stance invites us to accept responsibility; and that occurs through a forgiving love that redraws the boundaries of our identity.[6]

Therapy began a year after Jeanine had radically changed their marriage. In some ways, the task was to "mop up" after the hard work had been accomplished. Jeanine had initiated a change in the direction of their marriage. She got angry enough to act—and the motives for her actions were not punitive or revengeful. Her tough-love declaration of valuing the relationship too much to allow it to continue in the same manner was the substantial change. They came to counseling to help them tinker with the details.

Now that Jeanine had stopped drinking, the rules of engagement had changed. Lloyd had to respond to the new demands. Jeanine chose not only to not drink but to not argue with Lloyd while he was drinking. This was just about every night. Lloyd did his best to provoke her to return to the old ways of interacting (it's always easiest to get the other to change rather than to change yourself), but Jeanine was too tough. She was determined to not let her or his addiction to alcohol direct the course of their marriage. She instead offered to meet him at work for lunch—dropping by to give him a gift or to ask if she could help him. She took advantage of a primary life rule that Lloyd had learned from his father: never mix booze with work. Lloyd later described the morality of this logic with a degree of pathetic humor—"If you drink at work you could lose your work, then you wouldn't have any money to be able to drink."

The essence of Jeanine's message to Lloyd was, "I have been a failure of a wife in too many areas. You have been a failure as a husband in too many areas. We are failing our children. I want your forgiveness for how I have failed to love you. And I hope that you will participate with me in marriage differently than how we have lived up to now." This was aggressive forgiveness; there was no passivity here. This forgiveness did not wait for him to say sorry, then continue with no change. This forgiveness did not turn a blind eye to the problems of the marriage and accept the unacceptable with a fatalistic attitude like, "I don't like it, but what can I do?" This forgiveness was tough, stubborn and unwavering in its commitment to make restoration.

With Jeanine sober, neither knew just how to fight anymore. The rules had changed, and they came to therapy to help them learn a new way to be together. Lloyd and Jeanine knew that they were not able to experience the kind of relationship that they wanted. They knew also that drinking was involved somehow. Lloyd did not want to go backward, to return to the old ways. But he didn't know what the new ways would be like.

Couples are usually quite quick to declare that they have forgiven each other. Such declarations usually reveal our shallowness. To say that you have forgiven your lover, your wife, your husband, implies that you possess power—you possess the right to declare emotional blessing or cursing, which is to reveal that the other still holds you at bay by the injury.

Forgiveness counseling with Jeannie and Lloyd contained aspects of forgiveness described by Worthington. Each carried the burden of pain, resentment, anger, bitterness and hatred. Ultimately, as individuals they had to let go of the right to retaliate against one another and against their parents, extended family, and present and past friends. There was an internal journey that each one had to make—realizing that they carried self-protective hate that, while having a usefulness in guarding against future injury, kept them a prisoner, forcing them to conduct all relationships through their own bitterness.

In addition, their forgiveness journey included relational healing with a focus on their Us. They did not think in terms of reconciliation; they had not seen themselves as so broken that they needed to reconcile. Rather, their relational forgiveness was demonstrated by acknowledging that each had failed the other in fulfilling their responsibility as a lover—agape, phileo and eros. They had conducted themselves as self-lovers who stayed in the marriage not out of a care for the other. They stayed because it remained personally convenient for each. They both expected little of themselves and expected less of the other. Once they became aware of the depth of life that they were missing, and once they realized that they possessed the internal resources to make change, forgiveness served to propel them toward growth.

RETURNING TO THE CIRCLE: FORGIVENESS TO GRACE

Forgiveness does not complete the restoration cycle. Rather, it feeds it. A forgiving marriage becomes empowered to offer grace again and again. When a couple's injuries are diverted away from defensiveness through grace, stabilized by justice, understood with empathy, shared with trust, and washed clean by forgiveness, couples are empowered and replenished to be gracious again and again and again. Forgiveness is a great force that restores, brings life, and when allowed, transports us back to grace. The idea that forgiveness is an act of contrition or an apology is minimally important in comparison to forgiveness as a disposition—a way of being for the intimate Us. Counselors can model, teach and value the humility and courage required to become a forgiving couple. A counselor must teach the forgiveness skill, but can also teach the attitude of life with another. This lifestyle forgiveness is in direct opposition to defenses and self-protection. Forgiveness is key to a life in which fundamentally inadequate and insufficient souls come together to become more capable at managing their limitations and enhancing their gifts to one another.

NOTES

[1]Jones, L. G. (1995). *Embodying forgiveness: A theological analysis.* Grand Rapids, MI: Eerdmans, p. 6.

[2]Enright, R. D. (2001). *Forgiveness is a choice: A step-by-step process for resolving anger and restoring hope.* Washington, DC: American Psychological Association.

[3]Hargrave, T. D. (1994). *Families and forgiveness.* New York: Routlege, p. 16.

[4]Jones. (1995). *Embodying forgiveness*, p. xii.

[5]Hargrave, Terry. (1995). *Families and forgiveness.* New York: Bruner/Mazel.

[6]Jones. (1995). *Embodying forgiveness*, p. 147.

Part Three

MARITAL COUNSELING APPLIED

IN THESE NEXT CHAPTERS WE want to consider what is happening with couples within the context of particular issues. While every couple is unique regarding their personalities and experiences, there are common events, circumstances and themes that have an impact on marriages with some form of pattern. By understanding crucial components of common issues, counselors and pastors are in a better position to guide couples through them successfully. In the subsequent chapters we will address sexual intimacy, children and parenting, infidelity, divorce and blended families, and substance abuse and behavioral addictions.

The following five chapters will attend to important themes along a similar outline. After the general introduction, we will offer special considerations for working with couples who are facing that issue. Then we will consider how the pastor or counselor can assist the couple in the process of redemption—changing pain, defensiveness and injury to healing and intimacy. To do this we will examine the theme in light of how an intimate couple functions, experiences relationship and creates identity. This structure of function, relationship and identity is drawn from McMinn and Campbell's helpful work *Integrative Psychotherapy*.[1] It is addressed in detail in chapter one of our previous book, *Family Therapies: A Christian Appraisal*.[2]

To briefly summarize these ideas, Couple Function refers to the roles that couples occupy in marriage—literally how the couple works together. The presence of each one of these issues alters the way that marriage partners work together to fulfill their Us. Couple Relationship considers the "rules" that define closeness and distance within a marriage. In the presence of pain and trauma, tension can be generated because of the relative dependence or independence that individuals exhibit. Finally, Couple Identity refers to definition. Events press on a couple and force alteration of their identity. Likewise, a couple's identity presses back on any circumstance and affects how the couple will respond to it.

In the last part of the following chapters, we will consider each of the issues in light of the Conflict and Restoration model presented in part two of this book. Counselors must consider with couples the process of pain-defense-grace as they develop interventions that will enhance marital intimacy.

NOTES

[1]McMinn, M. E., & Campbell, C. D. (2007). *Integrative psychotherapy.* Downers Grove, IL: IVP Academic.

[2]Yarhouse, M. A., & Sells, J. N. (2008). *Family therapies: A comprehensive Christian appraisal.* Downers Grove, IL: IVP Academic.

10

THE EXPRESSIVE ART
OF SEXUALITY

She had secluded herself from a
thousand natural and healing influences;
That, her mind, brooding solitary, had grown diseased.

CHARLES DICKENS, *GREAT EXPECTATIONS*

YOU MAY NEVER HAVE THOUGHT ABOUT prayer and sex in the same sentence, but they share a unique expression in our common language. We speak of them both in terms of life. Christians speak of having a "prayer life." Clearly, prayer is a unique experience—we do not have "Bible study life" or "church life," and certainly not "tithe life" to describe our spiritual vitality. We have a prayer life.

Similarly, couples do not speak of "recreation life," "communication life" or "weekend chore life," but couples speak of their "sex life." Sex, like prayer, is something shared. Sex and prayer are communication or exchanges that occur on the most personal and intimate level. In fact, it is so intimate that we attach the word *life* to it to provide its context. We have placed sex and prayer in a special affiliation with our selves. It is our life.

It should be no surprise then that conversation about a couple's sex life is often avoided. Take Kathy and Ted. They come to see you for pastoral counseling. When they sit down across from you, Kathy speaks first and says that they have felt they needed to speak to someone for quite a while. She shares that they've grown distant and that it doesn't seem like Ted is as interested in sex with her as he used to be. "He goes to work, comes home, eats dinner and then watches TV or gets involved in some other project. He just doesn't seem to pursue me the way he used to. I don't know; it seems like something is wrong, but he says nothing's wrong. I'm confused. Now when we are together, I am not able to enjoy being with him the way I should."

You look at Ted, who has been looking away. He turns and catches your eye, explaining, "I don't know; it's not that I don't want to, but I'm tired. I work all day, usually getting an early start on the day, and then I don't get home until evening, and if we are not driving the kids around to this event or that show, it seems we have other things we have to do in the neighborhood or the church. It's been this way for a while; I guess it's been the last thing on my mind, but it's been that way for so long that I know it is frustrating to Kathy. It's not that I'm not interested; I am. It's that I guess I don't think about it the way I should."

How would you respond to Kathy and Ted? Does it seem unusual to hear the wife talk about wanting more sexual intimacy while the husband seems less interested? Is there a sexual dysfunction here? If so, at what point would a referral be appropriate? How would you know? To whom would you refer either Ted or Kathy individually, or Ted and Kathy as a couple? What if there is more anger and resentment beneath their words? How would you as a pastoral counselor work with them to extend grace to one another in this area?

When couples come to see a pastor or counselor to discuss their sex life together, the counselor has a unique opportunity to share the concepts we have been reviewing in part two of this book. Indeed, discussions of sexual intimacy provide ample opportunity to discuss with couples the concepts of grace, justice, empathy, trust and forgiveness. These themes are not the direct motivation for couples to discuss their sex life with the counselor; rather, they are the platform or the environment around which a mature sexual life grows. Just as in procreation, couples will conceive an Us that will be defined by rules, expectations, restrictions and freedoms that govern and guide how intimacy is experienced. For the most part, these rules are unspoken, yet still possess great power and control of intimate experiences. Counselors work in this environment—helping couples make known the influences that have been hidden. It is the quakes in this foundation of intimacy that lead to disruption in the sexual life of couples.

SPECIAL CONSIDERATIONS IN ADDRESSING SEX

When you think about meeting with a couple who discloses their concerns about sex in marriage, remember that talking about sex can be difficult for couples—and for pastoral counselors! As Penner and Penner[1] note, couples may have a number of concerns about discussing sex with a pastor or counselor. To have a real conversation on sexuality is to approach central aspects of personhood. There is no topic that triggers potential pain and provokes our defenses as does our intimate sexuality. Place this in a context of a couple's real life hurt and disappointment, and you have a dialogue that is easily avoided. Sometimes couples are nervous about what terms to use or about having an explicit discussion about sex at all. They might use words from TV shows they've seen or words they use when they talk about sexual anatomy with their children. Sometimes they default to slang terms. We encourage pastoral counselors to use the correct terminology rather than made-up terms or terms used with young children. Try to avoid *woo woo* or *bam bam* or slang terms or any other word or phrase open to interpretation or that might detract from the discussion itself.

Couples may also be nervous about talking about behaviors they are not sure are okay or talking about something they fear will not be understood by their pastor or counselor. If they use fantasy and role play, they may wonder if that is okay, and they may be anxious to mention it to their pastoral care provider. Or if they have been using a vibrator, they may hesitate to mention it to their pastoral care provider. This anxiety about what is okay to discuss, or about talking about something they worry might not be understood, is normal, and it is good for a pastoral counselor to be aware of this and to even talk to the couple about it, as it can help reduce the initial anxiety that often comes with discussing sex.

We have also found it helpful to use "ubiquity" statements. These are statements that let the couple know that while they may feel they are talking about a concern that others would not understand, they are not alone; they are not the only ones who have struggled with this issue. For example, a pastoral counselor might say: "Many couples find it difficult to make sexual intimacy a priority when they are at this stage of life with young children, demands on their time from work and other commitments—how about you?"

If you are starting to get uncomfortable as you read this introduction to language and how to help couples share more openly about their sex lives, that is also to be expected. You might find it helpful to reflect on your own knowledge and attitudes about sex, as attitudes in particular will come across in a pastoral counseling meeting. There are a number of helpful resources[2] that can guide you in this kind of self-evaluation. We turn our attention now to the three central themes of identity, functioning and relationship. We will draw on these to help us organize how a pastoral counselor can discuss sexual intimacy with couples.

COUPLE IDENTITY AND SEXUALITY

Recall that marital identity is an opportunity to "locate" the couple you are working with. We think it is helpful to place each couple you work with in a context. You can do this by reflecting on aspects of who they are, such as their age, cultural background, race, religious perspective (recognizing the range of differences even among Christians and how their faith informs their concerns), region of the country and so on. In particular, we want to understand how these characteristics inform their understanding and expectations for sexual intimacy.

Often related to age is the stage of life[3] a couple is in. For example, are you meeting with a young couple with no children? Their lives are quite different from a couple with young children, whose lives are different from a couple raising teens or a couple launching teens into young adulthood. The couple with no children is likely at the earlier stage in their relationship. They are trying to form a new family identity, one that is distinct from both of the families they grew up in. In the area of marital sexual intimacy, they may be more likely to benefit from discussing expectations for sex in marriage, getting into good habits, and communication in general and in the area of sex in particular. They may appreciate some additional education about sexual intimacy in marriage, perhaps books on the sexual response cycle and sexual technique, as well as help with being together rather than focused on past relationships or making comparisons to others they may have been intimate with prior to marriage.

Couples with young children are adjusting to a new person in the home. Young children can be physically draining, and changing diapers and constantly doing laundry do not tend to add a spark to a couple's sex life. They may benefit from reflecting on how they are staying connected to one another while learning to build a family identity that now includes children. Taking care of themselves as the central relationship in the family will often take a backseat to focusing on their children, and if they are not careful, unmet emotional needs can be taken to children, even young children, rather than worked out between the couple. This is an important topic to raise and discuss with them and to reflect together on how these changing priorities and relationship dynamics may impact sexual intimacy.

As children grow into adolescents, the couple faces new challenges associated with finding new ways to relate to teens who have more of a say in expressing themselves and their interests and preferences than ever before. Couples can often become polarized with teens, as one person in the couple ends up representing love and support or fun and good times while the other person in the couple ends up representing limits and rules or discipline. Couples benefit from understanding that they can both express love/support/fun and limits/rules/discipline, and that it is not good for any one person to become a caricature of these positions in a family. If these challenges are not navigated successfully, hurt and frustration will likely follow, and it would come as no surprise if negative emotions like these end up leading to more drift for the couple in terms of sexual intimacy. Finding time to be intimate can also be increasingly difficult. It may be helpful to find practical solutions to keep the marriage and sexual intimacy from being neglected.

In addition to these family life cycle considerations, each person in the couple brings to the marriage unique experiences and cultural and regional backgrounds that may fuel expectations or even myths about marital sexuality.

Expectations and myths of sexuality. Expectations, for instance, may include sex roles. For many couples, their sexual script is written well before they ever make it to the bedroom. What we mean by this is that cultural messages may permeate their marriage, telling them about who initiates, what men want, what women should be like, how often to have sex and so on. Often these messages take the form of sex roles: women should be passive; men should initiate; wives should not refuse sex to their husband; husbands will always want sex, and their wives may not; women should not enjoy sex.

This raises the issue of myths about sexuality and sexual functioning in marriage. Lisa McMinn has a helpful discussion of several such myths in her book *Sexuality and Holy Longing*.[4] For example, one myth relevant to the case of Kathy and Ted is that men are always ready, interested and capable of sex. Sexual desire concerns are often thought of as problems that women may face, and insofar as one's culture or religion reinforces the myth, there may be heightened expectations for how the husband is to show interest in sexual intimacy.

Another myth is that marriage is all about sex. We know that couples range considerably in how frequently they report sexual intimacy, with the highest percentages being once per week, then more than once per week, then once per month. So that is quite a range! Moreover, the frequency of sexual intimacy in marriage tends to be higher early in marriage and declines some each year until the forties—then it can remain rather steady for many years past that point if health problems or other concerns are not a part of the picture. This brings us to a myth about sex in older adulthood not discussed by McMinn, that older adults are not sexually active. While there does appear to be some decline in sexual activity in older adulthood, the majority of older adults continue to experience sexual desire, and one of the best predictors of sexual activity and interest in older adulthood is marital status.[5] Older adults more often than not remain sexually active if they have an available partner.

Another myth worth keeping in mind is that good women do not enjoy sex. This myth can be seen especially in conservative Christian circles where sex is often not discussed and where men tend to be the focal point of discussions of sex when they do occur.

We would add this myth to Lisa McMinn's list: If I do everything right before marriage, there won't be any difficulties in this area. This myth can be a hard one to shake. Many Christians can fall into the habit of bargaining with God. We might do this to pass a test, get out of a speeding ticket or win the lottery—*I would give 10 percent (no, half!) of my winnings to the church if you just let me hit the lotto!* If we are honest about how often we are prone to bargaining with God, it should come as no surprise that we do it in the area of sexuality.

Tammy and Ron came to see their pastor, and Tammy was nearly in tears. She talked about how painful intercourse was for her since they had tried over two years ago. She was particularly frustrated because she had no previous sexual experience and very little dating experience before she and Ron met. Ron shared that he had dated a little more than Tammy, but that he, too, had not been sexually intimate before their wedding day. Yet she struggled with painful intercourse, and each time Ron tried to enter her, she felt a tightening of the muscles around the outer third of her vagina. Through her tears, Tammy said, "I've been a good girl. I've always done the right things, even in this area. I haven't gone and slept around or crossed the line. Why would this be so difficult for me? Why would God make sex such a struggle for me?"

Even when people recognize that they have been bargaining with God, they can find it difficult to work through the feelings of disappointment, confusion and frustration with God. We have found it helpful to name and discuss these negative feelings, not only because they are a part of the couple's experience—that is, they are truly happening—but also because couples may be reluctant to share these with a pastor or Christian counselor.

A collaborative approach to sexual concerns. It can also be helpful to think about how the sexual concerns have come to "define" either one in the marriage or them as a couple. Couples often think in linear terms: *this* event caused *this* outcome. So when it comes to sexual problems, it is typical for one spouse to blame the other spouse, seeing the problems as a direct result of a particular behavior or event. A pastoral counselor would do well to keep each person from blaming the other and instead to get more of a team or collaborative approach to the concerns. One way to do this is with a sports analogy: If we think about a game of tennis, the couple can either be playing against one another while discussing their sexual concerns (they are then on the opposite side of the net) or they can be on the same team facing the sexual concerns together (they are then on the same side of the net). Then, we can ask them to reflect on which side of the net they are on with each conversation they have with their partner. The words they choose, the tone they take, the attitude they convey, the timing they select—do they convey to their partner that they are on the same side of the net (working together) or the opposite side of the net (often laying blame)?

Even in cases when we might be able to identify an individual sexual concern, that concern still occurs in the context of their relationship, and that means how it is discussed, how one's partner responds, and so on, can ease the problem or exacerbate it further.

With Tammy and Ron, for example, it will be important at some point to ask them how they have discussed the challenges they face together to get a sense for whether this has been about blame or about collaboration. This is a great opportunity to encourage each partner to extend each other grace, as they have both been confused and disappointed by their inability to consummate their marriage. But they share a common goal, one that can be facilitated by mutual respect, education and a plan for counseling a specific sexual dysfunction.

Identity, or the idea of locating a couple and each spouse in that couple, is an important first step. It is something that is part of getting to know them and understanding how their unique stories and experiences inform the concerns they bring to pastoral care or counseling. The next step is to think about functioning.

COUPLE FUNCTION AND SEXUALITY

Couples may come to see a pastoral counselor with questions about function or, more accurately, dysfunction, when they have concerns

about sexual intimacy. They want to know why something is not working the way they think it should. They could be interested in discussing
sexual desire and why it may seem absent, or orgasm and questions they
have if one partner is anorgasmic, or pain if intercourse is painful for
one or both of them.

Sexual dysfunctions. Before we discuss how to address these particular issues in counseling, we want to introduce you, the counselor, to the
main sexual dysfunctions.[6] They tend to be classified with reference to
problems in the sexual response cycle. Although there are a couple of
ways to conceptualize the sexual response cycle, it is most commonly
understood as beginning with sexual desire and followed by the stages
of excitement, plateau, orgasm and resolution. Common sexual dysfunctions, then, are the sexual desire disorders, sexual arousal disorders, sexual pain disorders and orgasmic disorders. Mental health professionals will also diagnose the dysfunction as *lifelong* (it has always
been a concern) or *acquired* (it has become a concern after a specific
event). Dysfunctions can also be classified as *generalized* (in all relationships or circumstances) or *situational* (in specific relationships or circumstances). Mental health professionals also distinguish between
sexual dysfunctions that are due to both psychological factors and medical factors, and dysfunctions that are due to psychological factors alone.
We will look now more closely at some specific disorders along the
sexual response cycle.

Sexual desire disorders include hypoactive desire disorder and sexual
aversion disorder. Hypoactive desire disorder refers to low or less-than-
normal desire and is characterized by a person's having no interest in
sexual activity. About 33 percent of women and 16 percent of men report struggling with sexual desire disorder.[7] Sexual aversion disorder is
a condition in which a person has strong negative reactions (for example, fear, panic or disgust) to sexual stimuli.

Sexual arousal disorders are different from sexual desire disorders.
Essentially, with sexual arousal disorders, the person has the desire for
sexual activity but is unable to experience arousal. Male erectile disorder
refers to difficulty achieving or maintaining an erection (as many as 50
percent of males report some difficulty with erections at some time, and

about 10 percent report complete erectile disorder), while female sexual arousal disorder refers to difficulty achieving or maintaining adequate lubrication (about 20 percent of women report lubrication difficulties, and this rises to about 40 percent of women following menopause).

Sexual pain disorders are reported more often by women than men. These disorders include dyspareunia, which refers to painful intercourse. It is reported by 10 to 15 percent of women. Vaginismus, which is reported by about 15 percent of women in clinical samples, is characterized by the involuntary clamping down of the muscles surrounding the outer third of the vagina in response to penile, finger or object penetration.

Orgasmic disorders include anorgasmia (inhibited orgasm) and premature ejaculation. Inhibited orgasm is a condition that is much more common in women than men, and it is diagnosed when a person has sexual desire and arousal but is unable to achieve orgasm (about 25 percent of women report having difficulty reaching orgasm). Although quite subjective to measure, about 30 percent of men report difficulty with premature ejaculation, which refers to ejaculation that occurs too soon in the sexual response cycle.

There are other problems that are beyond the scope of this chapter but that may come to the attention of a pastoral counselor. One concern is sexual addiction or compulsion.[8] This is a kind of habitual or driven sexual behavior. Examples include compulsive masturbation, sexual promiscuity, pornography dependence, telephone sex dependence and cybersex.[9] Another concern might be sexual identity or gender identity issues in which one partner reports same-sex attraction in the context of their marriage.

When to refer. Many pastoral care providers or counselors will work with couples who discuss, at least at some level, sexual concerns. What is perhaps more challenging is to identify what a particular pastor or counselor can offer and when a referral is appropriate. Doug Rosenau and his colleagues[10] have a helpful model, the DEC-R model, that a pastoral counselor could use to aid in determining when a referral is appropriate. The four-step process is intended to help those under our care deal with their sexual questions or concerns. The steps are (1) dialogue, (2) education, (3) coaching and (4) referral.

It is important that pastoral counselors prepare themselves for *dialogue*. Such preparation may mean reflecting on and addressing issues that come up with one's own sexuality, being somewhat desensitized to the topic so that you are able to discuss it constructively, having created an emotionally safe place to do so, and having a more clearly delineated theology of sex. The dialogue is to engage the couple in descriptive language regarding their sexual experience, holding close the importance of checking with both spouses as to the internal reactions in the conversation.

Furthermore, counselors provide a level of support through *education*. This is accomplished by answering questions accurately and dispelling myths that a couple may bring to pastoral care. As we discussed above, education may entail describing the sexual response cycle, pointing couples toward reading resources and so on. It is also important in this context to be able to identify and address any unrealistic expectations.

For most pastoral counselors, this will be the extent of what they feel they are competent to provide. Others who have additional education and training might move on to *coaching*. Coaching in the DEC-R model refers to guiding couples into improved sexual functioning. This might involve identifying and assigning specific exercises for an identifiable problem. Beyond identifying a good self-help resource, coaching also involves more bibliotherapy in which a specific assigned book is discussed and processed in the pastoral care meeting, so that the couple can begin to make application of what they are reading under the guidance of the counselor.

Lastly, the pastoral care provider will want to be prepared to make a good *referral*. This might occur to address medical issues that are part of the couple's presenting problem, or when it is clear that the pastoral care provider lacks training to address the issue competently. Referrals might be to gynecologists or urologists, general physicians, specialized peer-support groups (for example, Sex Addicts Anonymous), or professional sex therapists.

Sexual functioning is, in some ways, at the surface of what a couple may sometimes bring to counseling. There may not be anything else underneath the concerns they are raising. In these cases, help can take the forms we have been discussing, through education, coaching or a proper referral. Sometimes, however, it will be necessary to go beneath the surface, and we refer to this as "attending more to the relationship." It's not that we haven't had the relationship in view this entire time; rather, we have been focusing more on what would help them function better. But relationship brings to mind both interpersonal (between them as a couple) and intrapersonal (within each spouse) considerations. It could also entail generational relationships and various developmental considerations.

COUPLE RELATIONSHIP AND SEXUALITY

We have an idea now of the kinds of sexual concerns that would warrant a referral to a mental health professional who is proficient in working with sexual dysfunctions and other concerns related to sexual expression. But there are many times when pastoral counselors meet with a couple and are determining whether the concerns expressed should lead to a referral or not. Throughout the course of this level of pastoral care, there are many principles the counselor can follow to help the couple.

Value teamwork. Like many marital concerns, sexual concerns can often lead to blame placing in the marriage. In many circles today, women may be socialized to take the blame and men to place the blame. This is changing, and you may find wives you meet with just as likely to place blame on their husbands, but in either case, you would want to communicate to both of them that there is something fundamentally destructive in identifying their partner as the sole cause of the sexual concern. Even in cases in which there is an identifiable dysfunction—for example, the wife has been diagnosed with a desire disorder—it will be important for the couple to work together so that the husband has a better understanding of that disorder in general, how his wife experiences it, and how his ways of relating can be helpful or hurtful to her and to their marriage.

Getting a couple to work together will be both the result of and lead to an important change in attitude. The attitude that is conveyed is now one of mutual respect, mutual appreciation, mutual learning and mutual gain.

Engage in lifelong learning. With all that is available to people today via the internet, and with the increase in sexual stimuli and themes in entertainment and the media, education about sex may be less necessary. People often know what sex is, how different major anatomy functions and so on. If anything, they may have been set up by industries that communicate how easy and uncomplicated sex is, and so couples may feel anxiety when their experiences do not match what they see at the movie theater. So education is important, but often not for the same reasons it would have been important even thirty years ago. Back then, many people seeking help may not have known much about the sexual response cycle or sexual anatomy or about what is normal in terms of size or color, and so on. Today, education addresses a different set of myths, which we will discuss below, and it can be a corrective of either ignorance on the one hand or potentially damaging misconceptions that lead to an idealized view on the other.

In education today, we often hear people talk about "lifelong learners" or people who continue to grow and learn well beyond the years of formal education. The same principle holds true with knowledge and understanding of sex in marriage: you will want to convey the idea that it is good for both people to continue to grow in their knowledge and understanding of themselves and their spouse in terms of sexual intimacy and what each person enjoys.

We discussed previously the sexual response cycle. We should note that couples are actually not typically that interested in the stages we outlined. We think it is good for them to know what the stages are, but it is probably most important that they get an idea about what each stage is like—what to expect or what is a person's typical experience in each stage, recognizing that there can be differences here too. They might benefit from reading about the major external anatomy and the sexual response cycle.[11]

Typically, a good indicator that you may be addressing a sexual dysfunction that requires more professional assistance is whether education is sufficient to resolve their concerns. In the case of sexual dysfunctions, education, while necessary, is not considered sufficient, and the couple will benefit from understanding the dysfunction better but also working with a knowledgeable professional who can conceptualize and implement a treatment plan to move education into a practical, workable reality for them as a couple.

Improve communication. What is equally important is to emphasize communication for them as a couple. What you want to convey is that it is important and normal to talk to one another about what each person likes and dislikes. It can also be helpful to encourage the couple to affirm one another about what they are doing together and working toward without placing emphasis on an outcome. This can be challenging. Often one or both partners are focused on the goal, so that if they have not consummated their marriage due to a sexual pain disorder or vaginismus, for example, consummation will easily become the focal point. We would want to keep that goal in mind, of course, but we want to focus more on what is being learned and on the process, in part to decrease anxiety that can spike when couples emphasize where they feel they *ought* to be but are not yet.

At a very practical level, it will be important to communicate constructively, both when they are discussing their sex life and when they are sexually intimate. Sara can say to Dan: "I don't like it when you give me a massage; it just doesn't do it for me. You think it's romantic or that it'll get things going, but it never gets me in the mood." How likely is Dan to receive this as constructive feedback? Not very likely. But we would want Sara to provide Dan with constructive feedback, something that is referred to as feedback-rich communication.[12] She could say: "Dan, I really enjoy connecting with you and having a time for us to be intimate. I think one thing that helps me move in that direction is when I receive touch or a massage that feels really romantic. What I especially like is if you can rub my back and neck gently and rub my back with short strokes, and I can show you what I mean later tonight or tomorrow."

What is different about this way of communicating is that Sarah begins with a compliment and an assurance that she enjoys being intimate with Dan. She then talks specifically about something that she can identify that would help her in terms of desire and potential arousal. She is specific about what she likes, and she is willing to name it and show

Dan what she likes in a certain timeframe. We think Dan can receive this—not as a personal criticism or a criticism of Dan as a person (in contrast to the previous global statement, "It never gets me in the mood") but as a specific, identifiable concern than can be improved.

Couples can identify with their pastoral counselor a range of topics that they may find helpful to discuss. We just illustrated what it would look like to talk together about how affection is expressed in touch and massage. Other topics might include how they each initiate sexual intimacy, what it's like when one or the other declines sexual intimacy, what it looks like for them to set a mood for sexual intimacy and so on. It is a good sign if couples are able to talk to each other constructively about these kinds of topics. If not, that may be an indication that they could benefit from seeing a professional with more experience working with these issues.

Revisit lifestyle priorities. In addition to education and communication, it is important to review their daily routine, both weekdays and weekends. Many couples are overextended; they may both work long days or be overcommitted to various projects in the community, including their neighborhood, their kids' activities and events, and their faith community. Indeed, by the end of the day or by the end of the week, they may feel that they have nothing left to give in terms of sex.

These routines are important to review, in part because it is not worth making other changes if the structure of their lives does not change. It's going to be difficult to receive education about sex, to improve technique and to work on communication, but nearly impossible to try to take these new skills into a lifestyle that has little or no room for their execution. Sexual intimacy needs some kind of framework within which it can thrive. That framework includes the time the couple gets to spend together, both quality time and quantity time.

Quality time refers to moments where the two of them can discuss their life together, how each of them is growing and some of their worries or concerns. It may also include times of joy and delight in one another. Quantity time refers to how much time they get together. It is hard to manufacture quality time. Usually, quality time comes out of stretches of quantity time with one another. This time spent together, especially quality time together, can be an important component to improving sexual intimacy.

Many couples may have difficulty in finding time to share a meal together, let alone finding time for sex. They may benefit from setting time aside specifically for sexual intimacy, at least during seasons in their life when it is difficult to make time for one another.

SEXUALITY AND THE PAIN-DEFENSE CYCLE

Problems in sexual intimacy can be tracked through the pain-defense-injury cycle and by understanding that conflicts manifest themselves on multiple levels. Let's consider the origin of sexually related issues. Recall from chapter two that misunderstanding, injury, misperception and conflict have three simultaneous sources. First, pain is experienced through the *immediate problem* felt by either spouse. This would likely be the specific issue related to the sexual concern, be it premature ejaculation, reduced sexual desire or something else. Second, there is the *historical pain* that is associated with the concern. Imagine the presence of the dysfunction over many months or years. During that time, shame, embarrassment, guilt, avoidance or many other possible response styles emerged. Third, both partners have a lifelong pattern of responding to this and any other issue, so these adult experiences serve as reminders of feelings from childhood and one's *family of origin*. There is a vulnerability to act out of a different time and place, like vulnerable children trying hard to manage events and emotions that are not understood.

In this three-dimensional environment, the counselor seeks to understand pain. It is obvious that sexual dysfunction "hurts," but hurt is not experienced by all in the same way. We understand and tolerate hurt at different levels and different styles. For example, a couple named Raul and Flora might address erectile dysfunction as a result of his diabetes. He says to the counselor, "Yes, that is very difficult for us, but difficult like we are growing old and the machine doesn't work as well. But I don't get mad at my car because it has 200,000 miles. I am just disappointed that I can't get a new one." Here, his pain is described in the form of disappointment and loss, but they do not convey a level of crisis or devastation. Whereas another person might be devastated by the experience, saying, "The first time 'it' happened, I couldn't figure out what was wrong. So, I lied my way through it. I said that I was too tired, and I had a lot of stuff on my mind. I didn't, but I needed to cover this one up. I didn't want to learn that I couldn't get an erection. How embarrassing is that?"

Counselors can track the pathway of pain-defense-injury that has been cycled many, many times within the marriage. Two important therapeutic directions emerge with sexually related issues. The first is to address the sexual dysfunction. This likely will be addressed by referring the couple to a professional sex therapist or psychologist who specializes in sexual dysfunction. The second task is to address the pattern of pain-defense-injury that has been inserted into the relationship aside from the literal dysfunction. With sexual dysfunction it is often the smoke, not the fire, that often proves most destructive for couples. Your task is not to address the actual sexual dysfunction but to help them comprehend reciprocal damage to the relationship caused by attachments to the problem that have formed over time, which frequently produce a greater negative effect on the marriage than the actual issue.

PLACING SEXUALITY INTO THE CULTURE OF US

We want to reemphasize that pastors and marital counselors don't need to be sex therapists to be able to have significant influence in assisting couples in this area. Pastors and counselors help couples build the foundation upon which a vibrant life of sexual intimacy is constructed. In thinking about the model of relational restoration, here is how we see it emerging in the offices of pastors and counselors.

A graceful sexuality. Cliff and Joyce Penner's classic book *The Gift of Sex* is more than just a resource that counselors can recommend to couples; it is a way of life. Sexuality, that intimate space between lifetime lovers, is a gift. A grace gift. It is an unmerited bequest offering our bodies as the package through which we access the psychological and spiritual center of the other. Sexual expression cannot be driven from duty or expectation. It is not performance based. "Great sex" is an oxymoron, for sexual expression cannot be measured and compared. When intimacy is measured—great, good, average, poor, inexcusable—it ceases to be an exchange of love. Instead it becomes a combination athletic event and beauty pageant. Counselors can help focus their couples' priorities.

A just sexuality. Sexuality must be fair. Counselors can create dialogue in which there is conversation about fairness—creating a balance between conflicting physical needs, fatigue levels, sex drives and personal preferences. We see unjust sexuality emerging in the misunderstanding of partners—spouses are offended by differences in cadence and rhythm of sexuality. Creating sexual justice extends grace. Couples are more apt to give to one another because they have greater confidence that gifts won't in turn be altered into demands. Counselors assist couples in building the space between them, their Us, to reflect this commitment for justice.

An empathic sexuality. An empathic sexuality is able to sit close to the hurt and injury emerging from our sexuality and not become defensive. Empathy permits a spouse to imagine the experience of the other. This is strengthened by the fact that spouses usually do not have to imagine the historical contexts. They usually know the parents, grandparents, siblings and extended family system. Empathy comes more easily when the history and the personality of those involved is understood. The effect of empathy is to disarm the need for guardedness. Empathy helps diminish defenses. Sexuality flourishes in the absence of defenses, when a couple in naked emotionally and psychologically by diminishing pretenses. Empathy invites couples to be real. Counselors encourage couples to build empathy by demonstration. By their actions counselors declare, "If I can do it with you, than you can do it with one another."

A trustworthy sexuality. Demonstrating trustworthiness invites trusting. While this truth is a generalization, its application to the sexual relationship is most evident. Sexual experience thrives in the environment of trustworthiness. It invites greater trusting that is experienced as vulnerability or intimacy. An important goal for the counselor is to build a couple's expectation that the purpose of their Us is to plant, grow, nurture and harvest trust.

A forgiving sexuality. At first blush, tying forgiveness and sexuality together would prompt us to assume the existence of a sexual indiscretion. While that may be a theme that is frequently addressed by pastors and counselors, it is not our intent here. Rather, counselors can create a culture of forgiveness between couples. Forgiveness should be the language or the ambiance of the Christian marriage. Forgiveness, not just as a discrete declaration but as a lifestyle, understands, acknowledges and accepts. Through forgiveness couples understand their broken nature. C. S. Lewis referred to this as "the bent ones"—our sexuality is affected by a host of influences emerging from the fact that we are bent. By acknowledgment, forgiveness opens dialogue and communication. Sexuality obstacles are frequently hidden and buried, but forgiveness allows them to surface and enter into discussion. Finally, forgiveness is acceptance. Forgiveness removes shame. It creates a condition of approval. Counselors assist couples in moving beyond mere declarations of forgiveness and toward forgiveness as a marital language or theme.

A FINAL WORD: MARITAL SKILLS AND SEXUAL EXPRESSION

In chapter one we concluded with four marital counseling skills that enhance the counselor's success with couples. Each of these skills have important application when a counselor is talking about sexual intimacy with a couple. We want to visit these four themes again and mention their unique application.

Marital skill 1: Accept what the individuals choose to do with their lives. This first skill can be easily disregarded by counselors because sexuality themes not only attach securely to the core persona of our clients, but the counselor's sexuality—thoughts, feelings, securities and threats—is easily provoked with this topic. Don't forget that the boundary and limitation of the counselor role is an essential insulation. Counselors must form opinions from the science of the profession and the security of biblical truth and sound theology, not from their own fear or projection.

Marital skill 2: Be comfortable in the front lines. The discussion of sexuality is the most sensitive of topics. The topic of sexuality is the most demanding of the counselor. Because of the vulnerability and intimacy of the topic, there will likely be intensity of emotions, thick entrenched defenses and pain that travels from the depth of their souls. To speak of mature sexual expression requires a mature counselor who can remain close to the depth of their pain and not intercede because of her or his discomfort with the topic or the process.

Marital skill 3: Have no dog in the fight. You might recall conversations or arguments with your husband or wife regarding sexuality. Or you can imagine what they would sound like if you are not married. The disagreement over differing expectations and needs is common. A counselor can easily impute understanding of "normal" based on the individual need or expectation that emerged from his or her marital relationship. Identification with the husband or the wife because of similarity to one's marriage is bad therapy.

Marital skill 4: See both the forest and the trees. Because of the vulnerability and intensity of sexual intimacy, it is easy to miss important details. Within sex therapy there is often a debate as to whether an issue is best addressed medically, mechanically (as in altering external environment or methods of arousal) or emotionally. Counselors have biases often coming from their presuppositions and their training. Sex therapists trained in behavioral techniques understand and intervene with a solution from the behavioral school of thought. Helping couples restore or experience sexual intimacy requires that you be competent in understanding the complexities of human sexuality and to offer multiple approaches to issues that have a diversity of causes and solutions.

CONCLUSION

In this chapter we focused on issues of sexuality. Among other things, we want you as a pastoral or lay counselor to understand the characteristics of sexual dysfunction in order to make proper referrals. Frequently, conflict in couples emerges around sexuality or can begin to affect sexual intimacy, and it can be helpful to provide accurate information and create a context for mutual understanding and respectful consideration. We see effective counselors as being able to wrap competent sexual therapy with the power of Christian identification. The Christian story contains dynamic themes that contribute to a couple's ability to face physical and psychological impediments in their sexual experience. Counselors create the culture and the conditions through which the theme of sexual intimacy is fully explored.

NOTES

[1]Penner, J. J., & Penner, C. L. (2005). *Counseling for sexual disorders.* (Rev. ed.). Dallas: Word, pp. 4-9.

[2]Ibid.

[3]Carter, B., & McGoldrick, M. (1999). *The expanded family life cycle.* (3rd ed.). Needham Heights, MA: Allyn & Bacon, pp. 1-24.

[4]McMinn, L. G. (2004). *Sexuality and holy longing.* San Francisco: Jossey-Bass, pp. 131-46.

[5]Dello Buono, M., Zaghi, P. C., Padoani, W., Scocco, P., Urciuoli, O., Pauro, P., & De Leo, D. (1998). Sexual feelings and sexual life in an Italian sample of 335 elderly 65- to 106-years-olds. *Archives of Gerontology and Geriatrics, 6,* 155-62. See also J. G. Bretschneider & N. L. McCoy (1998). Sexual interests and behavior in healthy 80- to 102-year-olds. *Archives of Sexual Behavior, 17*(2), 109-29.

[6]Yarhouse, M. A., Butman, R. E., & McRay, B. W. (2005). *Modern psychopathologies: a comprehensive Christian appraisal.* Downers Grove, IL: InterVarsity Press.

[7]The largest sexuality study conducted to date was by Edward Laumann and his colleagues and is referred to as the National Health Social Life Survey. Most prevalence estimates in this section are drawn from this work. See Laumann, E. O., Gagnon, J. H., Michael, R. T., & Michaels, S. (1994). *The Social organization of sexuality: Sexual practices in the United States.* Chicago: University of Chicago Press.

[8]There is debate in the field as to whether the proper term is sexual *addiction* or sexual *compulsion.* Neither term is recognized as a mental disorder in *DSM-IV*; however, most professionals recognize a condition characterized by driven sexual behavior.

[9]Kafka, M. P. The paraphilia-related disorders: Nonparaphilic hypersexuality and sexual compulsivity/addiction. In S. R. Leiblum & R. C. Rosen (Eds.), *Principles and practice of sex therapy* (3rd ed., pp. 479-80). New York: Guilford.

[10]Rosenau, D., Sytsma, M., & Taylor, D. (2001). Sexuality and sexual counseling: Learning and practicing the DEC-R model. In T. Clinton & G. Ohlschlager (Eds.), *Competent Christian counseling.* Colorado Springs: Waterbrook.

[11]See Rosenau, D. (2002). *A celebration of sex* (Rev. ed.). Nashville: Thomas Nelson.

[12]LoPiccolo, J. (1980). Low sexual desire. In S. Leiblum & L. Pervin (Eds.), *Principles and practice of sex therapy* (pp. 29-64). New York: Guilford.

11

THE PRODUCT OF ART

CHILDREN AND PARENTING

*Children are the living messages
we send to a time we will not see.*

NEIL POSTMAN,
THE DISAPPEARANCE OF CHILDHOOD

THE NOVEL *THE JOY LUCK CLUB* begins with an allegory. An old woman is recalling her experience as a subjugated wife in Shanghai, her escape and her emigration to the United States. She carried a swan, which, she was told, actually was a goose that became beautiful by "straining its neck." The woman hoped to give the goose to her future daughter to teach her that she too can become perfect if she strains her neck toward achievement, just like the swan. The novelist Amy Tan writes, "I will make her speak only perfect American English. And over there she will always be too full to swallow any sorrow! She will know my meaning, because I will give her this swan—a creature that became more than what was hoped for."[1]

But upon arriving in the United States, a customs official tore the bird from her arms. The woman grasped only a single feather as a memory of her past and her hope.

Now the woman was old. And she had a daughter who grew up speaking only English and swallowing more Coca-Cola than sorrow. For a long time now the woman had wanted to give her daughter the single swan feather and tell her, "This feather may look worthless, but it came from afar and carries with it all my good intentions." And she waited, year after year, for the day she could tell her daughter this in perfect American English.[2]

The underbelly of parenting can be measured by good intentions. Husbands and wives, joined in marriage, carry hope for the next generation as they become parents. The stories from their childhoods, the mistakes and inadequacies of their parents, are "supposed to be" corrected through offspring. That expectation is universal. The pressure to do everything correctly, to raise children who "speak only perfect American English," is a relentless burden placed on parents, which is passed on to children.

The biblical narrative frequently depicts a similar subtext, seen in the shame that is carried by the childless husband or wife, and the expectations extended to the offspring to carry out the life purpose of the previous generation. It is abundantly clear that in raising children, parents are indeed blessed by God. Yet the ideal in Scripture—this blessing—is often not realized in the way that we might interpret or fantasize it to be. The twenty-first-century interpretation of *blessing* is success, happiness and ease. Just as the old Chinese woman came to understand that she, like her daughter, could not strain her neck far enough to become all that is hoped for, people in all cultures realize that, no matter how good we are, we just can't become good enough. Our cultural mentality has made God's favor to be the equivalent of success, beauty, wealth, power, prestige and especially the absence of hardship. To be blessed by God is to have an easy load. Then kids grow up and express their own will, opinion and pursuits. They become pregnant; play too many electronic games; get average, below-average, or failing grades; choose unapproved friends; drop out of college; fail to clean their room or help around the house. Something has gone wrong. Parenting doesn't feel like a "blessing."

Marital counseling is often initiated by parents because of their perceived or real failures to nurture their children, or their inability to work together to foster offspring into adulthood. Attending to the perceived sense of failure might be the most difficult challenge that marital counselors face. It is so difficult, in part, because our culture—both Christian and secular—places responsibilities and expectations on parents to control all of the factors and circumstances of their children's lives. These expectations are both high and unrealistic. No parent can succeed at their internal expectation, in spite of their best intentions. Enter the pastor or marital counselor whose profession carries some responsibility for the unrealistic expectations. We have created, from our pulpits and through our books, video productions, articles, and radio and television spots, the idea that if parents follow steps A, B and C, then the sorrow swallowed by previous generations, or the tragedies which have beset families in the next neighborhood, will not come to visit our homes. These interventions given and promises made about how to be a successful family are offered not as general principles, which increase the odds for success, but as implied promises that if the couple manages their circumstances "as they are supposed to," then they are, in the words of Dr. Seuss, "going to succeed, 97.9 percent guaranteed."

In this chapter we will examine the marital conflicts that emerge as a result of children's presence in the family system. For most, the introduction of children into a family was a far more radical change for couples than was their decision to marry. Yet the Christian literature has thoroughly neglected this change. Books and other resources are readily available to ease the transition from singleness to marriage. Similarly, there is an abundance of literature offering suggestions and advice as to how to raise children. However, there is precious little consideration of the changes that occur in the marriage when the couple becomes a family. Failure to understand these changes—the gender role expectations placed on both spouses, and the expectations imputed from our families, our cultures and our private fantasies about passing the swan feather—can increase the tension within the relationship between otherwise devoted and committed lovers.

SPECIAL CONSIDERATIONS IN ADDRESSING PARENTHOOD

It is important for counselors to remember a frequently neglected experience of a parental team. The American Christian culture often provides a discrepant message regarding their work as married parents. The first message is clear: children are a blessing from God. They should be valued and cherished. Jesus said, "Let the little children come to me . . . for the kingdom of heaven belongs to such as these" (Mt 19:14 NIV). It is the frailty and dependence of children that produces our value to care for those who cannot care for themselves. The value of children and the duty to provide for them is the Christian metaphor for God's care for humanity. To care for children is to be blessed by God because God cares for us—because we are like little children. We are vulnerable, dependent and needy.

But there is another message. It is not preached from the pulpits, but through conversations at the church potluck, in the foyer or as a joke to bring levity in an adult Sunday school discussion. This message is that children are a bother, a burden and a frustration. It is contained in statements such as: "Enjoy these years of freedom—once kids come you won't have a moment to yourself" or, "Well they're cute at this age, but just wait till they get to be ____ (fill in the appropriate age)" or, "I tell you, what we told our kids was, 'We're going to do the best we can to raise you right, then when you're eleven, put you in a box and nail it shut for ten years, then let you loose at age twenty-one when you are not our problem.'" These and other off-handed and often off-color remarks suggest ideas quite contrary to the Christian theology of family blessing.

Pastors and marital counselors often find themselves needing to reconcile with couples the first theologically real statement with the second experientially real statement. It is not an easy task, which is why, in our opinion, it is far easier to deliver a sermon about God's ideal plan for the family than to sit with a family of parents, children, adolescents and adults and resolve an entangled knot of boundary violations, misplaced priorities, misunderstood intentions and failed efforts. The task is complicated by the idealization of God's blessing, which states: if it's a blessing, then it ought be easy, uplifting and fulfilling. Blessings are not supposed to be work; they are supposed to be more like a vacation! Parents might be coming to the counselor's office feeling smitten rather than blessed.

THE MILLER FAMILY

Consider the circumstances of the Miller family. Jeff and Denise were very happily married, but now they describe their marriage as hard and heavy instead of happy. Jeff was an accountant/business manager. Denise was a nurse practitioner. They were both twenty-eight when they married after a four-year courtship and engagement. Any outsider would have said that they did everything right. Two years after their marriage, they were blessed with a girl, Twila. Three years later a son, Daniel, was born.

About the same time as Daniel's birth, Twila began preschool. Up until that time, Denise had worked part time and most of that at home as an on-call nurse. It was when Twila went to school that behavioral concerns emerged. She could not form successful social relationships. She could not stay focused on the teaching activity. She would wander out of her seat and then throw a tantrum when corrected by very gentle and capable teachers. After about three months of daily outbursts, her parents and teachers determined that maybe she just wasn't ready yet for school. But the next year was no more successful; neither was kindergarten or first grade. Psychological testing and psychiatric evaluations diagnosed her with an extreme form of childhood onset bipolar disease. Year after year her problem steadily worsened. Twila could not be left with any adult other than her parents. They could not have a babysitter, and they could not go to church together. No one could control Twila. Once, when she was seven, the family was riding in the car and Jeff was pulled over for a routine traffic violation. The physical presence of the motorcycle policeman sent her into a fearful state. She opened the passenger door and ran down the street. Denise, Jeff and the officer went running down the street after her, leaving little Daniel buckled in his car seat. Two blocks away, Twila stopped because she was too tired to keep running. Neither Jeff nor Denise were comforted by the fact that the officer decided not to write the traffic citation.

The strain in the home was difficult for both Jeff and Denise. But their stress emerged differently. Jeff was your classic introverted techie-accountant-computer geek. It was very difficult for him to be at home, though he tried with devotion and commitment. Then he got fired.

The engineering firm lost a bridge contract, so the company needed to reduce its staff. "Bean counters" were expendable, especially because Jeff had the highest number of work-related absences and interruptions. He frequently had to leave work to help with Twila at school or at home. There were doctors, specialists, medications and in-patient hospitalizations during the day. Then at night, Twila's nightmares and fits of rage kept him awake. At work he was frequently absent and consistently tired. Though he got another job, the wound from being fired lingered. Jeff became less available. If he didn't keep his job they would lose both income and insurance. He had to stay focused on his primary responsibility as provider. The cubicle became heaven. The family could not provide joy or fulfillment for Jeff. The phrase "home is hell" was a silent life motto that he often thought but would never vocalize to Denise. His commitment to Denise, Twila and Daniel remained as strong and resolute as ever. But his image of the family as a respite from the strife of life had been destroyed. He mused over his marriage, recognizing that he and Denise rarely fought and rarely even disagreed. Actually, they had more frequent "conflict" before children. Now he had no energy to care. There was no fight left in him. He was not angry with anyone, especially not with Twila. Jeff understood that it was not her fault. Nor was he angry at Denise. He had pity and sorrow for her. If anything he was angry at God, but would catch himself, not allowing himself to go there. His theology didn't permit the freedom to yell at his Creator. When asked what he felt in place of the anger that was not present, his one-word reply was, "Empty."

Denise's journey through Twila's illness was equally devastating. She carried the weight of helping a suffering child while protecting and providing for a second child, who was daily being robbed of the attention of his mother because of the demands of a needier sister. Jeff's needs lagged far, far behind. Her personal needs, such as time with friends at Starbucks, a pedicure, or just a quiet, unrushed hour at the grocery store, were distant memories. Denise had no life of her own. And in all her effort, she could not save her family. She envied her husband for his privilege of going off to work. They had no marriage. She stopped taking birth control years ago. "Why bother, I have no interest in sex" was her rationalization. They both saw their marriage as a plight. It was their private plague for which there was no escape.

Denise was very well suited for the role that she played—organized, precise, forceful, assertive and strong, with a medical education. She kept exact records from the dozens of physicians and psychologists. Her analytical mind was capable of demanding from doctors explanation and elaboration of their diagnoses and treatment. What she received from the demands was a medical consensus: "We don't really understand what is wrong with Twila." Denise's response was to become more fused with Twila and Daniel, and more separated from Jeff. He seemed happy to just go to work, and she was happy to send him there. He was one less person for her to take care of . . . except when she needed him at 3:45 in the morning when Twila was having a tantrum and Daniel was awoken by the night screams of his sister and was matching her, decibel for decibel. It infuriated Denise that Jeff would sleep. He used to wake up and ask if he could do anything. She would say, "No, I've got it, go back to bed." Now it seems that he doesn't even notice the chaos. She feels alone. Though she is with her children day and night, she feels alone. In spite of the fact that Jeff is there for them in a pinch, and his loyalty and commitment never waivers, Denise feels alone. And she is. They both are.

Now twelve years into parenthood, Denise and Jeff look at one another with a perplexing confusion. They are not enemies or opponents. They recognize, intellectually, that their problem can't be simplified into the good guy and the bad guy. They are still friends, even lovers. They are committed to caring for Twila and Danny, to helping them into maturity as adults. But the image of family joy, harmony and delight has been squashed by an eight-hundred-pound gorilla called family illness. In church (Jeff at the 8:30 service, Denise at the 11:00; someone stays home with Twila because she is too disruptive in Sunday school), it is hard for them to remain when their pastor preaches on family bliss. Jeff has thought, "The Christian family that he describes was what I used to fantasize about—before we became a family." The reconciliation of their experience with the simplified message is difficult.

We find that their story is everyone's story, only exaggerated. The weights and burdens of making a family work leaves a couple isolated from each other as they seek to become insulated from the weight and pain of life. Couples who come to counseling because of family issues know that to be in family is to be in challenging relationships. Jeff and Denise's bipolar experience with family as being wonderful and difficult is confirmed in the social science literature. The research indicates that children provide significant meaning to their parents. Life satisfaction increases for those with children compared to those without children. Parents live longer and live more securely than nonparents. Yet the research also indicates that parents report greater stress, greater fatigue, less free time, more anxiety regarding financial demands and less sleep, compared to couples without children.

Now the couple comes to you, the counselor, and you are well prepared. Taking Jeff and Denise Miller and their family as a case study, you are in a unique position to be an administrator of grace—which is not to be misunderstood as passive encouragement or religious platitudes. Rather, the Christian story applied to the Miller family can explain cause and provide freedom to stimulate creativity for the family to resolve their complicated situation.

COUPLE FUNCTION AND PARENTING

Your first task in understanding Jeff and Denise is to think about how the couple functions together—how does their Us dance? Articulated in family systems theory, the first task is to think of how to shore up the marital subsystem. In order for the couple to extend grace to both Twila and Daniel, teaching them to cope with challenges and complexities, they have to be strengthened as an Us. The marital couple is the fundamental holon, or unit, according to Minuchin. He writes, "Above all, the spouse holon must learn to deal with conflict, which occurs inevitably when two people are forming a new unit—whether the issue is closed or open windows in the bedroom at night or the family budget."[3] With the Miller family, marital conflict is the natural outgrowth of severe stress, threats to job, loss of individual freedoms, isolation from other adults, and experiences and complex medical decisions brought on by Twila's physical condition.

The external world is pounding their Us, causing them to turn against one another. Their survival as a couple hinges on the ability to defend themselves against this external threat. If they perceive each other as a secondary threat, or as an obstacle in addressing their primary threat, they will be actively working against their marriage rather than utilizing it as a positive force against the real threat brought on by Twila's disease. In counseling, the first task is to insist that Jeff and Denise locate one hour a week where they could be away from Daniel and Twila to see you for counseling. Imagine that there is initial resistance but you hold to this demand. They eventually settle on Saturday noon, for twelve weeks—a neighbor would watch Twila and Daniel.

Now imagine that you ask, "What is a family supposed to do? What purpose is a family supposed to fulfill or accomplish? And how are they supposed to function?" In their conversation, Jeff and Denise determine that the purpose of family in general, and their family specifically, is to work as a team to meet the challenges that are faced in normal life. These include the obvious things like eating, sleeping and staying safe. Further, they identify that families are to teach children how to grow up and become mature adults, and that families are to be active in creating joy, contentment and happiness.

> Counselor: Okay, so we know how families are to function—now let's look at how you two are doing and building your family.

> Jeff: Well, obviously not too good. We are so focused on caring for Twila that it takes up every bit of our attention.

> Counselor: Okay, what I have heard from both of you is that Twila's needs are so great that you have had to jettison many essential family functions so that you can care for her. To that I will advocate the most difficult task for you to accomplish successfully: "The officer has to sleep first." What that means is, on the battlefield, the person who has to make decisions for the rest of the company must get sufficient rest to be able to make smart choices. If he fails because of fatigue, people die. Likewise in a family, if the adults are so worn that they do not think and act wisely, the family suffers. So here is an order, coming from the doctor. When we meet next week, I would like you both to come with a list of four essential family functions that have been neglected, ideas as to

how those can be addressed, and concerns for the obstacles that might thwart your success.

Denise: But we just can't do that. I mean, we never know when Twila will be out of control. She goes into a panic when we are not with her. There is no one that we can lean on who is able to manage her when she is out of control.

Counselor: No one has the experience and the relationship with her as you both do. I want you to think of your situation this way: Imagine that you manage an estate and the great house has a very serious termite problem. You make it your mission to eradicate these pests. You focus all of your resources to eliminate termites from the mansion. After three years you succeed with that task, but the building is condemned because you neglected to repair the roof. Water leaked into the structure. The termite-free building has to be torn down.

The point being, you will need to redirect your resources in order to be fully functional. Clearly, you have functioned with the highest commitment toward caring for Twila, with significant costs to other aspects of the estate. Twila's needs will continue to be met, but you both recognize that without such a reordering, your marriage will not sustain this pace. Divorce, cardiac arrest, anxiety and depression will not serve her or either of you very well.

In this discussion you have initiated functional change. Prior to your conversation, Jeff and Denise were "fully dedicated" to caring for Twila—even if it destroyed them all. But your work is helping them redirect their efforts in revising their Us.

COUPLE RELATIONSHIP AND PARENTING

The second theme to be addressed with Jeff and Denise pertains to the way that the Miller family relates to one another. Imagine the following conversation occurring a few weeks later. You, the counselor, focus on the withdrawal and control behaviors that the couple describe as their natural defenses. The positive components of each of their actions are affirmed. For Jeff, it is his commitment to work; and for Denise, being on top of every detail of Twila's care is an essential family need. You turn the tone of the dialogue to address what is missed as a result of their mutual tendency to remain focused on their respective job and distant from the other's responsibility.

Denise: One effect that it has on me is I start entertaining all of these paranoid ideas like "Jeff doesn't care about me . . . Jeff is going to have to have an affair with an attractive coworker . . ."

Jeff: All my co-workers are accountants! An attractive accountant is an oxymoron!

Denise: True. See how crazy these thoughts are! But these thoughts are there, so I end up all the more protected from you and possessive of Twila and Danny because I think, eventually, you are going to abandon us.

Jeff: The fantasy is always out there of "the grass is greener." But I am smarter than that. I'm in this for good. Denise knows that. I guess for me, I escape to work because I don't know what to do at home or I am locked out of helping at home—I'm sort of in the way when how I handle a situation is different than how Denise handles it. That just really confuses Twila. I think that I miss being able to do all the fun things associated with being a dad. You know, going to soccer games, even just playing at the park is a major ordeal that leaves everyone tense. It's easier just to give up, stay at home and work on a budget project on the computer.

Counselor: What I am hearing from you is that there are some advantages in being separate and insulated from one another. You are more efficient and productive and you don't aim your anger and frustration at each other because you are not together often. But it leaves you both isolated.

Jeff: Yep, that sums up how we relate right now.

Counselor: Okay, so let's play a game this week. Well, you two will play; I will be an offsite referee. Because both of you tend to move away from the heat, I want you both to encourage the other to escape to isolation. Such as, Jeff, you are to say, "Denise, you are better than me at all of the activities to be done today. You should do them alone." To which, Denise, you say, "No, no, I want you to do them with me." In your case, Denise, the easy (and cowardly) thing to do is for you to do "whatever" all by yourself. But instead I want you to plead for Jeff's company. And then, Denise, you are to say the same thing to Jeff—"Wow, you are under a great deal of stress from work. Take more time this evening to work on those projects." And Jeff, your reply is, "I have done enough work today. I will abandon it to be with you."

Jeff: I don't get it. What is the point?

Counselor: Here is the relational dance—each of you push the other away, and you happily comply because absence makes each of your lives a little bit easier. And you both can be bitter and resentful for being isolated, misunderstood and taxed until you have nothing left.

Jeff: Yeah, that part I get.

Counselor: Okay, instead of that I want you to break that relational pattern—instead of running away, I want you to run toward. And I fully expect the tension to rise when you do this. Think of your independence as an addiction—it keeps you going at the same time it's destroying you. So you need to turn this process around.

Your efforts in rebuilding the relationship are in creating dependence, rather than encouraging isolation and separation. Ultimately, your effort is to create the message, "I need you," rather than the message, "I am better off without you."

COUPLE IDENTITY AND PARENTING

Couple identity is the culmination of the marital Us. It is the code. It is the constitution that defines existence. It is important for marital teams to address their identity with intention. If it is not, then the theme or identity of the family will be defined by its lowest common denominator—their suffering, pain and defenses. It will be defined thoughtlessly, which means that it may be controlled by their least mature emotions.

Counselor: Jeff and Denise, here is another game. It's called, "Name the identity." I am going to name a few things, people or families, and I want you to label them with a descriptor or an identity. When I say Albert Einstein, you would say, what?

Jeff: "Brilliant."

Denise: Yes, that and, what is it? "$E=MC^2$."

Counselor: Okay, good. Now, "Superman."

Jeff: "Faster than a speeding bullet."

Counselor: "The Simpsons."

Denise: "Completely worthless."

Jeff: "Us, the Miller family? Oh, Marge!"

Counselor: Okay then, "the Millers."

Denise: Oooh. That one will take a moment.

Jeff: I'd say it would be "tense" or "stressed."

Denise: Yeah, something like that. Maybe "exhausted from caretaking."

With this exercise, you located the identity. Some families are baseball families. Some are into swimming or homeschooling or soccer. Some center their lives around the church. But the Millers have defined themselves by their stress source, not by their commitments, resources, interests or values. Bringing this reality to their attention was both undeniable and sobering.

Counselor: When you define yourself by your problem, or your problem becomes so large that it permeates every aspect of your life and therefore controls you, it is difficult to find joy in anything at all. Everything is tainted by the "problem." Here is the task that I would like you to consider. Do not dismiss your problems and challenges you have as parents, but think beyond that. Given who you are and what your tasks in life will be, come back with a description of who you are and how you will define yourselves.

A week later Jeff and Denise came back with their identity. It read:

We acknowledge that as a family we have both limitations and strengths. We will define ourselves by our assets, acknowledging that they are gifts from God for which we must answer. The Miller family exists to honor the name of Jesus by supporting, encouraging and correcting each other so that each member is able to experience the grace of God to its fullest.

Family therapy with this couple and with the full Miller family takes a turn at this juncture, away from the primary focus of "we are spent."

The same challenges remain and the fatigue level is still high. But the focus and proportions of life are reoriented. You, the counselor, do not provide solutions to their problems, but redirect their focus, encourage them to apply the tenets of their Christian faith to their real problems, and serve as a sounding board for creative solutions. The key to this success with the Miller family is that you are not pulled into the emotional quagmire of despair and hopelessness. Nor do you build an artificial "Pollyanna reality" of trite, simplistic solutions with religious verbiage. You take the resources that are provided—namely, their commitment to succeed—and show them how to build with that resource to become effective parents and intimate partners. This puts Denise and Jeff in a position to look at their pain and defenses and to move through grace toward intimacy.

PARENTING AND THE PAIN-DEFENSE CYCLE

The pain, defense and injury that Jeff and Denise faced was not caused by self-centeredness, infidelity, manipulation or any other act that is known to destroy marriages. They exemplify the fact that life brings hardship and heartache. In the face of such hardships it is the most natural reaction to make the spouse the face of suffering, and then channel anger, resentment and bitterness toward the one who is the safest and the closest.

Pain. The research of the effects of children on marriage has revealed a trend or pattern of parental behavior that parallels the conflict cycle of pain-defense-offense described in this book. The cycle begins innocently with the unexpected reality of parenting—that it is way harder than what was planned, despite the fact that everyone said it would be so. It is not that couples are not prepared for parenting—they read, plan and learn about the demands of children by close association with siblings and friends who commenced down the road to parenthood before them. But nothing prepares them for 3:00 a.m. trips to the emergency room when there is an important work demand the next day at 9:00. The experience of negotiating life with children, accommodating their unique needs, cannot be anticipated, planned or prevented.

The result of this is pain in the form of tension and stress from the increased life demand for both spouses. These freedoms are taken for granted prior to children. The loss of personal freedoms, sleep, activities and interest and pleasure, predictable life patterns that aided healthy diet and exercise are altered. It becomes harder to be a "successful" adult as is common in earlier and later life stages. The effect of this change is experienced uniquely for each spouse. And it may pale in comparison to the overwhelming joy and enthusiasm for parenthood. But pain is there, obviously or clandestinely, spoken or muted, and the effects of pain in the form of defenses are also present.

Denise: I am just tired, exhausted and discouraged. The work never stops.

Counselor: I hear that, Denise, and I see it in your story and in your face. You are worn out.

Jeff: And it's not fatigue like the tiredness from running a marathon or working too hard in the yard. It's a relentless feeling. This situation takes all of her and all of me and there is no letting up.

Though the severity of parenting pain is unique to Denise and Jeff, it is not unique in terms of form. Most parents speak of being completely taxed of resources at various stages of family development. This strain changes as children go through their stages of growth. The exhaustion may be from a lack of sleep during infancy, to a need for constant supervision in early childhood, to defiance and rejection in adolescence. The effort expended to nurture children into mature adults typically exceeds expectations, and can prompt intense discouragement. Parents can succumb to the view that, because of the pain associated with family growth, someone is at fault and life should not have to be this difficult. While demonstrating empathy with the real pain, counselors can normalize the process of parenting by encouraging parents to read and talk with others who are in the process. That does not remove the pain; it normalizes it. Empathy and the realization that others have had similar experiences does not take away colic at 3:00 a.m., or insert an attitude of gratitude in fourteen-year-old middle schoolers. It does, however, alter the perception that parents are isolated from the normal challenges of parenting, or that there is something deviant about their family circumstance.

Defense. The defenses that emerge from the pain-induced challenges of parenthood will have a correlation with the specific role that the spouse occupies in the family. Frequently, these fall on typical gender lines but they will vary dependent upon the degree of "caretaker" and "breadwinner" responsibilities held by each partner. When the breadwinner encounters stress related to the parental role, the common response is to become more occupied by the responsibility outside the home. This "working parent alienation" has been frequently documented in research on marital behavior. Similarly, the caretaking parent tends to occupy greater responsibility and decision-making for the children. At times these role changes are unilateral—that is, the husband or wife independently moves toward isolation or control without the support, consent or even awareness of the other. However, most times it is a coordinated shift with both spouses moving to their respective "battle station" as the tension and the demand in the home increases. This brief dialogue reveals the process of defense to injury.

> Counselor: Denise, if I were a fly on the wall in your home, what observations could I make that would tell me that you were at the end of your rope, that you were tired, worn-out and exhausted?
>
> Denise: Well, I am ashamed to say it, but you would see me scream at the kids, at Jeff, at just about anyone or anything. At other times I feel withdrawn, sort of depressed and just lost.
>
> Counselor: I hear you say that you react to all of the "stuff" with two extremes—you might be full of rage or you might implode emotionally and just have nothing to give.
>
> Denise: Yep, that is me . . .
>
> Counselor: Jeff, what do you feel when she shows either of these patterns to you? What happens to you on the inside?
>
> Jeff: Well, when she's angry I want to head for the hills. So I stay at work or piddle in the garage or the yard, just about anything to stay under the radar.
>
> Counselor: What is the injury that you are wanting to avoid?
>
> Jeff: I am feeling pretty helpless, both about the situation with Twila

and compounded by my wife's anger. So, I think that I am afraid of being attacked.

Counselor: What about when Denise is feeling depressed? What do you feel then?

Jeff: I am not as fearful then, well honestly, I am fearful in a different way. When she is angry I fear for myself. When she is depressed I fear for her, that she might be so depressed that she commits suicide or something. Now she hasn't talked like that but that is what goes on in my mind. Either way though I think that I do the same thing, just withdraw into my own space or my work space and stay away from her.

Antagonistic defense. Marital tensions usually go underground when children are present. And, because children are present almost all of the time, it is common for marital tensions to take on a "permanent suppression style." The frequent result is that tensions percolate and are eventually transformed into deep-rooted bitterness. This active antagonism becomes the defense magnified or exaggerated. It becomes easy for the alienated spouse to feign an oblivious presentation. It's like the logic follows this path: (1) The stress is high in the home; (2) the stress is beginning to affect my work performance; (3) I need to pull away from the home stress in order to maintain success at work; (4) the stress has increased as a result of my pulling away but if I notice or change I will get sucked into the stress vortex; and (5) I concentrate more fully on work, leaving the home issues to my spouse to address.

Similarly, the caretaking spouse might use a similar logical path: (1) The stress is high in the home; (2) I need to attend to the children to ensure that they are not negatively affected by marital tension; (3) support in caretaking and home-management roles is insufficient, unreliable or unacceptable; (4) I am better off just doing it myself; and (5) I concentrate on attending to home and child issues because my spouse is unsupportive and/or uninterested in being in partnership with me.

Offense. The accidental effects of normal defenses and the malicious effects of antagonistic defenses usually result in either spouse feeling offended. The offense is experienced in the form of being manipulated, unappreciated, unaccepted, isolated and/or controlled. It puts husbands and wives on edge. They are alert and sensitive to the other's taking advantage. They are prone to interpret the actions through the lens of pain and defense rather than through grace and forgiveness. Being overly stressed leans a person toward additional defensiveness rather than excessive graciousness. Parents get worn out. And fatigued parents are made vulnerable by their exhaustion and therefore make decisions that use their defenses rather than decisions that are drawn from grace.

EXEMPLIFYING GRACE IN COUNSELING AS MODEL AND MENTOR

We believe that pastors and marital counselors possess significant power to help couples transform their families. It comes through your administration of grace, modeling justice, exhibiting empathy, encouraging trust and embodying forgiveness. When parents are in a depleted state, they fail to exercise the relational skills articulated within the Christian story. They know it intellectually, but they lose the capacity to live it experientially. They are like two castaways clinging to a life raft, deprived of food and water. All they can do is hang on. Your pulling aside and throwing them a rope may not be enough—they may lack the creativity and decision making to reach for it. Counselors often have to jump in and rope the family up.

The first task in this is to prompt them toward the restoration cycle with the gift of realistic hope. Many counselors will offer hope in terms of words of Christian encouragement. In working with Jeff and Denise, the counselor tries to take that a step further by acknowledging what they already know but will not freely articulate. He says:

> Because we do not know the future, we should remain humble in our projections and interpretation. But it is probable to think that Twila's physical condition will not get better, and could even become worse. That is "likely truth number one." And "likely truth number two" is that though her condition does not improve, it is entirely possible for you to have a full, meaningful and satisfying marriage and family life. You can teach, nurture and love Twila into adulthood, even with her challenges and disabilities. And Daniel does not have to live in the shadow of a sister who draws all the energy to herself so that there is nothing left for

him. In other words, the two of you have more than enough intelligence, material resources, social support and faith in a loving God to pull this off.

His message is clear, emphatic and even forceful: "You two can pull this off, if you are smart, insightful and you work as a team."

The second task is for the counselor to walk through the relationship restoration cycle. Grace, justice, empathy, trust building and forgiveness are taught, modeled and integrated into the discussions. The couple identifies their defensive withdrawal patterns and defines them for what they are—tools for self-protection. Furthermore, they realize that the use of their defenses, though providing immediate payoff, only serve to magnify the problem because their use will undermine the Us, the team strength needed to win in the game they are playing.

Finally, the counselor must examine the three elements of family redemption: functioning, relationship and identity. His purpose is to move the couple from their entrenched identity as a family in despair and retreat, to a family that possesses sufficient resources to face the challenges ahead. As a marital counselor, he believes that the biblical promise "And my God will fully satisfy every need of yours according to his riches in glory in Christ Jesus" (Phil 4:19) is a declaration of God's provision that requires parents to actively consider how God will see that need met. Each element serves to reorder and prioritize how Jeff and Denise will work together to alter the current family path. Counseling with the Miller family likely will include challenging the couple to garner resources from extended family, the community, government programs and especially the church, so that the promise of God's provision and supply is more than just a trite spiritualism, but a reality. The goal is to help Jeff and Denise reconstruct the family and marital identity from the image of "hanging by our fingernails" to a family and marriage that is stable, secure and sufficiently resourced, in spite of the challenges that must be faced because of disease and developmental challenges.

A FINAL WORD: MARITAL SKILLS AND THE ART OF PARENTING
There are few challenges to married couples as valuable and demanding

as parenting. Good parenting impedes the transmission of psychological immaturity to the next generation. Counselors play a very crucial
role in assisting couples in developing mature children. However, it is
easy to be pulled into the parental quagmire by offering opinions about
child care and development that is outside the bounds of established
knowledge. Consider the following marital skills when discussing issues pertaining to parenting.

*Marital skill 1: Accept what the individuals choose to do with their
lives.* It is common to be asked your opinion about parenting in the
form of these age-old questions, for example: "Should you let an infant
cry it out or pick him up at night?" or "Will you spoil a child if you . . . ?"
or "Should we start our daughter in kindergarten at age four and a half
or wait a year?" or "When should our son be allowed to date?" These
questions and countless others will feed your ego as the "family expert."
But unless you know the factual information and unless you understand the background in their asking the question, restraint is likely the
best path.

Marital skill 2: Be comfortable in the front lines. A good family counselor is difficult to find. Most counselors and pastors opt to offer sage
advice in the safety of conversations with one or both parents. It is
easier to critique the game rather than enter it. We encourage pastors
and counselors to become learned, trained and supervised in the art of
family therapy. Working with whole families or subsystems of parents
and children, as well as extended families, is a most valuable ministry
and service.

Marital skill 3: Have no dog in the fight. Parents, children and adolescents with differing views will actively seek to persuade you to join
with them against other family subsystems when conflict is occurring. Listen for that "loud sucking sound" as people seek to pull you
to their side. We recommend that you honor it by verbally acknowledging the pull by all sides and how that to take a side would be to
destroy trust and credibility. You can suggest that the opposing forces
instead consider a different strategy in working through conflict, returning to the pattern of pain and defense, and the potential for grace
and restoration.

Marital skill 4: See both the forest and the trees. Both parents and children are growing, adjusting, changing, accommodating and maturing. It can be said that parenting is too important to leave to parents . . . but no one else felt qualified for the position. Counselors working with parents with variant ideas, expectations and aspirations for their children can easily forget that the children, like themselves only decades earlier, are emerging individuals with their own minds, abilities and gifts, and that God calls them for a unique mission.

CONCLUSION

Bruno Bettelheim offered sage advice to parents and to counselors who work with parents by saying, "The fear of failure is so great, it is no wonder that the desire to do right by one's children has led to a whole library of books offering advice on how to raise them."[4] Often the greatest contribution made by a counselor for a couple challenged with children is hope, security and reassurance that children, like cats, usually land on their feet, in spite of the predicaments that they often find themselves facing. That being said, counselors are a vital resource for parents who wish to be linked to the libraries of knowledge and insight into child development, systemic behavior, motivation and maturation.

NOTES

[1]Tan, A. (2006). *The joy luck club*. New York: Penguin, p. 17.
[2]Ibid.
[3]Minuchin, S., Rosman, B. L., & Baker, L. (1978). *Psychosomatic families: Anorexia nervosa in context*. Cambridge, MA: Harvard University Press, p. 23.
[4]Bettelheim, Bruno. (1988). *A good enough parent*. New York: Vintage Books, p. 16.

12

SEXUAL INFIDELITY

No adultery is bloodless.

NATALIA GINZBURG

BEFORE HE DID IT, ROBERT KNEW what would happen. He calculated the devastation. He lived in secrecy for years. Only a few people knew his activities. His best friends and his family didn't even know he was involved. Very few could even imagine what he was up to. They noticed that he traveled a lot. They found him evasive when they asked what he was doing. His wife had some idea, but he couldn't tell her. He had to keep it a secret. Everything was denied; there were no accidents. All details were calculated. On paper, he knew the devastation that he would create, but when he experienced it, he was still stunned. Not surprised, but truly stunned. In witnessing the great fireball and mushroom cloud of the first atomic explosion, Robert Oppenheimer, the director of the top secret Manhattan Project, quoted the Bhagavad Gita: "I am become Death, the destroyer of worlds."

We see the married men and women who make public to their spouses and families their own "Manhattan Project" sit with a similar stunned look. After they confess or have their affair discovered, it's as if they are saying, "I knew that it would be bad. Oh, my God, what have I done?"

Carrie and David were like that. They sat down in the office. David started to share that they were meeting with their pastor because he had "blown it" in the marriage—that he had made mistakes previously, but that he was at fault for doing something that was really destructive.

David admitted that over the course of the past year, he had had two affairs. He said that neither lasted long—one for about three weeks; the other one, more recent, closer to seven weeks. He ended it after Carrie found out about it and confronted him.

Carrie began to tear up. She shared that they have been drifting apart for a while, but she didn't know that this was going on.

David went on to share that he probably got into all of this because of a long-standing habit of looking at internet pornography. He shared that he had been looking at it two to three nights a week now for well over seven years. He said he didn't think it was a big deal. He thought it was just something that some men do, perhaps most men, and that it didn't mean anything.

Carrie said that the pornography alone was a surprise, and that pornography itself was "like an affair." She said that it was like she wasn't good enough for him, like she wasn't pretty enough, and that the physical affairs just confirmed what was going on in his mind for years now. The conversation was nuclear. The explosion didn't just leave a big hole in the ground—like the energy released from an atomic bomb, everything near them melted. Nothing looked the same. Carrie was not sure whether there was anything left. She wondered what was there in the first place.

Carried wanted to know details—who, when, what, where, how many times and especially, why. She threw these questions toward him one after the other. Her mind raced faster and faster with every thought. Dave wanted to crawl into the crater that the explosion had created. He was being asked to defend the indefensible.

There is no topic more difficult to address than infidelity. Pastors and counselors must be prepared for it. In this chapter we discuss the unique characteristics of marital conflict that emerge subsequent to infidelity. The essence of this challenge is to conduct two therapeutic interventions. The first is to attend to the breach of sexual faithfulness by one of the spouses. The second is to address the nature of relational conflict prior to acts of infidelity.

SPECIAL CONSIDERATIONS IN ADDRESSING INFIDELITY

About 15 percent of married women and a little less than 25 percent of married men admit to having had an extramarital affair.[1] These are lifetime rates of infidelity. In a given year, we are talking about somewhere between 1 to 4 percent of married persons, with more men than women admitting infidelity. These rates are even higher among those who have been divorced; that is, over 40 percent of divorced men and women reported extramarital sexual relationships during their marriage.[2]

Affairs are a significant breach of faithfulness that can have a devastating impact on the life of a marriage. In fact, most models for responding to marital affairs in counseling or pastoral care presuppose that the affair causes great damage to the marriage. Affairs are often thought to "parallel some aspects of recovery from more general traumatic events."[3] Indeed, Donald Baucom and his colleagues refer to affairs as "interpersonal trauma."[4]

One image that might be helpful to our understanding of the impact of marital unfaithfulness on marital trust is this: that the fabric of the marriage can feel torn by marital infidelity. The marital cloth consists of threads woven over and under one another, combining themselves in strength and function. The rip of infidelity weakens the entire garment. The tear doesn't remain static; it runs, and the threads unravel. What was once a small tear has enlarged, making the garment useless.

How do affairs parallel other traumatic events? According to Baucom, an affair "violates basic assumptions about how the world and people operate."[5] The assumptions include that one's partner is trustworthy or that the relationship is a haven for both partners, the one place where a person is safe and protected. When these assumptions are violated, as is the case in an affair, it is more than just something unfortunate or difficult to get through; rather, it can affect a person at a fundamental level of what they hold to be true about the world and about their relationships.

> An extramarital affair is not merely a very negative event; instead, the injured person often experiences the shattering of core beliefs essential to emotional security. Common statements reflecting such turmoil include, "I don't know you; you aren't the person I thought you were, and our

relationship isn't what I thought it was" or "This just makes no sense; I can't understand how you could do this; I thought I could trust you."[6]

This is especially true if the injured spouse does not have an understanding of why the affair occurred. The more it is a mystery or seemingly irrational, the more confusing and potentially traumatic.

The case of David and Carrie. Let's return to David and Carrie, the couple mentioned at the outset of the chapter. Carrie was surprised to learn about David's struggle with pornography, as well as the two affairs. She did not understand why the affairs occurred; she had no framework for making meaning out of it. We are not talking here about justifying the affair, but just providing some way to make sense of it in the life of their marriage, based on Carrie's previous understanding of David and their relationship.

Experts on helping couples respond to affairs tend to offer frameworks that draw on principles for working with people who have experienced trauma. The models that have been proposed parallel some of what has been understood in the forgiveness literature. In forgiveness-based models of care, counselors or pastoral care providers help people gain insight into the offense, why it occurred, and eventually develop or gain a better sense of control over what has felt out of control in recent weeks or months.

How does this occur and how is it translated to marital affairs?[7] Typically, the spouse who has been injured is, over time, able to have a more accurate view of the offending spouse—so that they are not thought of in black-and-white terms, all good or all bad. This accurate evaluation of the offending partner often leads to less intense negative feelings toward him or her. Sometimes a decrease in anger or resentment can also mean an increase in understanding and even empathy. This is not the same as excusing the affair or rationalizing it or explaining it away. Rather, this can contribute to the act of forgiveness, in which the partner who has been hurt by the affair offers the offending partner forgiveness.

Carrie might come to a better and more accurate understanding of David and, specifically, how he got caught up in a pattern of looking at pornography. In this particular case, David did not have a healthy view of sex. His own sex education was at the hands of his peer group in school. He was exposed to pornography during middle school and used it to some extent through high school and college and beyond. With the advent of the internet, pornography was only that much more accessible to David, and he was able to take advantage of his tendency to isolate from others, including Carrie and his children. At times he could spend hours on the internet looking at pornography.

Pornography use, unlike many other sexual issues, is something that rarely stays at the same level of use. Rather, people tend to seek out variations of images, moving from softer pornography to harder pornography to violence and other depictions over time. This is not true for everyone, but it is a general tendency to need more stimulation, more exposure to more and diverse images to get the same out of it.

In David's case, his use of pornography eventually led him to want to have similar experiences in real life. Given his leadership position in his organization, he had ample opportunity to interact and flirt with women who looked up to him and saw him as rather powerful in the organization. This contributed to some of the fantasies in his own mind that ended up making the two affairs that much more likely and attainable.

The affairs did not occur in a vacuum. Instead of turning toward Carrie and developing their relationship and sense of intimacy, David tended to drift into virtual, imagined relationships, often keeping to himself and preferring (by his own temperament and personality) to have alone time. While not excited about this, Carrie was unable to find ways to connect with David, and she had her own interests, primarily her life with her growing children, so she invested a lot of herself in them and in their many and varied interests.

Given the demands of three children in elementary school and middle school, David and Carrie found less and less time set aside for one another. Both found other opportunities more interesting than building a life of greater transparency and intimacy. There was drift. While they had sexual intercourse every few weeks, they tended to have ample reasons why it was not an ideal time, especially given David's heavy work schedule and the children's demands of Carrie's time and energy.

Carrie would occasionally raise concerns with David, asking if he was okay and what he thought of their marriage. He would say that they were "fine," and that it was "normal" in their difficult stage with children and young adolescents. This made sense to Carrie, but she was still troubled at times by what felt like "emotional drift" away from one another and to a place where inertia was setting in.

With this additional information, Carrie was better able to see the circumstances that led up to David's pornography use and eventual affairs. Again, these circumstances and the habits that David got into do not justify his use of pornography or the affairs, but they do provide a context for understanding the emotional drift they experienced as a couple. They placed the affairs themselves in a context for insight and mutual understanding, which itself set the stage for the gift of forgiveness to be extended from Carrie to David.

We will return to this understanding of the place of forgiveness in responding to affairs. We want to further our understanding of it and consider a specific model for facilitating forgiveness and reconciliation in marriage. For the time being, however, we want to focus on the nature of the relational conflict prior to infidelity. We want to come to a better understanding of the kinds of conflicts that occur in marriages before an affair occurs.

Marital conflict prior to infidelity. It is difficult to predict affairs.[8] We know that couples who have affairs report lower satisfaction with their marriage. This can take many different forms, whether it is sexual dissatisfaction, emotional dissatisfaction, less time spent together, less trust, more self-centeredness and so on. Based on what we know about individuals who have affairs, we will discuss some of the nature of relational conflict prior to infidelity.

Men tend to be more likely to report affairs than women, as we noted above. And men who have affairs tend to be older than women who report having an affair. Men who have affairs tend to report being more sexually dissatisfied in their marriage than women who report having an affair. So when men are unfaithful, it appears to be tied more to sexual dissatisfaction, and the affair itself tends to be more about sex than about meeting a particular emotional need. And differences in expectations and preferences in sexual desire and frequency may be part of the relational conflict prior to infidelity. We have both counseled couples in which the husband has justified his sex outside of marriage by pointing to his wife's unwillingness to provide him with sex at a frequency that was satisfying to him. Christian men are not immune to this tendency to justify extramarital affairs; they too will point the finger at their spouse if they feel she is not meeting their sexual needs the way they feel she should.

In contrast, women tend to have affairs that are more about the emotional connection than the sexual connection. Women whose husbands have had an affair tend to be more upset by their husband's emotional connection in the affair than by the sex (whereas men are just the opposite: more upset by the sexual connection between their wife and someone else). So for women we may see that the nature of relational conflict prior to an affair on their part may have to do with unmet emotional needs.

In the case of David and Carrie, we saw David turn first to pornography and then later to two affairs in response to the drift in their marriage. Had Carrie had an affair, it might have very well been due to her emotional needs being unmet over time. As it was, Carrie essentially poured herself into her children and their interests and activities and her role as a mother to meet many of her emotional needs and to form a sense of her own identity.

In addition to what we have covered, couples who have later reported affairs report less time spent together. There is a kind of relationship drift, or even inertia, that can set in. Two people end up living side by side in their relationship rather than together. They begin to have and develop separate interests that keep them apart and offer them less time to be together.

This was certainly true of David and Carrie. At a very practical level, David shared during an individual meeting how they had been sleeping in separate rooms due to his sleep apnea. This had been going on now for over two years. Both said they slept better when they slept apart. It's not that this is wrong per se, but it led to a habit of going to bed at different times, of not closing out the day with one another, of spending evenings in separate activities—all of which over time added up to living two parallel lives.

So couples often begin to develop other interests and activities. Soon these other activities and relationships may be more interesting or rewarding to one or both partners. Couples at risk of having affairs also tend to enjoy the time they spend together less than those who do not have an affair. They might talk about having little in common: "We just don't have anything in common anymore." That may be exactly how it feels, too. But marriages do not begin there. They can get there over time, but it is important to recognize that couples drift to these different places—far apart from where they began and from one another. The fact that they now do little together and enjoy what they do together less and less only confirms in their minds that they prefer others or find other people or relationships to be more fulfilling to them.

Such couples also report difficulty with trust and dishonesty in their marriage. This could begin with small things—keeping secrets, having different interests and activities that one's partner doesn't know about. It could also look like compartmentalizing one's life, so that certain experiences are for your spouse, while other experiences are for others in your life, and not sharing those and being more transparent about one's activities.

David and Carrie experienced some of this. David was a private person. He liked his "alone time," and he gravitated to it time and time again. Some of this was because of his introverted personality—he "recharged his batteries" by taking some time to himself. But it became more than that. He began to prefer his time alone to time with Carrie, and he would find ways to put up an emotional wall in the relationship that eventually functioned to keep Carrie out.

People who are more self-focused or place greater emphasis on meeting their own needs are more likely to have an affair. Ours is a culture of getting our own needs met. We talk a lot about what we need, and this can quickly become a justification for behavior. After all, if a person feels that they have certain "needs," whether they are emotional or sexual, and that they have a right to get those needs met somehow, whether within their marriage our outside of their marriage, it is a short step to rationalizing an affair.

David began to get some insight into this during individual counseling. He admitted to his counselor that he was selfish. He liked to get his own needs met, and if that meant removing himself from emotional intimacy with his wife by "shutting down," he would do that. If it meant finding time to look at pornography, he would do that too. Eventually it meant having the two affairs with the women he met at work.

While it can be difficult to predict affairs, we have a better idea of some of the relationship dynamics that may be in place prior to an affair. These can be examined to help prevent an affair and to enhance marriages. But it is important that we consider ways to mend the fabric that is torn by infidelity. We turn our attention now to that topic.

The case of Lamont and Jess. Lamont and Jess had been in counseling for over a year. They had been referred to counseling because of an affair Jess had with her immediate supervisor at work. She talked about how Lamont was "boring" and kind of "lifeless." She indicated that her staff would go out for fun after work, meet up for happy hour or do other activities. She would "always" invite Lamont, who would "almost always" decline. Lamont said that he didn't know the people that well and that he preferred to be home after his day at work. Jess went on to talk about the things she would like to do—the travel she would like to enjoy, the events and activities that she would like to be a part of but that they do so little of now that they are married. Lamont shared that some of what Jess mentions in terms of travel sounds fine to him, but that he doesn't feel the same drive to do it that she does. But he would go and enjoy himself on occasion if she would like that. Jess went on to talk about how she wished Lamont would "take the lead" and show more "initiative" in liking the kinds of things she likes. She wished he were different that way—more adventuresome and exciting.

When asked about the affair, Jess was able to make the connection between the drift in her marriage and the tendency to do different activities that left Lamont out of the picture. She defended that choice: "I would ask Lamont all the time, and all the time he would say, 'No, you go ahead. I'd like to unwind at home.'"

Jess said she regretted the affair, that she knew it was wrong, but that it was exciting at the time to be with someone who was more like her in terms of taking an interest in her interests and show her more attention and wanting to spend time with her.

Lamont was initially shocked and angry to learn about the affair and had explored some kind of retribution. Specifically, he spoke early on in counseling about having an affair to "get even" with Jess.

Fast-forward over a year and a half later. Lamont and Jess are able to renew their commitment to one another. They have weathered a very difficult storm in Jess's affair. They have prevented even more damage, as Lamont eventually chose not to get even with Jess by hurting her in the same way. He had begun an emotional relationship with a colleague but chose to end it. He gave up on revenge and chose instead a different path for himself and for their marriage. How did they manage to make things better? Why didn't Jess's affair spell the end to their marriage? We will look now at specific factors of marital restoration.

COUPLE IDENTITY AND INFIDELITY

The primary issue with couple identity is locating the plural self in the world. *Who are we—together?* After the breach of an affair, this question is asked with greater intensity. Not only *Who are we?* but *Who are we now as a couple since who we were has been broken? And what will it look like to form an identity as individuals and as a couple on the other side of an affair?*

Keep in mind that both the offending spouse and the nonoffending spouse are asking these questions. There is shame in having acted out and having been the one to tear the fabric of the marriage. The person can feel bad not just for what was done but also for who he or she is. Helping that person walk through what it means to regret their behavior and make changes is important; it is also important to safeguard their sense of identity as a person who is loved by God in the face of decisions that are now regretted.

The nonoffending spouse is also trying to find their place in all of what's transpired. Their life may have revolved largely around the relationship that is now on life support. This affects a person's sense of self and identity. You can help them grow in their own sense of themselves as a person and, eventually, you can help them grow in their sense of themselves as a couple. The strength of identity in the individual should not be seen as competing with an identity as a couple; rather a firmer sense of self as an individual can strengthen and foster a stronger sense of identity as a couple once the foundation is laid for healing and reconciliation in the relationship.

An analogy might help the pastor understand what this is like. Think of marriage as being on an exciting expedition—perhaps it's like exploring the Amazon basin or climbing the summit of a mountain. The couple is a team. Each trusts one another with their lives, but there is a certain sense in which the couple is naive about the dangers that exist and are to be expected in any such expedition. But again, each must trust the other, and this is true in terms of marital identity. There is a sense of Us that exists and grows more and more with shared experiences. Each stamp in the passport signals another way in which the team is building a life together.

An affair derails the expedition. It threatens the sense of Us, as well as the trust that was necessary to be a part of exploring new terrain. Infidelity feels like sabotage. It's like someone has been draining much-needed water and throwing out what limited food was available for the team. Now it is also possible that this was happening before the affair and that the affair signals a fundamental problem in the expedition.

So identity is a casualty in an affair. The sense of Us and of trust is lost. That does not mean it cannot be recovered or that a new sense of Us cannot emerge or that trust cannot be rebuilt, but it will take time and effort. Both spouses have to find their footing again, having lost a sense for where they are, what they were heading toward, and who they are as a couple. One of the biggest changes after an affair is that the trust in one's partner changes. The nonoffending spouse may still decide to be part of the same expedition, but everything changes when it doesn't feel like one person can trust the other the way they could before the affair.

COUPLE FUNCTIONING AND INFIDELITY

Lamont and Jess did not magically arrive at a place of reconciliation.

There is nothing like the days and weeks following the admission of an affair. Impossible as it may sound, people still have to function. They get up in the morning; they have breakfast; they go to work; they get their kids ready for school; they take their kids to ballet rehearsal and soccer practice. They see themselves going on and they see the world going on when all of what they have known is in a jumble.

While all of this is going on, they have to deal with one another, and this is painful. Relating can often be strained, as you can imagine, as simple activities can be occasions infused with indirect expressions of pain and anger and confusion. Some people compartmentalize their feelings and believe that any expression of anger is an act of intimacy that they no longer offer their partner.

A first step is to acknowledge this, to talk about it with each of them and to recognize that the threat to their marriage makes relating diffi-cult right now. There are no shortcuts past this. We cannot pretend that nothing happened, but that is often how it feels when life goes on as usual. All the while, a couple's whole world has turned upside down.

In the area of functioning, the person who has had the affair has to decide what to do with the relationship and whether to curtail destructive patterns of behavior. For those couples who decide to work on their marriage, this means the offending partner must break it off with the person they had an affair with. This does not have to happen in person or be a long or extended goodbye. But it would be final, not leaving a door open for something else if reconciliation proves too difficult.

Also, the spouse who had the affair would benefit from understanding the context of the affair. What we mean by this is not what caused it—we help the person take responsibility for their actions—but what was going on that served as a backdrop to the decision to behave in ways that seem so out of character to the person they have been up to this point?

The spouse has to decide how he or she is going to function in rela-tion to the partner who has had the affair. Sometimes couples decide on a separation to work through some of the initial reaction to the affair. They find that the physical distance creates a space for them to work through the emotional pain.

COUPLE RELATIONSHIP AND INFIDELITY

Functioning is an important initial consideration. If a couple decides to work toward reconciliation, they have to do more than change destructive patterns of behavior. In other words, if the fabric of marital trust can be torn by infidelity, we have to look at what constitutes mending. How do couples recover from affairs?

Kristina Coop Gordon and Donald Baucom offer a three-stage model that fosters reconciliation after an affair. It is a model that is based on the importance of forgiveness following marital infidelity. The three stages are *impact*, a search for *meaning* and *recovery*. We see this model of forgiveness as relying upon and addressing the relationship theme in our work.

The first stage, the *impact* stage, is a time of great distress. It is during this time that a person's prior understanding of the relationship is shattered. People tend to feel powerless and may want to do something to get even. This overlaps considerably with what we just reviewed about finding ways to improve functioning. What makes this difficult, of course, is the strong emotional reactions, such as confusion, anger, resentment, grief, loss and so on.

The second stage, a search for *meaning*, is an attempt to place the affair in a larger context for understanding what's happened. The person is trying to answer the question, Why did the affair occur? Attempts to answer this question can provide the person with some sense of meaning and also a sense of control. "This increased understanding also aids individuals in reconstructing their violated assumptions and creating new beliefs and expectancies for the future of the relationship."[9]

This work has to be done by both the person who had the affair and the spouse, although much of the literature emphasizes the work that is done by the spouse who did not have the affair. In other words, the person who would at some point in the future offer forgiveness has to first come to a place of understanding. Insight or understanding into what happened—finding meaning in the event—provides a bridge to compassion. It is not the same thing as excusing the affair.

We also say that the spouse who had the affair also has to come to a better understanding of his or her behavior. We mentioned this above under the theme of functioning, as the offending spouse has to make change in behaviors that are destructive to the marriage. As we move into the theme of relationship, we see that changing patterns of destructive behaviors is important, and that moving to the next level of improving the relationship both capitalizes on these changed behaviors and anchors those changes in a possible new future together.

The third stage, *recovery*, is a time of moving forward in which the spouse "must move beyond the event and stop allowing it to control his or her life."[10] People tend to let go of anger during this stage. They tend to see holding onto the anger as damaging to themselves and not particularly helpful.

Many things can happen to the relationship at this point. The relationship could end. The spouse can forgive and attempt reconciliation. He or she could forgive but not reconcile. Females tend to be more forgiving than males.[11]

For couples who decide to attempt reconciliation, both spouses at this point of recovery have an opportunity to foster restoration by mending the relational space between them. This is often done by being trustworthy and by trusting. The offending spouse can be trustworthy through changes in behavior and relationship that are sustained over time.

We often talk to the offending spouse about a framework for rebuilding trust. This involves commitments to the counseling or pastoral care that they are a part of, as well as attending other meetings (for example, a local men's or women's group or self-help group) or being in other relationships that are fostering reconciliation (for example, an accountability partner or sponsor). Specific steps mentioned earlier are also part of a framework for rebuilding trust. Steps like breaking off contact with the other person, closing out relevant email accounts, installing software that tracks websites and so on.

Actively participating in these steps creates opportunities for the spouse to trust the other without having to function as the accountability partner. Once the nonoffending spouse has to function as an accountability partner, they are no longer free to rebuild trust; they take on a different role in the life of their husband or wife.

As we mentioned, many things can happen to the relationship at this point. It is crucial that neither counselor nor couple rush the process by seeking closure prematurely. This is a frequent tendency because relational life at this point in the marriage is very painful. Making short-term decisions to end pain—either by extinguishing the marriage or by foreclosing on the natural healing process and denying the significance of the violation—will ultimately impede the process. Men and women process pain at different speeds and patterns.[12] Giving due consideration to understanding what is occurring within the relationship and within each partner will be crucial to the healing process, whatever the outcome they decide.

As we have introduced the concept of forgiveness, we are getting at a key Christian idea that can be a part of mending the fabric of marriage torn by an affair. The cycle of grace and justice lends itself naturally to couples in this process. While we encourage counselors to utilize the model, we do so emphasizing the importance of time. Time is the friend of the healer. Use it.

INFIDELITY AND THE PAIN-DEFENSE CYCLE

As we have suggested throughout this chapter, marital infidelity tears at the fabric of marriage. It can confirm a person's worst fears and insecurities they may hold about themselves and about their marriage. The pain can be so profound and isolating that the nonoffending spouse feels nothing, but puts up a wall in the marriage—just to feel emotionally "safe." Counselors, *do not* try to dismantle that wall. It is a core psychological protection. Infidelity creates the most complicated manifestations of pain-defense-injury. At its core, infidelity is a violation of contractual trustworthiness established in marriage. Sexual fidelity is the basic and central to the marital contract. The pain that emerges in the aftermath of the revelation will be different for both spouses. For the one who has violated the marital vows, he or she typically feels shame for the event and wants to see that removed by the immediate repair of the relationship. For the spouse who learns of the violation, he or she usually experiences the pain of distrust and wants insulation, distance and time to sort out the mixture of emotions; this spouse wants answer to why, what and how this has occurred. Both of these responses are protective defenses to marital injury. A difference that is essential to understand as a counselor is that their defenses come from different injuries.

GRACE, JUSTICE, EMPATHY, TRUST BUILDING
AND FORGIVENESS AFTER INFIDELITY

It is the characteristic of any suspenseful book or movie to tempt us to fast-forward to the end to find out what happens. This urge is also true with infidelity. Couples overcome by shock waves want to know if the marriage is over, if there is hope for the future, if he or she will ever be trustworthy again. The topic of forgiveness might imply that we do just that—rush the process of healing so as to predetermine the outcome. Forgiveness is the most crucial of themes that counselors will address with couples, especially couples that have been stunned by the infidelity of one or both partners. There is an abundance of helpful material regarding the forgiveness process, written from the perspective of individual and relational healing. Central to the process of sorting out many conflicting needs and demands, there is grace, justice, empathy, trust building and forgiveness.

Grace. The purpose of grace in the presence of infidelity is to provide the needed balm to the wounded. But the nature of each person's wound is different, so the gifts that can instigate the long process of healing must be unique. Shock, devastation, confusion, rage, desperation and despair are common responses to the discovery of infidelity. The counselor's first task is to encourage the wounded spouse who has learned of the husband's or wife's infidelity to seek safety, support and security.

First, safety is the most important gift given to the wounded spouse to make him or her free from future threats. Safety is usually experienced as space and separation. Trust has been nuked. Thinking must prevail. Such thinking cannot occur when the one who has wounded the other is seeking to bring about the healing before the other has had time to process the events. Often the physical presence of the offender, and almost always the efforts of the offender to make things right, only inflicts greater wound. The offended can't be sure of motivations. Responsibility and culpability must be clarified and claimed. If the injured spouse asks for space, the grace gift is to grant it. Such space is needed to think, to reorient and to accommodate the new dimensions of the marriage. The unfaithful spouse has ruminated, considered and contemplated the marriage in light of the affair. The other spouse needs the same mental space to consider his or her options. Counselors can help the injuring spouse understand and provide that gift.

Second, the injured spouse will need the gift of support. Like safety, support cannot come from the injuring spouse. The community of friends and loved ones who are known and trusted play an essential role here. The unfaithful spouse may offer resistance in the other's need to have this story known to others. The gift to be offered from the offender to the offended is, "I have broken your confidence and now must charge you to enlist others to help you heal, while I demonstrate to you a repentant commitment to earn your trust again." The counselor can communicate to the offending spouse that his or her best course of action is to not beg that the other accept and forgive. Rather, the best course of action is that the offender releases the other to find healing, as the offender seeks to demonstrate that he or she has been broken and is committed to self-repair. The future will include the repair of the Us, but the present must be focused on the repair of self. The offending spouse needs to be released to establish his or her journey toward healing. It may be valuable for the husband or wife who has revealed the infidelity to witness the suffering of his or her spouse, but he or she cannot be the one to provide healing at this time. An important aspect of the marital healing is to identify with the pain that both must endure as part of being married. While the individuals should witness the pain, participating in the solution is not recommended early in the process. He or she has a vested interest in the outcome, usually wanting reconciliation to occur with a minimal cost. The injured spouse usually needs to think through the effects of his or her choices on all involved, without carrying the burden of trying to make it easier for the offender.

Third, there is a need for security. While safety is an immediate need, security looks into the near future and asks, "What will become of Us, of me and of you?" Here the counselor can provide needed stability, not in being able to answer those questions for the couple, but in holding them for the couple, to be addressed at a later date when the immediate issues are resolved. The counselor can say, "Amidst the chaos that exists, there is a pull to claim solutions before either of you are clear as to what you want and need. Sometimes decisions are made so that the pain that is felt right now will go away. This is true whether you are the offended spouse or the offending spouse. The former might say, 'Just get out of my life, I hate you, I won't forgive you. You made your choice, now so have I.' The latter might say, 'I want to come back to the marriage, and I want to make it right, and I want these changes this week, or I am leaving.'" It is imperative for the counselor to communicate that long-term decisions are best made when both spouses are not in crisis mode. Further, the counselor can say, "Trust me to hold those questions for both of you. Lend them to me and focus on the tasks at hand. I promise, we will return to them with you in the very near future."

A crucial task for the counselor to address with both husband and wife is the marital needs related to the offending spouse. Affairs occur within the context of an individual's story—some of which was written with his or her family of origin. Some of it is written with the marital partner. The needs and concerns of the offending partner should be acknowledged as a part of the essential topics that must be addressed once the traumatic recovery period has been stabilized.

Infidelity begets injustice. Breaking one's sexual vow is a blatant disregard that, outside of grace, cannot be undone. Just as Robert Oppenheimer set off an atom-splitting chain reaction in physics, infidelity sets off a chain reaction by splitting the power balance in the marriage and then provokes a series of perpetual power grabs by both spouses.

Counselors can teach that marriages exist on the integrity of sexual faithfulness. When that fundamental principle is violated, all other principles that define the relationship are questioned. Both spouses tend to see themselves as the "true victim" in sexual infidelity, and then become self-justified at acting unilaterally because the other person is not reliable or trustworthy. The spouse committing the affair will usually cite as justification some inadequacy with the other, such as, "You were never there for me." In return, the offended spouse will question whether anything in the past, present or future can be reliable. And because the reliability is questioned, actions are taken toward self-protection and self-interest. In infidelity, both sides must fight for themselves—the Us is seen as the other's concern, if they want to try to rescue it.

Justice. Justice, above all else in marital restoration of infidelity, is humble, contrite and not self-serving. When the priority becomes, "What have I done?" the other can become receptive to hearing what the spouse has done. Initially, this falls on the unfaithful spouse. Counselors in this stage may act as arbitrator. This role emerges because trust has been decimated, and boundaries that regulate motivations and behaviors have been crossed. Someone that is a trusted confidant to both sides needs to set the rules and establish safety. Counselors serve an important function in helping a couple understand the priorities, processes and timetables required of either party. Emotions run hot. Frustration is frequent. Counselors can be the active enforcer of limits, because they carry power because of their position, expertise, character and integrity.

Empathy. Empathy can be understood as, "Do you really get it?" The question implies that many people think that they understand themselves and their spouses, but their understanding is superficial and ever-so-subtly deluded. Spouses often say, "I think that you understand me from your vantage point but don't understand me from mine . . . and my vantage point is the one that really matters to me." Many times marital infidelity is never understood in its fullness. The explanations given are commonplace: "I was lonely . . . I was working too hard . . . I was away from you on a business trip . . . he seemed to understand me . . . we never intended to go as far as we did . . . I just got caught up in something . . ." These explanations reveal a lack of self-understanding and an absence of empathy. Most couples really don't get it. To pause long enough to listen and understand, to integrate the messages of need with a thoughtful assessment of personality style and family-of-origin narration, to include a thoughtful accounting of individual history and experiences takes more energy than most are willing to invest.

Counselors pass along the capacity for empathy through modeling. In essence, a pastor or counselor declares, "Watch how I treat your husband or your wife. You follow my lead." People can never be forced to offer an empathic response. They must be "felt" into it. It emerges through the identification of pain—that is, they make a connection between pain that they know and pain that the other knows. Empathy can be understood as striking the tuning fork and then locating the piano string that sings the same tune.

Trust building. We turn our attention now to what it means to rebuild trust. Each spring, every gardener anticipates the arrival of their spring flower garden. The crocus is the first cutting flower to break the winter frost. In the relational garden, becoming trustworthy breaks through the chilled ground and precedes every other color and scent. Counselors can encourage couples to listen for the cues from each spouse as to how trustworthiness can be demonstrated within the marriage. In its most simple form, trustworthiness is evident in someone when that which is needed is delivered. Trustworthiness answers in the affirmative the question "Can I count on you?" The process of trust building will be gradual. Usually counselors must warn couples of the time required to rebuild trust—most likely we are speaking of months and years, rather than days and weeks. It is very important that the one who is to build trust understand the sense of time.

It is equally important to convey that the process of trust building is a two-way street. The offending spouse cannot stay in the doghouse perpetually. If that is the experience of the husband or wife, the process will fail. Infidelity creates an untenable disruption in the balance of power in the marriage. While engaging in the affair, the offender has taken power from the relationship. Life decisions are being made that affect both but are made by only one. Conversely, after the affair, the power balance is often tipped in the other direction. The offending spouse may be willing to do whatever is necessary in order to restore the marriage, but the offended spouse may become stuck in her or his wounding and make "what is necessary" a moving standard—which the other can never satisfy. Both are vulnerable to being warped by the manipulation of power during and after an affair. To prevent this destructive process, trust building must be reciprocated with trusting, which is a gradual situation-appropriate restoration of confidence and interdependence. We use the word *dependence* to convey a reliance and a neediness. It may be that such dependence is not a restoration but an original creation, with couples never before knowing how to form emotional bonds based on disclosure, empathy, fairness and grace. The effect of trust building is a stability and security from which marital intimacy can emerge.

A counselor's task in this stage is to help translate the expressed needs of each. The couple remains vulnerable to derailing the process as, frequently, they each see themselves as trustworthy and can't understand why the other will not take the risk to trust. And they see themselves as having taken the risk and are demanding that the other demonstrate greater capacity to give. Couples can easily miss one another. The pastor or counselor who does not carry the wounds from injury in the marriage is in a unique position to translate the tasks for each of the loved ones.

Forgiveness. In the minds of many, forgiveness is the place to start the healing process, and they are surprised that we place it at the end. Often couples think of forgiveness as the end—the apology—that makes everything right. "Forgive and forget" and "Let's go back to how things used to be, like nothing ever happened" are two fantasies that should be decimated by the counselor. There is no such thing as forgetting, and events that affect relationships cannot be undone. Forgiveness must be an important component in the healing of a marriage, but it is never done in reality without difficult and honest conversations about the effects of the actions that each has exhibited toward the other.

Healing from infidelity may lead to reconciliation of the marriage. It may lead to divorce. Whichever path is taken, forgiveness is an important component for healing. Everett Worthington's REACH model and Terry Hargrave's family forgiveness model offer two different but similar tools for addressing forgiveness. With either, it is important not to superimpose reconciliation as the primary objective. Clearly, it is a worthy goal to pursue with spouses—once they have declared that that is their desired outcome because of the demonstrated faithfulness of the spouses to one another.

The REACH model is described in detail in Worthington's *Forgiving and Reconciling*. In it he encourages a five-step process by which the injured seek to become forgivers. The steps include: R: Recalling the hurt; E: Empathize; A: Altruistic gift of forgiveness; C: Commit to publicly forgive; and H: Hold on to forgiveness. This is an individual process model with the explicit goal of eliminating unforgiveness, the rumination of bitterness, resentment and hatred. Worthington views reconciliation as a separate and distinct process which may be the decided path of some who have successfully forgiven.

Hargrave's model focuses on couples working together through the stations of forgiveness. With each station there is a greater degree of forgiveness commitment required. Hargrave's four stations are insight, understanding, trust building and giving overt opportunity to forgive.

We see these two models being used by the counselor concurrently, as forgiveness contains aspects of individual decision making and commitments, and relational decision making and commitments. Spouses must approach injuries to the Us and injuries to the individual with the same respect and regard. Counselors can emulate the quality of "forgivingness" first described by Roberts[13] and developed by Worthington.[14] Forgivingness is to possess a quality of mercy as a way of life and it is an individual act of letting go of bitterness, resentment and malice.

Furthermore, forgiveness, to be experienced in its full strength, involves a restoration of relationship. Both individuals must collaborate in defining what that relationship will be. To restore cannot mean to return to the condition that was present before the injury—that is not possible. The relationship will remain different because events that occur cannot be "unoccurred." The Hargrave forgiveness model can be an effective tool in helping couples work through forgiveness themes— from the initial stage of insight, which is designed to protect each from the perpetuation of injury, to overt forgiveness, which involves an interrelational restoration of love and trust.

CONCLUSION

The truth is often buried under untested assumptions and explicit deceptions. To the surprise of most, infidelity is not the kiss of death for marriage. Healing is possible. But it is not a given. Choices must be made by both husband and wife for the marriage to be mended. Pastors and counselors play a unique role in facilitating the restoration. We recommend that the best position to take is quiet optimism— that is, to convey that the restoration of marriage is, in most circumstances, the path that most likely leads to the greatest potential for individual and relational happiness. But that process requires a new commitment to honesty, integrity and trustworthiness that will come at a high and demanding price for both. Should both partners be willing to exhibit the courage and the stamina to reconfigure their relationship, there is real potential for marital intimacy beyond the quality of the relationship that existed before the affair. There is significant risk as neither can control the willingness and capacity for integrity in the other. This is the leap of faith that each made when they married, and must make again.

NOTES

[1]Laumann, E. O., Gagnon, J. H., Michael, R. T., & Michaels, S. (1994). *The social organization of sexuality: Sexual practices in the United States.* Chicago: University of Chicago Press.

[2]Gordon, K. C., & Baucom, D. H. (2003). Forgiveness and marriage: Preliminary support for a measure based on a model of recovery from a marital betrayal. *The American Journal of Family Therapy, 31,* 179-99.

[3]Ibid. See also Gordon, K. C., Baucom, D. H., & Snyder, D. K. (2005). Forgiveness in couples: Divorce, infidelity, and couples therapy. In E. L. Worthington (Ed.), *Handbook of forgiveness* (pp. 407-21). New York: Routledge.

[4]Baucom, D. H., Gordon, K. C., Snyder, D. K., Atkins, D. C., & Christensen, A. (2006). Treating affair couples: Clinical considerations and initial findings. *Journal of Cognitive Psychotherapy: An International Quarterly, 20*(4), 375-92.

[5]Ibid., p. 376.

[6]Ibid.

[7]Ibid., p. 377.

[8]There is relatively little research on this issue compared to how to respond to an affair. We discuss some of the findings reported and discussed by David Atkins and his colleagues. See Atkins, D., Yi, J., Baucom, D. H., & Christensen, A. (2005). Infidelity in couples seeking marital therapy. *Journal of Family Psychology, 19*(3), 470-73. Interestingly, in their discussion of the literature, Atkins and colleagues noted that "conscientiousness, religiosity, and marital satisfaction are negatively related to potential infidelity" (p. 470).

[9]Gordon, K. C., & Baucom, D. H. (2003). Forgiveness and marriage: Preliminary support for a measure based on a model of recovery from a marital betrayal. *The American Journal of Family Therapy, 31,* 179-99

[10]Ibid., p. 182.

[11]Miller, A. J., Worthington, E. L., Jr., & McDaniel, M. A. (2008). Gender and forgiveness: A meta-analytic review and research agenda. *Journal of Social and Clinical Psychology, 27*(8), 845-78.

[12]Ibid.

[13]Roberts, R. C. (1995). Forgivingness. *American Philosophical Quarterly, 32,* 289-307.

[14]Worthington, E. L. (2001). *Five steps to forgiveness: The art and science of forgiving.* New York: Crown House Publishing.

13

DIVORCE AND
BLENDED FAMILIES

Divorce is like an amputation.
Sometimes it's necessary but it should be avoided
if at all possible because it brings about a permanent disability.

BILL DOHERTY

When there are kids involved, there's no such thing as divorce.

CARL WHITAKER

FOR MANY WITH SENSITIVE EARS, the blight of any neighborhood is the pack of middle school or high school kids who have just started a garage band. Groups that gather to "make their own sound" have only one essential criteria: *loud*. Whether it is Guitar Hero fantasy or the next emerging sensation to sign for a record company contract, loud is essential. The music is so loved inside the four walls of the double garage that it must be shared with others. Amplifiers can share the sound with neighbors blocks away. A kid might say, it's not loud enough until we see the garage door move by the force of volume.

Like a garage band, divorce is loud! It is conflict with an amplifier. Marital conflict already exists and has contributed to the decision to separate or divorce, but the emotions involved in divorce can often amplify existing conflicts and make the process a cacophony. The sound is so loud people can't hear themselves think. At the time where thinking is most needed, it is often the most difficult to accomplish.

In this chapter we want to discuss some of the challenges of conflict resolution in cases of separation and divorce, as well as additional complexities that emerge with blended families.

Counselors, for the most part, earnestly seek to prevent divorce. Unfortunately, about half of the couples who come to counseling for marriage help end up divorcing within only a few years of therapy. Indeed, marriage counseling is difficult work. Divorce counseling is even harder. But it is counseling that we as Christian counselors and pastors are called to do. It is often at this most crucial point in a family's history—at the time and place where the greatest injury is occurring— that the church and the influence of the gospel is most absent. Couples can move to a place of not feeling loved or valued, not feeling like there is much hope for the future of their marriage, and not feeling like putting effort into something that feels like a lost cause.[1] Although counselors may do all they can to prevent divorce, we do need resources that address the reality of divorce. Counselors are often under-prepared to address marital conflicts after the decision for divorce has been made and after one or both have established marital relationships subsequent to the divorce.

In addition, pastors or those in Christian ministry who try with all of their energies to keep marriages together may be the last people that couples turn to if divorce is decided. Couples can come to feel as though the church or their pastor was there to help try to save the marriage, but then rejected them if a path was chosen that was contrary to their guidance.

We turn our attention now to the special considerations in addressing divorce. One way to approach these considerations is to reflect on some of the myths that exist about divorce. These myths could be held by one or both spouses when we see them pursuing divorce. These are the kinds of things that they may be thinking divorce will settle for them, and pastoral care or lay counseling can at least provide a place to explore these myths, where they came from and the fantasy of an easy solution.

SPECIAL CONSIDERATIONS IN ADDRESSING DIVORCE

When working with couples or individuals processing a divorce, marital counselors are "loan officers." They loan their ego strength. Couples are in need of clear, unbiased, objective decision making at a time when they are least likely to be able to possess that resource. So they borrow it from you, the counselor. During this time of radical transition, lawyers are advising, parents and adult siblings are opinionating, friends are expressing their views based on what happened in their divorce. The dissonances of advisors compete with the internal voices speaking for justice, self-interest, grief and hope. Individuals often get to the point where they no longer think or even care. They just want it to be over so they can begin to rebuild. But though individuals and couples may want to go away or disappear (or wish their spouse would), they cannot. Counselors can play a crucial role in helping them think—providing for them the resources to make sound decisions. Myths, fantasies, obscurities and deceptions abound in these contexts.[2] Your objectivity, in the form of reasoned, wise, godly counsel, is important.

Fantasy myth 1: It will all be better. In our experience, couples can sometimes have unrealistic expectations for divorce—that it will make everything better. This is the myth that "All of the problems I am having will be solved." This is probably the most basic myth around which a couple may build a fantasy. This fantasy emerges when the whole of life's frustrations are embodied in one's spouse. He or she can be made into the devil incarnate. The counselor can help individuals discern fact from fantasy. Indeed, after divorce abuse, vulgarity or financial mismanagement may be ended. But other challenges not anticipated might emerge. These could include changes in relationships, loneliness, added fatigue from being the sole caregiver, financial challenges and others. The key theme will be helping individuals process the divorce with eyes wide open—not deluded, avoidant or exaggerated, but realistic, courageous and honest.

Fantasy myth 2: It will be better for the kids. This is a myth based on popular psychology that permeated culture in the 1990s and still lingers around somewhat today: that it would be better for the kids if they didn't see their parents disagree or argue. And we agree that it would be good for the kids not to see parents fail at problem solving and fail at respecting each other in their disagreements. However, unless there is violence in the marriage, the data seems to support staying together in spite of the marital partners' failures or immaturities.

The challenges that children face in parental divorce is very well documented and described in Elisabeth Marquadt's book *Between Two Worlds*. In it she documents the experience of children who must learn to navigate the bicultural existence as children of divorce. Children literally live in two orbits in the joint-custody existence.

That divorce is a relief and is a tragedy for children is poignantly depicted in the movie *City Slickers*. Recall Mitch (Billy Crystal), Ed (Bruno Kirby) and Phil (Daniel Stern) on horseback in a midlife-crisis vacation driving cattle through the Southwest.

> Mitch: Alright Ed, your best day—what was it, twins in a trapeze, what?
>
> Ed: No, I don't wanna play.
>
> Mitch: C'mon, we did it.
>
> Ed: I don't feel like it.
>
> Mitch: Uh, okay.
>
> [*pause*]
>
> Ed: I'm fourteen and my mother and father are fighting again . . . y'know, because she caught him again. Caught him . . . This time the girl drove by the house to pick him up. And I finally realized, he wasn't just cheating on my mother, he was cheating us. So I told him, I said, "You're bad to us. We don't love you. I'll take care of my mother and my sister. We don't need you any more." And he made like he was gonna hit me, but I didn't budge. And he turned around and he left. He never bothered us again. Well, I took care of my mother and my sister from that day on. That's my best day.
>
> Phil: What was your worst day?
>
> Ed: Same day.

Parents will likely come to see the decision to divorce as both the best day and the worst day of their lives. Spouses divorce; parents cannot. Parents will not have the freedom to live where they might choose or seek employment where there are opportunities. They will be dealing with their spouse again, and often for years, as they have to negotiate time with the kids during the week, weekends, church attendance, sports, and other extracurricular activities like drama and band, as well as vacations, holidays, time with grandparents on mom's side of the family, time with grandparents on dad's side, and so on. The one thing a person going through divorce *won't* be free of is the father or mother of their children. Therefore, a reasoned discussion of the effect of divorce on children, on future family existence, is crucial. Where spouses may divorce, parents may not, and the relationship with one's ex-spouse continues through parenthood and eventually grandparenthood.

Fantasy myth 3: I will not make the same mistake next time. If we take this to mean that their next marriage will succeed, we certainly hope so. However, the research suggests that most people will remarry following a divorce, but that most of those remarriages will end in divorce. The work of Harville Hendrix in *Getting the Love You Want* is worth examining. Hendrix's thesis is drawn from psychodynamic and intergenerational thinking on relationships. Fundamentally, it states that we are drawn to and we marry those who resonate with underdeveloped or unresolved issues. After divorce those same needs become magnified rather than diminished. This places both divorcing spouses in a position of relational vulnerability. Wisdom here says, "You will likely make the same mistake, unless there is time dedicated to building life patterns of honesty and integrity in how you address the challenges in life."

Without a doubt, there will be other challenges that will obscure the individual's or couple's ability to think clearly and make decisions that are best for everyone's long-term benefit. These should be addressed in a tactful manner, showing empathy for what is difficult for them in their marriage and what they are hoping will come from divorce. But we would be remiss if we didn't identify and discuss with couples some of the fantasy that comes with the idea of divorce, as the reality often does not match the fantasy.

We turn our attention, then, to the three central themes of *identity*, *function* and *relationship*. We will draw on these to help us organize how a pastoral counselor can work with divorcing couples and blended families.

COUPLE IDENTITY AND DIVORCE

Throughout this section of the book, we have been discussing how marital identity is an opportunity to "locate" the couple. The fact that they are going through a divorce does not change the importance of reflecting on family identity. Perhaps more than most experiences, divorce reminds us of the importance of family identity, in part because so many family identity questions are raised. The counselor is trying to understand the couple in a context by reflecting on aspects of who they are: their age, culture, race, religion (recognizing differences among Christians), region of the country and so on.

As we have done in chapter ten, we want to begin by locating the family in terms of what stage they are in. Normally a family goes through predictable stages that are referred to as the family life cycle.[3] Although we can think of each person leaving their own family that they grew up in, the beginning of the new family begins as a couple gets married, leaves each of their own homes and forms a new family together. Christians refer to this as *leaving and cleaving,* thinking of the passage in Mark 10:7-8. There are actually two family life cycle stages that can be identified here: *leaving home* (leaving) and *the new couple* (cleaving). Taken together, these are considered the first two stages of having a shared identity as a couple.

The next stage for most couples is called *families with young children.* This can be complicated by decisions about whether to have a family, how many children to have and concerns with infertility, among other things. Once a family has young children and faces the unique challenges involved in incorporating new family members into what has so far been a couple, the family eventually moves into the stage of *families with adolescents.* This is a time of increased independence, as teens tend to move in and out of the family as they do more with friends and others outside of the home. Over time, older adolescents are positioned to leave home. This stage is called *launching children and moving on.*

Couples who do not separate or divorce can struggle with any number of issues in each of these stages. They can struggle to balance attending to their marriage while also pouring into the life of a young child. Couples can wrestle with how to give their teens greater independence during adolescence. Couples can struggle, too, with how to launch older teens into young adulthood, and the anxieties that often arise. So the family life cycle itself, while identifying predictable stages, can be challenging for couples who do not divorce. Imagine how couples can be impacted by the additional strain of separation and divorce and the ripple effects of the disintegration of the marital relationship on the family. It leads to "profound disequilibrium" on the entire family and on existing family relationships,[4] perhaps best conveyed in this analogy:

> If we visualize a family traveling the road of life, moving from stage to stage in their developmental unfolding, we can see divorce as an interruption that puts the family on a "detour"—an additional family life cycle stage—in which the physical and emotional losses and changes of divorce are put into effect and absorbed by the three-generation system. The family (now in two households) then rejoins the "main road" and continues its forward developmental progress, though in a more complex form. If either spouse remarries, a second detour occurs—a second additional family life cycle stage—in which the family must handle the stress of absorbing two or three generations of new members into the system and struggle to define their roles and relationships to existing family members. When this task of merging in mid-journey with another three-generation system has been completed, the new, highly complex system rejoins the "main road," and individual and family development continues.[5]

Counselors might benefit from keeping this analogy in mind. Indeed, we are not now seeing the divorced couple do their own thing. Rather, they are still on a common path heading in a common direction.

Marriages, while often resilient, can also be vulnerable at key stages, and each of these stages presents different concerns that could contribute to a couple's decision to divorce. For example, it can be challenging to introduce a baby into a young couple's experience of family. If they haven't yet formed their own sense of who they are as a couple, either one of them or both can turn to a newborn to meet their emotional needs.

There are also unique challenges as older children enter into adolescence. The stress during the teen years can really amplify existing differences in parenting beliefs and values in ways that are different than what a couple experienced with young children.

Some couples may drift apart emotionally but choose to stay together until their children are grown. As they launch their children into young adulthood, sometimes one or both spouses may be ready to move on from the marriage. Perhaps their purpose and identity has been primarily about raising their kids, and once this responsibility is met, they may feel the next chapter in their lives is for them to fulfill their dreams or explore other options that felt closed to them previously.

So it is important to "locate" the family in terms of what might be a normal stage of life together. This at least gives you a sense for what to ask about. You might ask about the challenges they have faced in becoming a family (if they have a newborn or young child), or you might ask about the stress they are under if they are dealing with teens who are having increased contact with and influence by their peer group.

We turn our attention now to what couples can expect if they take the next steps toward divorce. Many couples do not know what to expect when they go through a divorce. It can be helpful to be aware of what might be thought of as important stages in divorce, just as we look at important stages in marriage. Recall that if this is a detour, you want to help them get back on the main road mentioned above.

COUPLE FUNCTION AND DIVORCE

When we discussed family identity, we discussed locating the family in the family life cycle. We discussed how there are predictable stages that couples and families go through over time. There are also predictable steps or stages or transition points for families who experience separation and divorce.[6]

Sometimes couples go through separations that lead to reconciliation and other times lead to divorce. Many pastors and lay counselors may wonder about the potential benefits of a separation, and we try also to be judicious in when we recommend a separation. A key consideration is to identify the purpose of the separation. For example, a separation can be helpful if it is about safety. If, for example, there has been violence in the home, a separation can be critical in providing safety to all those involved. A couple can decide to come back together when there is consensus that it is safe to do so and when they have in place a safety agreement and plan should warning signs present in the future.

Transition points in the divorce process. One of the leading researchers[7] on separation and divorce has identified several predictable steps that couples going through divorce experience. Of course, every divorce is unique, so we want you to use this framework with appropriate caution. But it can be helpful to identify what couples can expect. This also gives you as a pastor or lay counselor an opportunity to identify important themes or issues that may emerge.

The first transition point for a couple going through divorce is actually the decision itself.[8] This decision can be made by one or both spouses, but it means that there is a kind of acceptance or coming to terms with the idea that they are unable to either resolve the conflicts or repair the damage they've experienced in the marriage.[9] Even if one spouse is against the divorce, the fact that the divorce is happening is something that both come to terms with individually.[10]

The next transition point in divorce is announcing the decision to divorce to the rest of the family.[11] Family members may suspect that a divorce is coming, or they may fear that as a real possibility. But this transition is the process by which the divorcing couple lets the family know about the decision.

Parents will often ask for suggestions or resources on how to talk to their children about their decision to divorce. This is one of the most difficult discussions for parents to have. There are a few general principles that may be helpful to keep in mind.[12] One principle is to tell each child what that child can understand based upon his or her age and maturity. This will be different for a younger child than for an older child or an adolescent. From a developmental perspective, children of different ages and teens are going to have different understandings of divorce and of practical matters like custody and visitation.

A second principle is that parents are to be honest with their children. It is important to tell the truth. This means being able to be in a relationship with their children so that they can ask and receive answers to questions that come up for them. It may also mean being aware of what a child can process. One challenge to truth telling is the question "If I don't want the divorce, should I tell the children that it is my husband's/wife's decision and not mine?" This question, and those like it, should prompt the counselor to dig a bit deeper as to its motivation. Is the question driven by an effort to triangulate and win the support of the children against the spouse? Or is the question prompted by the effort to bring healing to the family with necessary information? Counselors should emphasize to divorcing couples that each should claim his or her story as part of the divorce, knowing that by telling the other person's story, particularly in a way that destroys the parental image the child has for the other spouse, results in injury to the child. Counselors can encourage couples to speak the truth to restore and heal rather than speaking the truth to retaliate.

A third principle is to approach children to discuss the divorce rather than expect children to come to the parents. Children can take their cues from their parents or quickly move into almost a caretaker role so as not to upset their parents, and this could be misinterpreted as children not having questions or not wanting to talk about it. Parents can often feel the relief that comes from not having to talk about an uncomfortable topic.

Lastly, following this idea of children moving into a caretaker role with parents, it is important that parents not turn to their children or confide in them for emotional support. Children may need to be protected from some information, including some of how a parent is emotionally handling the divorce.

There is more involved at this transition point than just communicating the decision to divorce to the rest of the family, as important as that is. Part of what it means to divorce is recognizing that this means breaking up the family, which involves finding ways to support workable arrangements for everyone affected by the decision to divorce.[13] This entails coming to agreement on custody, visitation schedules, financial matters and other relevant issues. This is where a pastoral counselor or lay counselor can be especially helpful. There is a need to work with each member of the divorcing couple on what is best for everyone involved.

The next transition point is the physical separation itself. Someone, either the father or the mother, leaves the home. Constance Ahrons shares that telling children about the decision to divorce, while significant, may not be as vivid a memory to children as the actual separation.

> Most people remember the day they separated—not the day their divorce was legally awarded—as the day their divorce began. Separation day is one of those marker events that divorced people never forget. For children, this is when they realize the enormity of what is going on, even though they may have suspected or feared the prospect for some time.[14]

This can be a painful experience for some family members, and it will be important to prepare them for it as well as create an atmosphere that allows for further discussion as needed.

There are many practical matters to deal with now: Who moves out and who stays in the house? How often are they going to see one another during this time of separation? Under what circumstances will they see one another? Will they both attend the same church? Pastoral or lay counseling can be helpful here; these are topics that can carry great emotional significance for one or both spouses, and it will be important to assist them in clear communication and practical problem-solving, so that the anger or hurt does not keep them from making decisions.

As a pastoral or lay counselor, you can expect that about half of families going through divorce work out a cooperative arrangement for co-parenting.[15] The other half of divorcing families will continue in a more adversarial posture, displaying conflict openly or passive-aggressively or simply not act responsibly to the demands of co-parenting at this point.

You can also expect that it can take between two and three years to move through these different transition points of divorce.[16] What does successful navigation of these transition points look like? It looks like parents being in ongoing contact with their ex-spouse to work out the different parenting responsibilities; it also involves both former spouses relying on and expanding their own relationships and sense of community. This has been referred to as "family redefinition."[17] Expanding relationships may mean remarriage for one or both ex-spouses. The pastoral or lay counselor should anticipate this, as most people do choose to remarry following divorce.

Remarriage. Although the focus of this chapter is on navigating potential marital conflict during separation and divorce, the challenge of remarriage is worthy of some consideration. The decision to remarry can bring up feelings that were thought to have been worked through previously. These emotions may include anger, hurt and resentment.[18] The non-remarrying former spouse may be surprised to have these feelings. Strong, unexpected feelings might be seen as telling them that they hadn't really faced their feelings about the loss of their first marriage. This can sometimes have to do with the loss of what had been (or the picture of an ideal family that is no more), or it can sometimes have to do with a sense that their ex-spouse is moving on sooner or is in some way now more "successful" in life following the divorce.

The ex-spouse who decides to remarry may also be dealing with ambivalent feelings. They may be excited about what lies ahead, but they may also have fears and anxiety about this new future, as well as a renewed sense of loss from their previous marriage. Expect that these feelings may come in waves. There is a need for patience and time to deal with and adjust to what will certainly be increasingly complicated emotional relationships and commitments, rules for relating to one another, expectations and signs of loyalty.[19] There are simply that many more people who have a stake in the family relationships. A protective stepfather can have strong feelings about the perceived unresponsiveness of a biological father to his children. These kinds of reactions can fan the flame of discord. But there are also opportunities to demonstrate mutual respect and consideration, to support each person's role with children and to more effectively coordinate co-parenting responsibilities.

The decision by one or both former partners to remarry can also squelch any thought or fantasy that they might get together again. This fantasy can be held by one spouse or even by extended family members, such as grandparents. It could go without saying that it is the fantasy of every child, even decades after the divorce. To mitigate the potential for harm, divorced parents should be very careful of time together. While divorced parents should both be present at the important events, such as birthday parties, they should be cautious and cognizant of the fact that others, particularly their offspring, will have other agendas that cannot be eliminated merely by words. A cordial, cooperative relationship with very clear boundaries that communicate the true intention of the divorced couple is paramount.

In addition, grandparents and other extended family members may have been "lost" in the process of divorce. These losses should not be underestimated, and counseling can be a place to discuss these relationships and the potential to maintain some contact when possible. Grandparents have no legal rights in a divorce proceeding. When Josh and Theresa divorced, they did not anticipate the effect that it would have on Josh's parents. Living one thousand miles away, Tim and Shelly loved to have vacation visits to their son, daughter-in-law and grandchildren's home. Christmas was spent with Grandma and Grandpa in the winter wonderland of the Northeast. Then came the divorce. The judge awarded Theresa full custody. Josh's addictions proved him to be incompetent as a parent. He was given limited visitation rights one day a week under supervision. Within two years Theresa remarried and moved away—effectively excommunicating the three boys from their father, and totally eliminating contact from Tim and Shelly. Christmas stockings are still hung, almost in loving memory of what once was and will not be again.

Noncustodial parents may experience a crisis in identity too. They may wonder what their place is with their own children if their former spouse remarries. Often there can be a complete cut-off or isolation between the noncustodial parent and his or her children. If the noncustodial parent is still working with a pastoral or lay counselor, issues of powerlessness, patience and hope may prove to be important themes. Practically speaking, it can be helpful to think about what they can and cannot have say over, so that they are not too focused on things over which they have little or no control.[20]

When working with the spouse who is remarrying, pastoral and lay counselors can ask about feelings that come up in the new relationship. Depending on the circumstances that led up to the decision to divorce (for example, an affair), the spouse may experience fears about trust and intimacy in a new marriage relationship.

This is a good time to work through what has been referred to as the "emotional divorce" of each former spouse.[21] Working through emotional divorce means coming to a better place with feelings of loss from the first marriage, if this remains a concern.

Consistent with the suggestion about parent-child boundaries, it can also be helpful to encourage the biological parent to take the lead in setting expectations and addressing discipline. This also gives the spouse the responsibility to establish more of a relationship with their stepchildren, so that in the future, expectations and discipline can be provided out of the context of a real relationship rather than a sense of "position," if you will.

Experts also discuss helping everyone involved tolerate emotional ambiguity that comes with the territory. This is the nature of divorce and remarriage. New families that feel safe or provide nurture and support do not magically happen; rather, they take time and patience, shared activities and healthy communication.

There appear to be differences between stepfather homes and stepmother homes.[22] Stepfather homes are more common and appear to experience less stress. As was mentioned above, they tend to succeed when stepfathers can provide support but less direct discipline while focusing on building relationships with stepchildren. Stepmother families tend to experience more stress, which could be due to the disruption in mother-child bonds, as these are families in which the children are not with their biological mother but instead their biological father has custody. Girls in particular report greater stress in these living arrangements.

What are the characteristics of successful stepfamilies?[23] They are stepfamilies in which:

1. family members have realistic expectations in light of changes and losses in relationships

2. family members are able to grieve the loss of and changes to prior relationships

3. the couple is able to work well together, providing a stable marital relationship

4. step relationships are satisfying over time

5. new routines are in place for the stepfamily

6. the children's separate households are able to cooperate

Pastoral and lay counselors can take these six characteristics of successful stepfamilies and develop an outline for working with stepfamilies to facilitate improvements in each area. It can be helpful to provide stepfamilies with information on what is possible, as well as what each step may entail, so that they are given time and realistic expectations, and so that they can extend one another grace as they begin to approximate these characteristics in their own homes.

COUPLE RELATIONSHIP AND DIVORCE

We have an idea now of the kinds of issues families face when they experience separation and divorce and, in many cases, remarriage. Throughout this discussion, we have pointed to the kinds of experiences that might facilitate a smoother transition, as painful as it may be. We close this chapter with a discussion of the general principles for enhancing existing relationships.

Work together whenever possible. Divorce can become an acute event in which one or both partners point the finger at the other. Most counselors know from experience that there is rarely one person to blame when a marriage ends in divorce. Even in situations in which a clear wrong has been done, an affair for example, it will be important that the couple learns to work together on behalf of their children.

Getting a couple to work together can be challenging. The fact of the divorce and all of the concomitant feelings of frustration, anger, hurt and resentment can amplify even the slightest obstacles to teamwork. But getting them to see the benefits of cooperative agreements can result in and lead to important changes in attitude. Independent of the focus on cooperation and teamwork, one or both of them can benefit from working through negative feelings, but these are important to monitor as they can quickly impede progress, and small decisions can become a 'stage upon which the drama of their divorce can be played out.

Education on transition points. Education is an important but often overlooked aspect of divorce counseling. As we have discussed throughout this chapter, there are predictable transition points with identifiable stressors that most couples experience. This can be presented to a couple and discussed together, so that they have a sense for what they can expect, and so they can begin to make a plan for how to proceed. Education can address some of the myths discussed above, but will most likely focus on reasonable expectations.

Improve communication. It is important to emphasize communication for them as a couple. Obviously, if communication was a strength, the relationship might not be ending. However, we have every reason to believe that improving communication will help them work together in difficult areas like visitation and custody concerns. This will likely involve some education, role-playing, and modeling of effective listening skills and assertive communication.

In the area of assertive communication, it can be helpful to distinguish assertive from both passive and aggressive communication. Passive communication does not take one's own feelings into consideration. Deference to the other person is given. Aggressive communication does not take the feelings of one's former spouse into consideration—it steamrolls over them. Assertive communication takes both a person's feelings and the feelings of the former spouse into consideration, the overarching interest being in working toward the best interests of the children.

Couples can identify with their pastoral counselor a range of topics that they may find helpful to discuss. This can include budget and financial issues, moving out, talking to family members about the divorce, talking to friends and extended family about the divorce, talking to those in their church about the divorce, church attendance and membership, visitation, custody, and so on.

Setting priorities in problem solving. In addition to education and communication, it is important to facilitate effective problem solving strategies. Better communication will go a long way in improving problem solving. But it may also be important to work on ways to compromise with one another, to share, to show empathy by seeing the topic from the former spouse's perspective. Role reversal may be an effective way to do this.

DIVORCE AND THE PAIN-DEFENSE CYCLE

Rob is a grown man, age forty-eight. He has been married to Lori for more than two decades. By every external measure, he is a high achiever. He is a committed Christian with a stable marriage, happy kids and a decent 401K account. He is a success story. But there does reside a shadow in his life.

> When I was thirteen my mom and dad divorced. They could not understand, and still don't understand, how much that injured me. I hated my parents for this—even while I loved them and needed them, I still hated them. I came to hate counselors even more than I hated my dad and my mom. My dad said that the counselor told him that divorce would be better for the kids, that the constant bickering was a danger. But the man didn't ask me what I thought. No one discussed this decision with me. While that counselor cashed his check and slept very well, he left a childhood destroyed.

Rob's story gives us pause. We can't confirm or deny the details of the story. We can pass no judgment as to the condition and details of the marriage and the promptings, both personal and professional, that led to Rob's parents' divorcing. We don't have the full story. But we do know of one side, which is that the remnants of family dissolution continue to affect the way Rob sees the world thirty-five years after the event. These are facts around which we can think about the counselor's role in bringing grace, justice, empathy, trust and forgiveness to a family that has continued even though the marriage was disbanded.

So, here is a radical recommendation—that we as pastors and Christian marital counselors continue to work with divorced couples and their children for years after the divorce has occurred. The adults move on, they may remarry, they start new lives. They have additional children. But families must continue to adjust. The mental health literature says that the adjustment usually goes poorly for many families, especially for the children. Assisting families in healing from the wounds of divorce is to address one of the most important mental health needs affecting children, and one where the church—and just about everyone else—is noticeably absent. Let's consider the role of grace, justice, empathy, trust and forgiveness applied to post-divorce family counseling.

Grace. In marital conflict resolution, our counseling focuses on helping couples provide unmerited gifts to one another. But in this new context, the focus of grace is no longer directed toward spouses; it is directed toward children. The couple can consider with the marital counselor what relational gift they each can provide to their children in the new relationship of a post-divorce family. These gifts might include precious commitments of integrity, availability, support and stability. Integrity might include the promise that each partner will not manipulate conditions to undermine the authority of the other as a parent. Availability could be the willingness to work through difficulties with the whole family whenever they emerge. Availability might also mean a commitment to unavailability when the children are in the custodial care of the other spouse. The children could try to manipulate living arrangements by pulling a mom or dad into circumstances that do not concern them. Support might mean that though the adults are ex-spouses, they are not ex-parents, and therefore they must continue to support each other's role in the life of their children. Stability might be the most important. One of the greatest questions is "What is going to happen to me?" These *what* questions include circumstances such as when a parent remarries, when I graduate from high school, when stepsiblings are born, when a parent moves out of the area—all of these are crucial questions for a child or adolescent that are not actively addressed during the divorce or in the new stages of family development. However, a clear, unyielding commitment to the continued care for the child is the most essential gift that former spouses can provide to one another and to their children.

Justice. When it comes to divorce, justice is complicated. That is why there are so many divorce attorneys battling each other in court for "her" rights against "his" rights. Counselors can encourage another level of justice—before things are fought out in court. Each partner can engage in dialogue about divorce focusing on the rights of the children as a common good. Such a theme can quickly unravel if the divorcing couple is not of the same mind about the divorce decision. Imagine a spouse saying, "If you cared about what is in the best interest of the children you wouldn't have filed for divorce in the first place!" Chaos ensues, and the counselor thinks, *"Never again!"* However, the counselor can oversee and direct the dialogue toward making wise and mature decisions for their children instead of acting out of the pain and defenses driven by self-protection and retaliation. Parents who are entering a new dimension as "divorced spouses" will continue to share children and grandchildren for the rest of their lives. Establishing a way to work toward the common good of others is a valuable step toward justice. It reduces the size of the "divorce crater"—that degree of collateral damage caused by the breaking of a family. In counseling, parents are asked and expected to set aside their legitimate hurt and injury in order to exist collaboratively for the well-being of their children. As an aside, they work for the well-being of one another, even though they are now divorced, because it is in the best interest of their children. Jonathan is a father who is divorced and remarried; he has a high-school-age daughter from his first marriage and describes it this way:

> I could easily remain angry and consumed with hate for what my ex-wife did to me (extramarital affair). I used to hope that she would get everything that she had coming to her. Then I realized, when she is depressed, it affects my girl. When she is depleted of resources, my girl suffers. When she fails, my daughter has to carry that burden, and I cannot change that. But I can be involved in a way that does not contribute to her struggle in life. I can be involved in a distant way—even though I am remarried and have my own family—that contributes to my ex-wife's well-being. In the long run, this is fair. I help her and she is more able to help Katie. I hope that she will help me also. But even if she doesn't, I still am the beneficiary.

Empathy. Empathy in the post-divorce world is very important for children. For parents, life usually gets easier after the divorce. Life stabilizes. They take up new residences, or paint and wallpaper the kitchen and bathroom to make it reflect their tastes alone. New routines are established and they quickly become the norm. But for kids, life becomes extremely complicated. They must dwell in two orbits, their father's and their mother's. At first, there is not much change, but with time, parental expectations grow further apart. Staying true to the rules required of one parent, which are different from those of the other parent, is complicated. Add to that challenge the insertion of stepparents, and there are four potential authorities to whom the child must answer, and each authority may be sending conflicting messages. On top of that there is the complicated challenge of friends. Two sets of clothes, two sets of toys, two sets of life that will change every week on Monday evening at 6:00 when the children are handed from one parent to another. *This condition requires empathy!*

By empathy we do not imply that parents should feel perpetually guilty. Circumstances are what they are. Guilt has no usefulness. Rather, our intent is to encourage parents to maintain understanding for the new set of difficulties that kids must now attend. Their lives increase rather than decrease in complexity and complication after the divorce.

Trust building. In addition to empathy, the ability to build trust is essential. Indeed, trust building in a post-divorce family might be more important than in an intact family because there has been some overt or covert threat of disintegration of support. There are ample reasons in divorced families to not trust one another—and very few influences that help form trust—all to the detriment of children's well-being. But the church can have a voice here. The Christian tradition is a "faith tradition." Faith is the placing of trust in God, who is committed to being trustworthy (Heb 11–12). Similarly, we are called to function with faith and faithfully toward one another within the community of believers. If this is to be done in the family of faith, how much more is it to be in the overlap of faith and family, when Christians share both a faith commitment and a family commitment through the parenting of children.

Trust is formed in complicated social structures like divorced families through the devout respect of boundaries and through the modest risk taking in which the other, with whom there has been previous injury, is cautiously given opportunity to become trustworthy. Counselors should remind participants who seek to build trust bonds between members that the suspicions toward each other are likely high, given previous experiences of injury. Therefore, caution and discipline are important commitments. Caution should be offered by counselors that couples should not overextend themselves in taking risks that are greater than the relationships can withstand, and discipline to ensure that as far as it depends on each adult, they will live in peace with all. Counselors can and should engage in dialogue with both divorcing spouses about how to build a new culture of trust and trustworthiness.

The overarching theme for counselors to convey is that it is in the long-term interest of everyone involved to learn to live peaceably with one another. Should they fail, there are serious negative effects that consume the family wealth, destroy the children's capacity to develop intimacy with their future spouses and affect the ability of each ex-spouse to proceed with new life goals.

Forgiveness. Forgiveness is not marital restoration. We do not advocate the conversation on forgiveness as a means to rescue marriages from divorce decisions. Rather, as Christians we extend forgiveness as the embodiment of our character.[24] Forgiveness is what Christians do because it is who we are. As we have been forgiven, we are to actively seek forgiveness with those with whom we relate. Furthermore, we see forgiveness usually as occurring only in a superficial manner—as in an apology—and a subsequent effort to contain and suppress residual resentment and anger. Christian counselors are in a unique position to broker a maturity of relationship with divorced families who carry the responsibility to parent the next generation with maturity.

We advocate a progressive model of forgiveness, like that presented by Terry Hargrave in *Families and Forgiveness,* Robert Enright in *Forgiveness Is a Choice* or Everett Worthington in *Forgiving and Reconciling.* Likely the most significant contribution to a couple's ability to experience forgiveness has been identified by L. Gregory Jones: "both parties (or all of the parties) come prepared to forgive, but are completely un-prepared to be forgiven."[25] As Worthington interprets this, family members are usually willing to see themselves as the victim, the one who has been wronged and then is willing to extend forgiveness to the wrongdoer, but we, and those we serve, are far less likely to ever see ourselves as the wrongdoer, the one who needs to be forgiven.

CONCLUSION

In divorce counseling, the church and Christian counseling has abdi-cated an important ministry—helping families heal. We have not done so with intention; rather, it has occurred through the unintended con-sequence of valuing marriage. Because of the church's unyielding com-mitment to seeing marriages survive and to prevent their disintegration into divorce, we have cast aside those who do divorce. As our culture has become more secularized, that divorced population has grown—leaving a very large segment of our society separated and disconnected from the Christian community and Christian faith. We believe that it is possible, and it is expected for pastors, to actively maintain their com-mitment to both marriage and to those who have divorced.

NOTES

[1]These are what Everett Worthington refers to as the three main causes of divorce today: loss of love, loss of faith, and diminished work. See Worthington, E. L. (1999). *Hope-focused marriage counseling.* Downers Grove, IL: InterVarsity Press.

[2]The three myths we discuss are mentioned in ibid., pp. 245-46.

[3]We are repeating here our understanding of the family life cycle first discussed in Yarhouse, M. A., & Sells, J. N. (2008). *Family therapies: A comprehensive Christian appraisal.* Downers Grove, IL: InterVarsity Press, pp. 373-81. In the discussion of the family life cycle, divorce and remarriage, we adapted material from Patterson et al. without referencing the adaptation itself and did not cite the relevant chapter from Carter and McGoldrick. We encourage the reader to see Patterson, J., Wil-liams, L., Grauf-Grounds, C., & Chamow, L. (1998). *Essential skills in family ther-apy.* New York and London: Guilford; Carter, B., & McGoldrick, M. (1999). *The expanded family life cycle* (3rd ed.). Needham Heights, MA: Allyn & Bacon, pp. 1-24. See also McGoldrick, M., & Carter, B. (2003). The family life cycle. In F. Walsh (Ed.), *Normal family processes* (3rd ed.). New York: Guilford, pp. 375-98; Carter, B., & McGoldrick, M. (1999). The divorce cycle: A major variation in the American family life cycle. In B. Carter & M. McGoldrick (Eds.), *The expanded family life*

cycle: Individual, family, and social perspectives (3rd ed.). New York: Allyn and Bacon.

[4]Carter & McGoldrick, The divorce cycle, p. 373.

[5]Ibid., p. 374.

[6]Constance Ahrons refers to these as "developmental steps." See Ahrons, C. (1999). Divorce: An unscheduled family transition. In B. Carter, & M. McGoldrick (Eds.), *The expanded family life cycle: Individual, family, and social perspectives* (3rd ed.). New York: Allyn and Bacon, p. 385.

[7]Ibid.

[8]Ibid., p. 386.

[9]Carter & McGoldrick, The divorce cycle.

[10]Interestingly, Ahrons indicates that in the U.S. most divorces are now initiated by women (60-75 percent), which she attributes to "the increase in women's economic independence." It is suggested that many women would have stayed in marriages due to economic dependence. See ibid., p. 387.

[11]Ibid.

[12]These principles are from Bonkowski, S. (1987). *Kids are nondivorceable*. Chicago: ACTA Publications. See also Bonkowski, S. (1990). *Teens are nondivorceable: A workbook for divorced parents and their children: ages 12-18*. Chicago: ACTA Publications.

[13]This is what Carter and McGoldrick refer to as "supporting viable arrangements for all parts of the system." See Carter & McGoldrick, Divorce cycle, p. 374.

[14]Ahrons, Divorce, pp. 388-89.

[15]Patterson, J., et al., *Essential skills in family therapy*.

[16]Ibid.

[17]See Ahrons, Divorce, p. 393.

[18]McGoldrick, M., & Carter, B. (1999). Remarried families. In B. Carter & M. McGoldrick (Eds.), *The expanded family life cycle: Individual, family, and social perspectives* (3rd ed.). New York: Allyn and Bacon.

[19]Ibid., p. 424.

[20]Bonkowski, S. (1987). *Kids are nondivorceable: A workbook for divorced parents and their children: Ages 6-11 version*. Chicago: Buckley.

[21]These principles and many others are discussed in McGoldrick & Carter, Remarried families, pp. 419-21.

[22]Visher, E. B., Visher, J. S., & Pasley, K. (2003). Remarriage, families and stepparenting. In. F. Walsh (Ed.), *Normal family processes: growing diversity and complexity* (3rd ed.). New York: Guilford, pp. 153-75.

[23]Ibid., pp. 163-69.

[24]Jones, L. G. (1995). *Embodying forgiveness: A theological analysis*. Grand Rapids, MI: Eerdmans.

[25]Ibid., p. 148.

14

SUBSTANCE ABUSE
AND BEHAVIORAL
ADDICTIONS

*What is necessary to change a person is to
change his awareness of himself.*

ABRAHAM H. MASLOW

THERE IS NO BETTER PLACE TO THINK about addictions than the
church. We, the community of Christians, are as Gerald May declares,
"all addicts, in every sense of the word."[1] Paul describes this addicted
state as the condition through which Christ rescued us, one in which
we were in "bondage to decay" (Rom 8:21). In other words, we were
addicted to that which is rotting, festering and decomposing. The
Heidelberg Catechism declares, "That I am not my own, but belong
with body and soul, both in life and in death, to my faithful Savior
Jesus Christ. He has fully paid for all my sins with His precious blood,
and has set me free." Having been set free from bondage—chemical,
behavioral, emotional, material, relational, physical and psychological—we must continually examine ourselves to ensure that we are experiencing all that we have been promised and provided.

Gerry and Carol came to counseling to accomplish that very goal. They
had significant marriage difficulties. Gerry shared that he had a history of

depression and was losing the fight with alcohol. For the past three years, beer had been his best friend. He is also now fighting with a new opponent: sexual addiction, particularly compulsive masturbation to pornography. They have been married five years and report that their "real" problems in their marriage began about a year ago. To use Gerry's words, he was "unable to function" with Carol. Gerry says that he hadn't given internet sex much of a thought. But he became aware of more of a problem with sex addiction to pornography about a year ago. He has been compulsively masturbating about twice a day for over one year. He describes being "compelled," as though it becomes all that he can think about. He states that he experienced impotence "against" his wife, to express anger toward her. He also stated that she "knew" when he masturbated and would insist on sex during those times, since he would be unable to function.

Carol initially denied insisting on sex when Gerry couldn't function, but over the course of the session, admitted that if Gerry found women on the internet more attractive than her, she had no problem shaming him into seeing how wrong he was. She went on to share how his use of pornography had an impact on her. She talked about feeling like it was "almost an affair" in the sense that he preferred masturbating over sex with her. She said she felt angry about it and frustrated. She also said she felt confused and wanted things to get better for them.

Gerry and Carol sit in your office, locked in a pattern of chemical, sexual, behavioral addictions. Gerry is the big target. It is very easy to focus on him, the "addicted one," as the problem. Addiction becomes synonymous with blame and culpability. But just focusing on Gerry will likely serve to simplify the complicated layers of pain and injury that exist in their marriage. And simplified solutions usually are temporary. The pastoral or marital counselor is in a unique position to understand and aid a family system that is manifested by addictions. It is in working with Gerry and Carol together—fully acknowledging both Jerry's and Carol's problems—that there is the highest potential for helping this marriage mature.

THE BIG PICTURE OF ADDICTIONS

Addictions have historically been associated with chemicals, such as alcohol, nicotine, heroin and so on—terms such as *alcoholic, drug addict* and *addicted to pornography* are useful in our common language. They are often terms without specific definition. Is a "chocoholic" essentially the same as an "alcoholic" but with a different drug of choice? Should the person who plays lotto every week and the person who spends $10,000 at off-site betting clubs join Gamblers Anonymous? When Michael Jordan or William Bennett lost millions of dollars gambling, does that mean that they were addicted? What defines addiction: the amount, the effect or the reaction of others?

Categories of addiction. Addictive disorders—both behavioral disorders like eating and sex, and chemical disorders such as cocaine and caffeine—are defined in the *Diagnostic and Statistical Manual,* the psychiatric text for mental health diagnoses. The *DSM* separates addictive disorders into abuse and dependence categories. The former is described as the continued use of a substance or a behavior in spite of its continued negative effect on one's ability to function in work, school or home; placing oneself in risk of harm while using the substance or engaging the behavior; experiencing legal or reprimanding consequences because of its use; or continued use or conduct in spite of harmful effects on relationships or social responsibilities.

In other words, *abuse* is defined as continuing to use the substance or involve oneself in conduct knowing that the actions have had and will continue to have negative consequences: "I know this is harmful, but I will continue to do it."

Substance *dependence* is a little more serious. It includes all of the characteristics of substance abuse stated above, as well as the continued use of the substance in greater amounts to obtain the desired effect (tolerance) and the experience of a negative physiological reaction when the substance is reduced or eliminated (withdrawal).

When people brag about how much beer they can drink without getting a "buzz," unknowingly they are describing tolerance. It means that their body has accommodated to the presence of the chemical and must receive additional concentrations to experience an elevated mood.

Substance abuse and dependence and behavioral addictions have reached a point of crisis in our culture today. From an economic standpoint, an estimated $148 billion per year may be lost in productivity, unemployment and the increased cost of health care due to these concerns.[2] From a psychosocial perspective, economic loss is only overshadowed by the strain on marriages, families and entire communities affected by destructive patterns of behavior and the lack of available resources to address such concerns.

The statistics on substance abuse are astounding. About 1 in 5 (21 percent) of the U.S. population smokes cigarettes.[3] About 10 million people in the U.S. misuse alcohol and another estimated 8 million people are alcohol dependent.[4] The most common illegal drug in the U.S. is marijuana—about 73 percent of those who use illicit drugs use marijuana.[5] It is commonly begun during the teen years, and in a sample, about half (48.7 percent) of 18-year-olds reported using it at least once. An estimated 20 percent of high school students who try it eventually use it daily.[6] Nearly 1.6 million Americans either abused or were dependent on cocaine in the past year.[7] We have seen a decrease in heroin abuse, although many still experiment with it.[8] As challenging as these statistics are, they do not reflect the costs related to the spread of HIV, which is associated with the abuse of substances.[9]

We have more recently seen an increased interest in behavioral or "process addictions."[10] A process addiction involves a repeated and habituated act that is conducted to bring pleasure but comes to dominate one's life and is continued in spite of negative consequences. Process addictions could include sex, gambling, religiosity, eating, work, shopping/spending, media use (television, computer, video games, internet), hobbies, exercise and so on.

Perhaps the most often discussed behavioral addiction is sexual addiction. Experts on sexual addiction estimate that approximately 8 to 10 percent of adults are involved with sexually related behaviors that they cannot control.[11] Addictions arise in a culture that is fascinated with sex. An estimated 40 million Americans regularly visit pornography sites on the internet, and over $12 billion dollars is spent annually on pornography in the U.S.[12] But it is more than pornography; our society shows many images of sex that do not rise to the level of illicit images. It has been estimated that on the average television network, there are fifteen sex acts, words or innuendos *each hour,* most often by unmarried partners who often have either just met or have no previous romantic relationship. According to some reports, the average American teenager hears or sees about 20,000 sexual references and images a year. The effect is that as a culture, we become tolerant to sexuality like we become tolerant to substances. It takes more and more exposure to obtain arousal, so we crave and pursue sexual fantasies with greater intensity.

The debate as to whether process addictions are the same as substance addictions continues. The similarities and differences are noted in the professional literature. In this chapter, we will be referring specifically to substance abuse and addictions, with the acknowledgment that many of the interventions might be applicable to families who are addressing process or behavioral addictions.

Addiction and marriage. The marriage relationship is deeply impacted by substance abuse and addictions. We mentioned above that the impact can be seen in the loss of money and resources spent on substances, loss of employment or under-employment from the lack of stability that surrounds addictions, negative health consequences from the misuse of substances, and risk of premature death. Add to that list of concerns the risk of increased violence, damage to the marriage relationship, and the risk of passing along to the next generation negative patterns of behavior and ways of relating.

Substance abuse and addiction often lead to deception. Whether an addict lies or minimizes or omits important information, there is a tendency with the misuse of substances to have ready excuses in place. The excuses typically place responsibility for any kind of consequence or outcome on others rather than the addict.

This lack of transparency and growing mistrust can lead to stress and conflict in the marriage. The conflicts might not be about the substance at first, but rather conflict could be about spending habits, time away from home and other concerns. The spouse struggling with alcohol or another substance may be unpredictable in what sets them off, and they may become more negative or critical of other family members, especially the spouse.

Substance abuse and addiction can also damage marriages by damaging other family relationships, particularly relationships with children and adolescents. When children or adolescents of a substance abusing parent struggle emotionally, behaviorally or academically, the strain felt in trying to manage that or respond constructively to those struggles will often be felt in the marriage.

All of this leads to decreased satisfaction in marriage. And in some ways the spouse who does not struggle with a substance or addiction is really competing with a "jealous lover." The substance the addict spends time with is enticing at first. It promises to take their mind off of the daily grind or a specific painful, frustrating or disappointing event. Substances are often reinforcing because they lead to increased pleasurable feelings; in some cases, such as with alcohol, they can also reduce stress. Addictive substances can be reinforcing at several levels, both positively (by providing pleasurable sensations) and negatively (by reducing stress or anxiety).

But substances are rarely content with the time an addict allots to them. An addictive substance wants more. Given the opportunity, an addictive substance will take everything from the addict. It will want the addict's time and money. It will want their time and attention at work. It will want their time and attention at home. It is rarely content with a few hours of a person's time, and given enough investment of time and energy, it will be increasingly difficult to say no to. It will become a familiar presence in the life of the addict. It will become a steady and reliable friend, something that never disappoints, never argues with them. Put bluntly, real marriages and real families will have a hard time competing with what an addictive substance promises the addict.

SPECIAL CONSIDERATIONS IN ADDRESSING SUBSTANCE ABUSE AND ADDICTIONS

Addictions live in the context of pain-defense-injury. Addictions are the attempt to solve a problem, but then they become a new problem that easily eclipses the original problem. Our cures are indeed worse than our diseases. Healing exists in the context of pain—through the administration of grace, justice and those qualities that lead to reconciliation. The counselor can utilize the pain and grace model as a template to understand the addictive process, to build the counseling relationship, and to work with the couple as a team to confront and collaborate together against the addiction.

Picture yourself interacting with a couple like Gerry and Carol mentioned in the introduction to this chapter. They are sitting in your office enveloped in shame, denial, anger, hopelessness, avoidance, confusion, numbness and a host of other conflicting emotions. Your task is to help them build an Us, from the ground up. The Us they bring to you is one that is centered around their addictive defenses. Addictive marriages operate through a perpetual failure identity. People don't start out addicted to substances or activities; they start out seeking solace, relief, comfort, escape or enjoyment. People involved in addictions live in a world where the trees have taken over the forest. The trees are those addictions that rest in the front of their minds—they are the foreground. But the foreground has become so dominant that it is all the couple can think about or talk about. Crucial to your establishing the essential relationship is to look beyond the addiction and validate the pain. The pain-defense pattern can be used to empathize with the current struggles that both partners feel, all the while confirming that the current patterns of action just maintain enslavement.

The grace response suggests a different way of interaction, a new language. It says that each understands the actions of the other as a habitual means to manage pain. The old way sort of works, but it fails at bringing the type of relief for which husbands and wives yearn. Grace, justice, empathy, trust and forgiveness are their real desire, but it requires insight, courage, commitment and especially patience to overcome entrenched patterns. The grace cycle functions as a new lens or paradigm through which everything is to be understood.

After couples have established a new understanding of rules to live by—a commitment to learn to live by grace and justice rather than by pain and defense—the counselor is in a position to attend to the very important behavioral and chemical addictions as well as destructive relational patterns. There are many models available for responding to substance abuse and addictions in the family. We like the model by

Juhnke and Hagedorn[13] in particular. It offers a helpful plan that provides counselors and pastors with a progressive, sequential approach that draws on the best of the different models available today. This substance abuse intervention model can be used in conjunction with the pain/grace model that can accommodate a wide range of needs.

Couples come to counseling to address addictions at remarkably different stations in life. Some couples are facing the shock and denial of additions. Husbands and wives are being confronted with a reality that leaves them stunned, dizzy, confused, fearful or in full-scale flight. Other couples have successfully managed addictive patterns. For example, a substance abusing spouse might have been in recovery as an individual for three, four or five years, but only now is wanting to work with his wife to talk about their Us issues. Or a couple could have a history of addictive actions and previous counseling but be addressing an experience of relapse that has left each person with bitterness, shame, anger and fear that with this recurrence the nonaddictive spouse might just say, "This game is over; I am getting out. She has broken one too many promises."

The stages include more short-term, brief approaches and can evolve to more insight-oriented models if that is appropriate or needed. They include aspects of motivational interviewing, an emphasis on solutions, ways to address the rules that govern family functioning and so on. The model also recognizes that spouses may potentially play an important role in recovery. This may have to do with the level of compassion for their spouse and the love and loyalty that they have.

In any case, these approaches are essentially facets of a larger framework for recovery. We organize them under the headings of family *functioning, relationship* and *identity,* in keeping with the overall themes of integrative Christian family therapy. The specific approaches under each of these headings can be addressed in a progressive manner, building off of the gains made as the family continues to receive help. When a couple or family is just starting the recovery process, they are more appropriate for the first few stages; couples or families that have been working on recovery longer may benefit from some of the latter stages.

COUPLE FUNCTION AND ADDICTIONS

One initial consideration that has to do with functioning is helping the addicted spouse take responsibility for treatment. *Motivational interviewing* is one way to do this as recommended by Juhnke and Hagedorn. The approach they advocate is an important contrast to the in-your-face approach that is often the caricature of the addictions counselor. Again, motivational interviewing has as its goal to help the addicted spouse take responsibility for treatment. The key is to gain insight into the addicted spouse's perspective, to listen to that perspective respectfully, and to encourage decision-making in the course of counseling or pastoral care. Because this occurs in a couples setting, the counselor is listening to the addicted spouse and to the other spouse, listening to the concerns of everyone involved and facilitating mutual understanding. It is in this context that the counselor or pastoral care provider might note discrepancies or inconsistencies while encouraging the couple to pursue a recovery plan that they can all agree upon.

Another response that is part of addressing functioning and follows motivational interviewing is referred to as *finding solutions*. This is typically time-limited, maybe fewer than ten weeks. The emphasis is first on defining the problem—that is, why the couple is asking for help. Even more specific than substance use, what about arguments, intoxication in the home and failure to attend specific events. For example, if the husband fails to attend a child's recital because of his drinking, it would be this specific event and others like it that would be seen as the motivation for counseling, as well as how his wife and others may have responded to the no-show.

What would happen next is the pastoral counselor would create an intervention that changes the way the couple or family interacts. The care provider would look to depart radically from what the spouse or other family members have tried up to this point. Any intervention now challenges the status quo, often by thinking about what nonaddicted people do. If non-substance-abusing families go on outings together, then this family should begin planning outings. If non-substance-abusing families speak directly to one another when there is a problem, then this family should begin to act in a similar manner. If after a time the problem is not reduced, then another method is employed. So this may take the form of a series of changes in the way the family does business.

The last approach that is part of a functional emphasis represents the major approaches to responding to addictions—that is, *addressing thoughts and behaviors*. This brings together what are called cognitive and behavioral approaches. The pastoral counselor guides the family to address the realm of individually and communally held thoughts, beliefs and values that encourage and maintain addictions as an acceptable response. This represents the cognitive aspect of intervention. The idea is to alter and replace unhelpful thoughts, beliefs and values with helpful thoughts, beliefs and values that foster more effective responses. This approach also considers ways in which existing exchanges in some way reinforce the misuse of substances. This is more of a behavioral consideration.

A hallmark of an approach that looks at thoughts and behaviors is that it examines what is going on before the misuse of a substance. For example, Margaret and Ivan are paying bills and balancing the checkbook together. The stress and tension between them is increased as they realize once again that each has spent money without the other's awareness, and they are forced to take money, once again, out of their savings. They deliver harsh words to one another to vent their frustration and to place blame on the other for the current financial condition. The words escalate into an argument and Ivan leaves—changing into sweatpants and running shoes and going off for a sixty-minute run. His energy to exercise exists on an addiction level—running at least an hour a day, and longer when there is tension at home or work. His running is fueled by the desire to escape the conflict at home. Margaret is fueled by another motivation. She turns her frustration into addictive eating, and consumes chocolates and pastries.

In this case the precursor to unhealthy behaviors is the financial concerns and the patterns that have developed around spending and bill paying. It would also be helpful to examine the individual and communal thought processes or the beliefs held regarding financial decisions, expectations of self and spouse regarding spending, views of self that are triggered when these expectations are not met, and finally, the thought processes of self and spouse regarding how to appropriately cope with disappointments associated with failure to meet economic expectations.

COUPLE RELATIONSHIP AND ADDICTIONS

The next major area for consideration and the first one that goes a bit deeper beyond family functioning and into family relationships is addressing *family boundaries*. Indeed, it is often common in substance abusing families to see the blurring of boundaries and the subsequent chaos that comes when family members assume responsibilities and tasks that belong to others. With couples, the blurred boundaries usually take the form of protecting the addicted spouse from the natural consequences of their addiction. It might mean the husband calls and makes excuses to his wife's employer regarding her absence from work.

After joining with the couple and perhaps the other family members, an appropriate intervention might help support healthy boundaries within the family, including the marriage relationship. The pastoral care provider would likely start with the couple and focus on the relational skills, boundaries and responsibilities needed for successful leadership of the family. If the addicted family member is one of the parents, the counselor would address the addictive behavior on that level first, before broadening to the others in the family.

Another point of relationship emphasis has to do with generational issues, or what some people refer to as the *sins of the father*. A popular Scriptural passage known to many family counselors is Exodus 20:5-6,[14] which talks about the Lord "visiting the iniquity of the fathers on the children, on the third and fourth generations" (NASB). This idea of the sins of the father brings to mind the kind of generational considerations in this next step in helping families.

Murray Bowen[15] considered the generational tension between individual and family to emerge out of the paradox of being separate from others in the family and at the same time together with family in a healthy collaborative relationship. He described how members of the family can feel pulled toward disengagement from others while also experiencing an opposite pull toward fusion.

It is in this constant processing of yanking and tugging that the inclination toward addictive behaviors emerges. The tension that is the result of enmeshment—others crossing boundaries and manipulating or controlling family members—is soothed and triangulated by the presence of a substance or a satisfying behavior.

In other words, a person is vulnerable to forming an addiction when the drug or the act functions both as a pleasure activity and as an intermediary between people—to calm or to soothe the tensions that exist in relationship.

Another model for addiction formation is as a replacement for a family member with whom there is an effort to create emotional cutoff. The person essentially says, "I will reject or cut myself off from you and love 'this thing' instead."

The main focus in this relationship level of intervention is to control the emotional intensity that would otherwise interfere with the couple's (and family's) ability to manage differences, solve problems and attend to each other's needs. A key task is to stabilize the relationships within the session—say, within the marriage, for our purposes—so that a healthy and functional dialogue can take place between the spouses. This can occur if the counselor is an active conductor of the process. Counselors can offset the common triangulation process found in addiction-affected homes by demonstrating an alternative to implementing a third party to manipulate or retaliate against others in the family. This "healthy triangulation" occurs when the counselor disrupts the conversation occurring in session and guides the family toward a constructive conclusion. In this case the counselor acts as a triangulating entity, but rather than taking sides between warring factions with the family, the counselor provides stability in the system and prevents the conversation from escalating into emotional defensiveness.

The third and related relationship theme is that of *family-of-origin considerations*. This way of approaching addictions in the family builds on the last one. It involves helping people injured by addictive patterns in their own homes to recall important events and details in their family history, usually with the family-of-origin members. This can help a person solidify the emotional boundaries between them and their parents, for example. A person can benefit from talking through these experiences from their now-adult perspective.

For example, an adult who harbors resentment toward a parent for alcohol abuse and being such an embarrassment to him or her during adolescence might have the opportunity to hear, understand and place in context the parent say, thirty years after the events, "I know that I wasn't there for you. I was so depressed, discouraged and defeated with my own stuff that I didn't go to your events, and I was often too drunk for you to have your friends over to the house." This element of recollection of events can serve to validate felt experience and clarify or correct assumptions about a parent's motive for acting through his or her addiction.

COUPLE IDENTITY AND ADDICTIONS

The final stage recommended by Juhnke and Hagedorn focuses on the person's ability to understand how they have taken in certain perceptions of themselves and of their family in a way that has contributed to their pursuit of addictive behaviors. This moves us into identity considerations. Identity can be reflected in culture, gender, socioeconomic status and so on. Identity is also about helping a family prompt growth or development in the couple and in the sense of *who we are*.

There are many ways in which struggles with substance abuse and addiction can impact identity. Substance abuse can be a response to pain, particularly pain that occurs between people in close relationship, and to be more specific, pain between people in close relationship where there is intimacy and affection as an expectation. Such pain has an effect on the quality of relational and emotional connections a person has. Whereas life pain would normally be addressed, managed and soothed within family relationships, the failure to accomplish the management of anxiety through these core relationships prompts people to seek solace through other means such as substances or behaviors. These originate as acts of self-soothing and gradually become a dominating and controlling component in a person's life as the substance or behavior is more and more frequently relied upon. The inability to connect with others to address life pain becomes a secondary effect of addictive substances or behaviors, thus producing another level of pain.

The task of counseling at this level is to form insight into how individual needs emerge from the earliest relationships to act in an emotional "dance" of undeclared interactions. To see the dance—to understand it, discuss it, accept it, change it and encourage growth through it—is the focus of treatment.

COMMON THEMES

One of the most challenging tasks for any counselor or pastoral care provider is to know what to do and with whom to do it. The model we have discussed is helpful in delineating the major approaches to family addictions counseling and providing a basic template for understanding the differences in the approaches to addressing family addictions. We organized these under the three headings of function, relationship and identity. Regardless of the approaches, there are fundamental skills required of the counselor or care provider in order to be effective.

The common themes for counseling or care provision are building trust, facilitating stabilization, providing education and preventing relapse. The task in joining with the couple is to acquire an understanding of each spouse's need and perception of family functioning. Patience in gathering family information and prudence in implementing interventions is essential in allowing for the family to reveal the complexity of its structure misaligned around the addiction.

Building trust. Counseling success is dependent on the quality of trust between counselor and clients. This need is amplified in situations with substance abuse, because there likely is a history of "trust abuse" so that both husband and wife may not be secure in trusting the other or trusting themselves to maintain commitments. While trust is such an obvious starting point, counselors must be clear as to *what kind* of trust. Couples in conflict must be able to trust the counselor to protect and support them if they enter the risk of therapy and put forth a good-faith effort. If a person revealing their vulnerabilities assumes responsibility for their shortcomings, sins and errors, are they secure from retaliation or manipulation? In essence, couples must trust the counselor that he or she will have enough authority or power to maintain safety the process of counseling.

Trust is maintained by the counselor's demonstration of understanding of both people, by the counselor's concern and by an unyielding commitment to mutual fairness. In many ways the counselor's relationship with the couple is similar to a parental relationship. There is a clear protective element with the greater purpose of creating autonomy within the couple. The message is, "You can trust me now to protect you, so that you can learn to control your need for retaliation for previous pain."

This kind of trust is crucial for the substance/addiction couple in that there is likely a history of deception, crossing boundaries and failure to maintain promises. Prior to the creation of stability in the marital system, the stabilization of the trusting relationship with the counselor is needed.

For a short time, the counselor exists as a stabilizing mediator, as if to say to both spouses, "Trust me for now while I work with your spouse to make him or her more trustworthy." This is an important, temporary role that serves to provide restraint because the counselor is there to enforce the rules, and it provides hope that the couple need not spend all their relational energy in self-protection but rather can focus on doing good to the marriage.

Facilitating stabilization. Stabilization refers to the family's capacity to create an environment that provides sufficient safety for everyone. The safety component applies most directly to the substance abuser, assuring that the potentially harmful, destructive or fatal aspects of continued substance use are controlled. Security applies most directly to those in the family who feel anxious about the dangerous behavior of their loved ones, such that they become inclined to disregard the boundaries necessary for healthy family functioning—creating a snowballing contribution by inciting adverse emotional reactions on the part of the abuser, which is often soothed by increased substance use.

Stabilization often includes the formation of agreements that define expected behavior over the short term, and what the result will be if the agreement is broken by any of the family members. The counselor often is charged with reminding the family of the contract as they commonly test the strength of the boundary that is placed on them.

Providing education. Counselors often occupy the role of educator for either spouse. The counselor or pastoral care provider can offer information about the addictive pattern and the recovery process, help the couple establish an agenda that is realistic to the problem, and serve as a coach as the family interfaces with other professionals.

Preventing relapse. One of the key areas of education is the topic of substance abuse relapse and relapse prevention. Relapse is often regarded as a "one-sided argument." While the family can easily recognize the relapse behavior of an abuser, they do not as readily acknowledge the relapse of their own behavior in disregarding boundaries or failing to render support as was contracted. Both relapse of the substance abuse and of the family pathology to which substance abuse is associated must be taught as serious violations of the family contract.

Regarding relapse, three ideas must be acknowledged to couples. The first is that all relapses are serious violations and insults to how the family has agreed to function. Second, not all relapses are equal. Likeness in kind should not be mistaken for likeness in degree. Third, couples must anticipate that the full and complete success over addictions is an arduous process. We will examine each of these important realities.

Relapses are serious. When they occur, they will threaten the future of the marriage. The nutrition of successful families is trust, honesty and support. Relapse behaviors poison families. There is limited ability for individuals within a system to act with grace when there are violations of trust. Some couples can survive relapses; many do not. We encourage counselors to discuss beforehand the meaning of relapse. Like natural disasters such as earthquakes, tornadoes or hurricanes that threaten the structures of our houses, so addictions threaten the structures of our homes. Like natural disasters, addictive families know that they live near fault lines. Safety plans and contingency strategies are important to reduce the risk of harm in the event of relapse.

Second, not all relapses are equal. Marital survival is dependent on the details, the answers to questions such as: "Was the relapse disclosed by the addictive spouse in the form of a confession, or was it discovered by the spouse or children? Was the relapse a single event in the aftermath of intense stress, or was it an ongoing deception? Did the relapse occur after a significant period of months or years of successful trust building, or was it weeks after the commitment to change?"

Finally, addiction recovery is a lifelong commitment. It is easy to think that addiction is a problem that is confronted, challenged and conquered. However, the real life experience of couples addressing addiction offers us different insight. We are familiar with the language of men and women who have confronted alcohol addiction, referring to themselves as "recovering alcoholics." The repeated group introduction of those who attend AA meetings is, "My name is _____, and I am an alcoholic." Couples should take wisdom from the experience of those who have gone before them. Some may argue that including contingency plans for failure opens the door and invites the perpetuation of abuse, to which all must agree. However, Scripture and theology, as well as the body of psychological literature, support the argument that all are vulnerable to setbacks and failure. Just as we are sinners—not former sinners—so too we are addicts, always prone to fall. In a study of alcohol recidivism among over a thousand addiction counselors—these are addicts who after their recovery come to help others overcome addictions—found that nearly 40 percent had returned to substance abuse at some time while they counseled others. This was a self-report study so the real number is no doubt much higher. The message to take here is *not*, "Spouses will fail, and that's okay." Absolutely not! The message is that failure, in the form of brief setbacks, must be anticipated by the couple, and that contingency plans for prevention and for restitution should be established beforehand. For example, those in recovery will use the phrase, "One day at a time." This means that they carry the identity of an abuser, who for today is sober or in control of his or her behavior, and by the grace of God and the support of those who love him or her, will complete this day as a former addict. Tomorrow, the commitment to continue the fight will resume.

CONCLUSION

Couples who take on the identity of confronting sin together, and build a marital culture in which there is shared dialogue about the threats to their Us, have the best chance for long-term success. Each spouse carries individual burdens—the weight of their own sin. When couples confront addictions together, neither are assuming that they are taking on the responsibility for the other's sin, but are sharing in each other's solution. There is a saying among Latin American cultures that translates to English as, "A burden held is a burden doubled. A burden shared is a burden halved." Marital counselors play a crucial role in helping couples halve their burdens with one another.

NOTES

[1]May, G. G. (1988). *Addiction and grace*. San Francisco: Harper & Row, p. 3

[2]Harwood, H., Fountain, D., & the Lewin group (1998). *The economic costs of alcohol and drug abuse in the United States, 1992*. Washington, D.C.: US DHHS, NIH, NIAA.

[3]Centers for Disease Control and Prevention (2006). Tobacco use among adults— United States, 2005. *Morbidity and Mortality Weekly Report, 55*, 1145-48.

[4]See Grant, B. F., Dawson, D. A., Stinson, F. S., Chou, S. P., Dufour, M. C., & Pickering, R. P. (2004). The 12-month prevalence and trends in DSM-IV alcohol abuse and dependence: United States, 1991-1992 and 2001-2002. *Drug and Alcohol Dependence, 74*(3), 223-34; J. C. Anthony, L. A. Warner & R. C. Kessler (1994). Comparative epidemiology of dependence on tobacco, alcohol, controlled substances, and inhalants. *Experimental and Clinical Psychopharmacology, 2*(3), 224-68; R. M. Julien (1992). *A primer of drug action* (6th ed.). New York: Freeman.

[5]Substance Abuse and Mental Health Services Administration (2008). Results from the 2007 National Survey on Drug Use and Health: National Findings (Office of Applied Studies, NSDUH Series H-34, DHHS Publication No. SMA 08-4343). Rockville, MD.

[6]Cooper, Z., & Haney, M. (2008). Cannabis reinforcement and dependence: Role of the cannabinoid CB1 receptor. *Addiction Biology, 13*(2), 188-95.

[7]Substance Abuse and Mental Health Services Administration, Results from the 2007 National Survey.

[8]In the past, heroin was abused by an estimated one-half million Americans and an estimated 1.9 million had experimented with the drug. More recent statistics suggest that heroin abusers have decreased from 338,000 in 2006 to 153,000 in 2007. See Substance Abuse and Mental Health Services Administration, Results from the 2007 National Survey

[9]Kalichman, S. C., Carey, M. P., & Johnson, B. T. (1996). Prevention of sexually

transmitted HIV infection: A meta-analytic review of the behavioral outcome. *Annals of Behavioral Medicine, 18*(1), 6-15.

[10]Juhnke, G. A., & Hagedorn, B. (2006). *Counseling addicted families: An integrated assessment and treatment model.* New York: Routledge.

[11]Carnes, P. (2001). *Out of the shadows: Understanding sexual addiction* (3rd ed.). Center City, MN: Hazelden.

[12]Preserving family values in a media driven society: pornography statistics. (2006). Retrieved from http://familysafemedia.com/pornography_statistics.html#anchor6.

[13]Juhnke & Hagedorn, *Counseling addicted families.*

[14]Exodus 20:5-6: "You shall not worship them or serve them; for I, the LORD, your God, am a jealous God, visiting the iniquity of the fathers on the children, on the third and fourth generations of those who hate Me, but showing lovingkindness to thousands, to those who love Me and keep My commandments" (NASB).

[15]Bowen, M. (1976). Theory in the practice of psychotherapy. In P. J. Guerrin Jr. (Ed.), *Family therapy: Theory and practice.* New York: Guilford.

15

A GRACEFUL CONCLUSION

We're going inside of 'em, we're going outside of 'em—inside of 'em!
outside of 'em!—and when we get them on the run once,
we're going to keep 'em on the run. . . . And don't
forget, men—today is the day we're gonna win.
They can't lick us—and that's how it goes. . . .
The first platoon men—go in there and
fight, fight, fight, fight, fight!
What do you say, men!

KNUTE ROCKNEY,
NOTRE DAME FOOTBALL COACH

NOW AT THE END OF THE BOOK, we feel like football coaches, having prepared you, the team, to perform. Now we are to give you the final charge culminating in a cheer ("Go, fight, win!") and then a grand rush out to the field . . . or to the office. Counselors can take this knowledge and with zeal launch community campaigns to "fight against fighting." Or, maybe not.

We all know that "winning" in the counseling domain does not mean eliminating conflict and creating a blissful, ecstatic marital existence. Instead of the last chapter pep talk motivating you to go "win one for the Gipper," we want to offer cautions regarding the work of helping couples restore marriage. We have found that those who are interested in this topic do not need to be motivated to become involved in marriage and family ministry. By reading this and countless other books, you have demonstrated your motivation to learn. That desire to learn is likely driven by the base motive to render care to others. Toward that end we join with you.

In this last chapter, we want to consider subtle messages about marriage that are often advocated within the Christian culture that have an initial appeal, but at closer look actually serve to undermine the efforts of Christian counseling and pastoral counseling ministry. We find these concerns emerging from the "law of unintended consequences"—when a principle or truth is advocated, additional ancillary effects or conditions emerge that were not part of the original intent, but still have an effect on outcomes and experiences. A simple example would be a church that names the new education wing of the building the "Family Life Center" but are surprised to learn in conducting a survey that single adults do not feel welcome at the church. Clearly, the church leaders did not want to convey exclusion in their ministry, but by emphasizing families, one important value of their ministry, they communicated an unintended message: "This church serves married couples with children."

THEIR GOAL, YOUR GOAL

It is nearly unanimous. Couples come to counseling to have problems fixed, or more specifically, to remove pain in the form of dissension, argument, benign neglect, chronic disregard or apathetic disinterest. Most of the time, marital efforts are short-term and immediate. Couples want to feel positive, content, hopeful and happy, and they want their marriage relationship to be a contributor to those positive feelings. According to Hargrave, couples experience pain—and in turn, counselors interact with couples as they address the pain that they feel—in different phases of their marriage.[1] Initially, couples in conflict are addressing pain because of the need for marital stabilization. The empirical literature on marital conflict is quite clear, particularly with couples married less than about a dozen years. The conflict centers around uncommunicated expectations, misinterpreted motivations, and blurred boundaries between marriage and the respective families of origin. But for couples established in their marriage, the counseling goals will likely have a different nuance. "It is important to remember that even though stability issues are the first developmental task in achieving marital "us-ness," security is next, and sincerity follows."[2]

By security, Hargrave refers to the "main tasks" in marriage—building and demonstrating commitment through love and trust. Security suggests that the couple has established the ability to be an Us. They have established routines, formed family and built traditions. Change can easily become the threat to couples in this phase. The husband or wife entering midlife and realizing that there are unfulfilled dreams from early adulthood—and it's not too late to claim them—creates a real threat to the security of the marriage. Unilaterally, marital patterns and habits are changed. Power over one another is attempted and exerted. Moves to counter efforts to control and to block the wishes of the other are examples of the subtle shift from the Us back to the Me. In most areas, the couple might be coordinated as a cohesive team, but perception in important areas such as finances, sexuality, career paths and parenting might prompt the team sport of marriage to be played more like the individual sport of self-interest. Counselors possessing insight into the couple—that this Us is not threatened by the perils associated with younger marriages—are able to transpose the experience of conflict into a language or a metaphor that the couple can comprehend.

Finally, Hargrave suggests that couples' conflicts might be emerging because of the call and the challenge of sincerity. He defines it as the "ability to learn about oneself in the context of the marital relationship."[3] The conflicts occurring may look more like our existential longing for intimacy in light of the presence of misplaced priorities. Life takes its toll. Over time the Us can be superseded by work, hobbies, children, other relationships or friendships, individuality and emotional separation, or simple selfishness. The conflicts regarding sincerity might be expressed by a sense of despair and hopelessness. To a marital counselor, observing this relational discouragement might feel much less intense than sitting with the flash of anger from couples who are destabilized by the lack of a common tradition.

Hargrave's identification of goal variation should remind us that the motives and forces that prompt a couple to seek our participation in their lives are an amalgamation of pulls and pushes, deficits and excesses, hopes and discouragements, potentials and losses. Wise counseling is seen as maintaining an open and receptive posture for new disclosures. The understanding of relationships and the formation of effective interventions is a fluid process. There is constant motion. The model we have presented should be used to allow the couple to be who they are and are becoming, rather than to be used to prescribe a definition of who the couple is or is supposed to be.

THE CULTURAL IMAGE OF A "HAPPY" MARRIAGE

Addison Hodges Hart in a short but thoughtful book, *Knowing Darkness*, examined the characteristics of faith through the lens of melancholy.[4] Not depression—the psychopathological condition that is derived from deprived levels of the neurotransmitter serotonin—but biblical melancholy as shown by David, Jeremiah, Ezekiel and especially Jesus. Hart writes, "The Bible, with its unvarnished picture of human life, its utter lack of sentimentality, its frankness and straightforwardness, never confuses faith with perpetual 'happiness' or 'living the victory' or 'the joy-filled life' or anything akin to a greeting-card, Precious Moments outlook. There is nothing even remotely cozy, in the dreamy 'Kinkade-cottage in the woods' sort of way, to be found there."[5]

Though Hart is thinking of the Christian journey in general, we believe that we who are involved in Christian marriage counseling ministry are guilty of perpetuating a destructive image of what constitutes a successful, God-honoring, Christian marriage. Amazon lists more than twenty thousand books on Christian marriage—that's right: *twenty* with three zeros after the comma. In the spirit of full disclosure, we have not read all of them. But many that we have read offer simplified and unrealistic paths to help couples discover that soul-level yearning of personal happiness and fulfillment that is believed to be manifested in marriage. There is a "happy Christian family" industry that markets a powerful idea: if one carefully follows prescriptive steps, marriage and family outcome can be predetermined.

The truth is that many couples will not experience the "happiness" for which they yearn. They wish that the pain and hurt from previous injury in life might pass from them, yet it stays. The sorrow from the death of an infant daughter, the childhood trauma of parental divorce, or the lingering pain of rejection or disregard by friends lingers in the lowland of one's soul like mustard gas in the farmland of a French battlefield. Gary Thomas asks this crucial question in his book *Sacred Marriage:* "What if God designed marriage to make us holy more than to make us happy?"[6] This question has serious implications for the Christian counselor who is charged with the superficial request offered by a couple to "help us become happy," and who understands that there may exist a much deeper and profound request that the couple does not know how to articulate at the onset of therapy, which is "help us learn to be content and at peace with our pasts, present and future."

The emphasis on marital bliss, frequently preached, written and broadcast throughout the Christian community, creates an expectation for success that marriage counselors cannot support with integrity. Furthermore, it creates an expectation for an outcome that couples will fail to experience. That failure leaves couples more vulnerable to perpetuating relational conflict. For example, the back cover of a marriage book written by a regarded Christian marriage and family therapist claims that his program "promises to: *Uncover the three key elements that can change your marriage forever; *Help you grow a depth of love that many couples never experience; *Leave no part of your marriage vulnerable; *Arm you with all the critical relationship tools that you will ever need; and *Guarantee a revolutionized marriage in a few short months."

We believe that these success messages can create expectations that are impossible to fulfill and will encourage the "happy Christian" syndrome in which acting happy is valued above being honest. Ultimately these unreasonable blissful expectations can create a logical process for both spouses: "We are supposed to experience a deeper marital joy . . . and we are not. And, since I am doing everything the counselor, pastor, book, tape, or radio broadcast has told me to do and it's not working, then the reason our marriage is not as fulfilling as the books say it should be is because *you* are not doing it correctly."

We believe that our objective as Christian counselors should not be to promote emotional states of happiness, contentment or satisfaction. Those are conditional characteristics that reflect immediate circumstances. Rather, we yearn to instill traits—long-term life characteristics. The apostle Peter suggests that the qualities of faith, goodness, knowledge, self-control, perseverance, godliness, kindness and love result in transformational effectiveness in Christians in society. We take note that happiness, fulfillment, satisfaction and nonconflict are not on the list for the Christian, married or otherwise. We believe that with maturity comes the capacity to understand one's self and one's lifetime lover with insight and service. The constructs of grace, justice, empathy, trust and forgiveness are characteristics for grown-ups, for the mature, for men and women who carry the burdens of life for one another.

COUPLES WITH WHOM YOU WORK MAY DIVORCE

Divorce rocks families. Husbands and wives are emotionally crushed. Children are spun into confusion. Faith communities take it like a kick in the gut. Pastors and counselors themselves are prone to feel defeated, rejected, hurt and dismayed. If there were a quantifiable "mental health survivor's guilt," it would manifest itself here. Questions of self-doubt abound: "Should I have done something different? If only I tried harder, met more often, challenged with greater forcefulness, encouraged with more compassion, attended more carefully to messages expressed . . . maybe this marriage could have been saved." Divorce hurts everyone close to the marriage—even the professional caregiver.

From our work with couples, we know how easy it is to be an advocate of a good thing (e.g., to resolve conflict) for bad reasons (e.g., to meet the needs of the counselor). It is because counselors can become so emotionally connected to their clients that a potential for "bad work" is created. While divorce does create significant risks to both spouses and to children, it should be remembered that they are risks, they are not causes. Divorce is a hardship, but it does not prescribe outcomes for individuals or for families. All too often we see pastors and Christian counselors not able to accept the fact that divorce has or will occur in the marriages to which they invest their emotion and devote their time. We have experienced within ourselves and have seen in counselors the powerful pull to declare a pox on their house—particularly to the one whom we may fix blame. We write ourselves out of the solution to the family crisis. Tragically, we see that the person needed at such a crucial time in a family's history—the pastor or counselor who could be providing compassion, insight, relationship, networking, community and guidance—is often not present once the decision to divorce is made or the process of divorce is instigated. When the call of the gospel is most needed, it is often muted by the ones who do not agree with it, then withdrawn by those in the church who are offended that the message is being disregarded.

There are a few important steps that pastors and counselors can take to reduce this trend. First, as was emphasized in chapter one, the most important skill to model and impart to couples is that of mature boundaries. Divorcing couples have created an environment where counselors can model the meaning of boundaries. We would expect for the counselor to feel a host of emotions when informed of the decision to dissolve the marriage. The therapeutic task is to manage that appropriate emotion in a manner that encourages human resiliency. In redefining the marriage through divorce, new boundaries are being drawn. When children are involved, partners divorce in marriage, but they do not divorce in parenting. They remain responsible to make decisions for the children that will be in the best interest of the offspring's growth and development.

Second, when couples do divorce, the change in family structure will suggest a greater and growing need for the continuation of counseling. At the time of transitions and emotional adjustment, we want to encourage the continuation of counseling under a different set of rules. We suggest that at the beginning of the counseling experience, pastors and counselors communicate that it is their understanding that the couple is enlisting expertise to reconcile and enhance their Us, and that that is the goal held by both spouses. In the event that the goal is no longer to build the marriage, then the couple is encouraged to speak with the counselor so that they can agree on a different goal.

Tragically, Christian counselors or pastors and couples frequently end their professional relationship at a critical time when a reasonable, respected voice needs to be heard above the cacophony of emotions and drastic change. A crucial question to ask the couple is if each will allow you to stay engaged with them as they transition into a new definition of the relationship, that of a divorced couple. The ethical position here is not to maintain contact in order to persuade one or both out of their decision. They have spoken, and out of respect for their autonomy, that boundary should not be crossed. However, knowledge of their patterns, history and individual family-of-origin experiences may prove to be a vital factor in the divorce adjustment. The crucial goal is for counselors to assist the couple in minimizing the negative effects of divorce on each of them, and on children and the extended family.

VALUE CONFLICT RECOVERY OVER CONFLICT ERADICATION

In the preceding chapters we have described a model of two marital paths—conflict and restoration. Our goal was to communicate how we see the counselor role in helping couples understand and experience relational harmony and intimacy. An errant interpretation of this model is that there are "just two paths" in marriage, and that a couple is on one and not the other. The error lies not in the conceptualization of the road but in the assessment of the position. Emphatically, we do not believe that there are "good couples" who exist on the path toward relational intimacy and "bad couples" who exist on the path of conflict. Rather, we believe, and the marital research supports the idea, that it is not the frequency of conflict or the level of emotional intensity that predicts marital success; it is the recovery time. Therefore, we think that counselors should focus their time on conflict recovery rather than conflict prevention. Imagine this example: Donovan and Estelle fight, on average, two times a week. But it takes them an average of three days to recover from each conflict. While only fighting two times per week, they are in a state of disagreement six out of seven days. On the other hand, Willie and Deborah find themselves in an argument four times per week. But they are able to recover the same day—usually within hours of the conflict.

IN CONTRAST TO BRIEF, TIME-LIMITED THERAPY, BE PREPARED TO STAY FOR A WHILE

The controversial Texas Senator Phil Graham delivered an illuminating rhetorical question to an advocate of an education-related bill that Graham opposed. He asked, "What is my son's name?" To which the opponent was a bit flabbergasted—of course he would have no idea the first name of Senator Graham's elementary-aged son. "When you know my son's name, when you care about him and have his long-term interests in mind, you will become qualified to make educational decisions for him. Until then, kindly leave it up to me." The point in communicating this illustration has nothing to do with federal education policy. It has to do with being known. We find that couples counseling does not fit well in the short-term brief-therapy world. The type of relationship that we are advocating for you as counselors doesn't work well in rigid "ten sessions—then terminate" structures.

It is common for couples to have long-term relationships with marriage and family counselors—such that the counselors do actually know the names of the children. Marital counselors can be actively involved in the marriage dynamic for a season, like ten to twelve weeks. In that time, the couple usually is successful in gaining insight into their conflict process and has established the ability to render grace and justice to one another. The other components of the model—empathy, trust and forgiveness—are stations that the couple should be developing together over the subsequent months. It is common to end therapy at that time, but not end the relationship. We advocate another check-in session about six months later. Furthermore, we encourage check-in sessions to continue about every six months or once a year. The purpose is to stay in contact and remain as an auxiliary support for marriage and family growth. The counseling relationship really doesn't terminate; it is put on pause for a time, then continues, then pauses again.

THE LAST WORD: GRACE

We enthusiastically support the work of counselors and pastors in their efforts to enhance the Us. When attending to the needs of couples, we think outside of *DSM* categories and beyond the circular fights of "he said . . . she said . . ." We think of building maturity, resilience, commitment, intimacy and love. We see the role of the counselor as crucial in instilling a vision of where marriage can go, providing a path to reach that destination, and offering encouragement and mentorship along the way.

The model presented in this book is built around the construct of grace. As Christian counselors, you are familiar with this idea as being central to our faith. But many of the couples with whom we work have only a superficial understanding of grace. For them, the idea of grace as a quality of marital Us can be revolutionary. Those outside of the Christian faith tradition often are drawn to the idea—they can imagine it occurring in their marriage because, in part, they experience it within counseling. Counselors instill a hope that the same acceptance they experience in the counseling relationship might be replicated within their marriage. In addition, those who have been raised in the Christian tradition and have familiarity with the idea often know of it as a theological idea, but it is not one that they have thought about as the basis for their marital commitment. Teaching couples that marriage is "graceful"—literally, full of grace—is a very powerful way for counseling to be explicitly Christian.

It is our hope that your work with couples will also be full of grace, justice, empathy, trust and forgiveness. We join with the apostle Paul when he writes the closing words of nearly all of his epistles: "May the grace of the Lord Jesus be with you. Amen."

NOTES

[1]Hargrave, T. D. (2000). *The essential humility of marriage: Honoring the third identity in couples therapy.* Phoenix: Zeig, Tucker & Theisen.

[2]Ibid., p. 180.

[3]Ibid., p. 179.

[4]Hart, A. H. (2008). *Knowing darkness: On skepticism, melancholy, friendship and God.* Grand Rapids, MI: Eerdmans, p. 34.

[5]Ibid.

[6]Thomas, G. L. (2000). *Sacred marriage.* Grand Rapids, MI: Zondervan.

Index

CAPS

An Association for Christian Psychologists,
Therapists, Counselors and Academicians

CAPS is a vibrant Christian organization with a rich tradition. Founded in 1956 by a small group of Christian mental health professionals, chaplains and pastors, CAPS has grown to more than 2,100 members in the U.S., Canada and more than 25 other countries.

CAPS encourages in-depth consideration of therapeutic, research, theoretical and theological issues. The association is a forum for creative new ideas. In fact, their publications and conferences are the birthplace for many of the formative concepts in our field today.

CAPS members represent a variety of denominations, professional groups and theoretical orientations; yet all are united in their commitment to Christ and to professional excellence.

CAPS is a non-profit, member-supported organization. It is led by a fully functioning board of directors, and the membership has a voice in the direction of CAPS.

CAPS is more than a professional association. It is a fellowship, and in addition to national and international activities, the organization strongly encourages regional, local and area activities which provide networking and fellowship opportunities as well as professional enrichment.

To learn more about CAPS, visit www.caps.net.

CAPS BOOKS
from IVP Academic

The joint publishing venture between IVP Academic and CAPS aims to promote the understanding of the relationship between Christianity and the behavioral sciences at both the clinical/counseling and the theoretical/research levels. These books will be of particular value for students and practitioners, teachers and researchers.

For more information, visit InterVarsity Press's website at www.ivpress.com, type in *Integrative Psychology,* and follow the links provided there to CAPS books.